1-25-64

DATE DUE

MAR 2 2 '68	
APR 1 8 '69	
May 16, 1969	
MAY 21 '69	
DEC 1 9 '69	
APR 16 '71	
Sept 3, 1971	
DEC 3 '71	

$7.50

1965-64

D0893795

THEODORE M. NEWCOMB is Professor of Sociology and Psychology and Chairman of the Doctoral Program in Social Psychology at The University of Michigan. He has also taught psychology at Lehigh University, Western Reserve University, and Bennington College. In 1951 Professor Newcomb was a Fulbright Scholar in London; he has been a Fellow at the Center for Advanced Study in the Behavioral Sciences, a Guggenheim Fellow, and is a past President of the American Psychological Association. He is the author of *Experimental Social Psychology* (with Gardner and L. B. Murphy), *Group Adjustment* (with W. I. Newstetter and M. J. Feldstein), *Personality and Social Change,* and *Social Psychology*. From 1954 to 1958 he was Editor of THE PSYCHOLOGICAL REVIEW.

THE ACQUAINTANCE PROCESS

Theodore M. Newcomb

THE UNIVERSITY OF MICHIGAN

THE **A**CQUAINTANCE

PROCESS

**HOLT,
RINEHART
and WINSTON**

New York

TO MARY
——————————— **who helped most of all**

PREFACE

Ideas, like individuals and nations, have histories, and so do the research enterprises that sometimes stem from ideas. The history of the research that is reported in the following pages is mainly one of indebtedness. The ideas out of which it grew have a remote ancestry in those of Charles H. Cooley and George H. Mead, and an intermediate one in some things I learned from my own research at Bennington College twenty years ago. Their more immediate ancestry can readily be traced to my former colleague, Professor Leon Festinger, and to the writings of Professor Fritz Heider. And from Dr. James G. Miller and his associates I have learned some of the advantages of treating these borrowed ideas in system-like terms.

The research enterprise really began in conversations with Dr. Joseph E. McGrath, then (in early 1953) a graduate student in social psychology, whose encouragement and imagination were indispensable to its launching, and who directed research activities during the first data-gathering period. My next, and heaviest, obligation is to Dr. Peter G. Nordlie, whose graduate years, I fear, were too much taken up with management of the Project House, with machine-processing of the data, and with helping me (through an entire year at the Center for Advanced Study in the Behavioral Sciences) to solve some difficult problems of analysis. Dr. Harry A. Burdick directed the second year's data-gathering and was responsible for many of the early analyses. These three, my first lieutenants, knew more than I about the project between 1954 and 1956, when other duties too often distracted me, but such shortcomings in planning and data-gathering as later became apparent were mine, not theirs. My use of "we" throughout the chapters of this monograph is not intended to divert to them the responsibility for its writing; it merely betrays the fact that I have always thought of it as a joint product.

H. Merrill Jackson, who, like Dr. Nordlie, lived for two years in the Project House basement, eagerly participated in nearly every form of research activity for two years. Other graduate students who devoted large proportions of their time to the project between 1954 and 1956 were Peter Houts, Ina Samuels, Harry Scarr, Clagett G. Smith,[1] and Alice G. Weinstein. And several other students—including Eugene Abravenel, Elaine Alter, Jane Jackson, Henrietta Klawans, Richard Louttit, Frederic Mosher, Richard Schmuck, Richard Wagner, and George Wieland—took on temporary, specialized tasks of analysis. Dr. Philip J. Runkel gave me informed and useful counsel on several occasions.

Far from least in this list of able and willing assistants were Mrs. Marion McGarth and Ruth Goldhaber who took over secretarial and many other duties. Mrs. Willodean Stalker, Secretary to the Doctoral Program in Social Psychology, came to my aid in a thousand ways, including the preparation of the final manuscript. Mrs. Joan Warmbrunn, of the Center for Advanced Study in the Behavioral Sciences, gave me similar help at an earlier stage; and Mrs. Norma B. Nordlie, then also of the Center, carried out several of the earlier analyses.

Two of my colleagues, Dr. Richard Savage of the Center for Advanced Study in the Behavioral Sciences in 1956–57, and Professor William Hays, of the University of Michigan's Psychology Department, provided statistical advice on problems beyond my ken; they bear no responsibility, of course, for my misapplication of their counsel. And a third colleague, Professor J. R. P. French, Jr., has paid me the high compliment of criticizing, astutely and in detail, the first draft of the entire manuscript. Though I have, as a result, almost entirely rewritten it, he is scarcely to be blamed for the fact that I did not adopt all of his suggestions.

The 34 men who, week after week, faithfully provided the bricks of information out of which this monograph is constructed were, of course, my principal benefactors. Not one of them ever lapsed, for even a single week, and my debt to them is most inadequately repaid by sending each of them a standard model of

---

[1] After the present manuscript was set in type, Dr. Smith's dissertation (1961), based upon certain data gathered during the course of the study reported in this monograph, has been completed. Some of his findings concerning adaptation to forces toward autism and reality would have been cited in the present study, had they been ready a few months earlier.

this monograph. Some of them, perhaps, will recognize an occasional individual in the following pages, although, by changed code numbers and by other arts of disguise, I have done my best to preserve their promised anonymity.

The not inconsiderable expenses of this relatively long-time project were borne, in the first instance, by the Rockefeller Foundation. Smaller but equally essential grants were later made by the Horace H. Rackham School of Graduate Studies at the University of Michigan and by the Office of Naval Research. The Foundation for Research on Human Behavior, together with the Center for Advanced Study in the Behavioral Sciences, made it possible for Dr. Nordlie to accompany me to the latter haven in 1956–57. This happy and productive year was an essential one in the life-history of the present research, and I am deeply grateful to the Center's Trustees, to Doctors Ralph Tyler and Preston Cutler, and to their many associates there. The Center's facilities were again made available to me for several months in 1959–60, when I was able to complete the manuscript.

The history of our execution of the research had its full share of cup-to-lip slips. We were aware, in our earliest stages of planning, that many of our procedures must be improvised, since at many points we had little published precedent to guide us. Before the end of our first four-month period of data-gathering we became aware of how inadequate some of our improvising had been. We then faced the age-old dilemma of would-be replicators: to sacrifice either known improvability or exact replication. In most cases we chose the latter alternative. In some respects, therefore, our first round of data-gathering must be regarded as a pilot study in preparation for the second. We sometimes wished, later, that we could regard the second as only a pilot to a third.

The writing of a research report, too, has its own history, and in the writing of this one I came to the conclusion that it would be a bare-boned research report, together with only such theoretical connective tissue as in fact inspired the initial planning of the research. I have therefore eschewed references to the published research literature—no matter how relevant, how supportive, or how contradictory—and to other theoretical contributions. There are other channels of publication for comparative studies, and this report is long enough as it is.

The reader will find, finally, that I have sometimes oscillated between the reporting of tests of theoretically derived predictions and the presenting of exploratory findings. Insofar as the latter are interesting or significant, I have no apology to make for them—especially as one who has often criticized students who, in their eagerness to find support for cherished hypotheses, ignore serendipidous findings. The phenomena of getting acquainted, like most others which one studies intimately for a period of years, are full of interesting surprises, and none of us is capable of anticipating all of them. If one were gifted with such prescience, where would one find the hypotheses for one's next research?

T.M.N.

Ann Arbor
June 1960

CONTENTS

LIST OF TABLES

List of Tables ———————————————————————————— xiii

PART ONE

*Problem and
Research
Setting*

Prologue

On Sunday afternoon, September 12, 1954, there arrived at 927 South Forest Avenue, in Ann Arbor, seventeen men who were transferring from other institutions of higher learning to the University of Michigan. Except for brief visits by one or two of them, none had ever been in Ann Arbor before, and no two of them had ever met or ever heard of each other. They had accepted invitations to live, rent free, at this address, in return for devoting four to five hours a week, as informants and as experimental subjects, throughout the fall semester—until the end of the following January. Among the many who had written to express an interest in the inquiry that had been mailed during the summer to a hundred-odd prospective transfer students, these seventeen had been selected primarily by the criterion of strangership. No two of them, according to information that they supplied, had ever lived in the same town or city, or attended the same school.

One year later, on Sunday, September 11, these men were followed by seventeen others, selected in exactly the same manner, with the single exception that the second population was matched, as nearly as possible, with the first, according to selected demographic variables. We had ample opportunity, during the four months following their arrival, to confirm our initial belief that in neither population had any two men had even the slightest previous acquaintance with each other.

Two essential conditions of our research were met only at considerable pain and expense: the recruiting of populations all of whose members were complete strangers to one another; and the providing of a setting in which the strangers so selected would, over a considerable period of time, remain in close contact with one another and have ample opportunity to become well acquainted. Why so much pains to create these conditions?

It was, essentially, the requirements of experimental method that dictated these procedures. The late Professor Kurt Lewin used to express the experimentalist's credo by saying that if you want to improve your understanding of something you will observe it as it changes, and preferably as it changes under conditions that you yourself have created. He might have added (and perhaps he did) that there are special advantages in observing it in *statu nascendi*— that is, in watching the emergence of variables that initially were not there. Basically, even if not in the restricted, laboratory-like sense, any procedure is an experimental one if it systematically observes the emergence of phenomena under conditions that have been designed to make them emerge.

Initial strangership represents the zero state out of which, given opportunity and motivation, various kinds of relationships among persons emerge. Given, in addition, a relatively long period of time during which such relationships can develop, we may expect them to become more or less stabilized. We shall have more to say, in the following chapter, about these relationships and how they may be conceptualized. Meanwhile, we may say simply that the central objective of the study, to which arrangements assuring initial strangership and subsequent opportunity for acquaintance were instrumental, was to improve our understanding of the development of stable interpersonal relationships.

Systems of Orientation _____ **2**

Any contribution, via a single bit of research, to the very broad and general objective of understanding interpersonal relationships must of course be based upon a restricted formulation of a specified sector of the general problem. This chapter is devoted to the presentation of such a formulation.

Social psychologists, like other students of human affairs, are dependent upon their observations of what people do—of people's behavior—for their source of raw information. But raw observations need to be refined in ways that can result in interpretations relevant to the questions that one is asking. When one is dealing with complex behavior, and in particular when one has only very limited control over the situations in which such behavior occurs, it becomes essential to distinguish between the transitory and the enduring, between (in Lewin's terms) the phenotypic and the genotypic. For present purposes this means that our observations must be so codified that whatever it is that makes for stability in human relationships can be detected, in spite of the fact that the raw behavioral components of these relationships are constantly changing. The quest for orderliness in things, here as elsewhere, imposes this requirement.

THE NATURE OF ORIENTATIONS

For such reasons our formulation centers on the concept of *orientation,* which is a useful way of taking account of the fact of individuals' persistencies in relating themselves to things in their environment. An orientation is a property of a person, inferred from his behaviors that have to do with the specified object of orientation.[1] The utility of the notion springs from the reasonable (and necessary) assumption that a given instance of behavior vis-à-vis a specified object is a resultant of specific, momentary influences in the immediate environment together with predispositions surviving from previous experiences with that object or with similar ones. Orientations are, by definition, persistent—not in the sense that they are unmodifiable by experience but only in the sense that in any immediate situation they are persisting residuals of experience with previous situations. As persistent phenomena, in this sense, they are more appropriate building stones for our needed formulation concerning stable interpersonal relationships than objectively observable behaviors, which necessarily vary with situational vicissitudes, would be.

The term *orientation* implies directedness and selectivity, as its etymology suggests; to be oriented toward something means, minimally, to direct one's attention toward it rather than toward something else. The major definitional properties, both conceptual and operational, of orientations include *sign* (positive-negative, favorable-unfavorable, approach-avoidant tendencies) and *intensity* (strong-weak, extreme-moderate). Orientations are labeled and distinguished from one another by their objects, which may be specific or general, concrete or abstract; an object is always express or implied—an orientation toward Adolph Hitler, toward citrus fruits, toward Christianity, or toward oneself. Objects "exist" for an individual, of course, as they are perceived by him and not as they "really are," though they commonly have (and more commonly are assumed to have) some correspondence with objective existence.

Orientations, though most readily measured in terms of sign and intensity, also have other properties of importance—especially cognitive ones. Sign and intensity are cathective properties that refer to approach-avoidance tendencies; cognitive properties of orientations have to do with the ordering, or structuring, of attributes as cognized in, or attributed to, their objects. A pair of parents, for example, may be indistinguishable in the sign and

---

[1] As here used, the term is identical with *attitude,* as conventionally used by social psychologists. For our purposes, it is convenient to restrict the latter term to a specific category of orientations, as distinguished from other categories to which other terms will be applied; see pp. 6–7.

intensity of their attractions toward their child, but the cognitive content of their orientations may nevertheless be quite different; for example, one parent's attraction toward the child may have strong cognitive components of pride and resemblance to himself, while for the other parent warmth of personal response may be a more important component. Since differences between orientations toward the same object are subsequently to be stressed, it is essential to note that cognitive differences may have exactly the same consequences as the cathective ones of sign and intensity.[2]

Categories of Orientations

Since our basic general concern is with relationships among persons, and since our elementary conceptual unit is a single orientation of a single person, it follows that our formulation will be in terms of *relationships among orientations*. Such a model, if it is to be generalizable across different persons and different orientations (that is, toward different objects), presupposes some sort of categorization that is sufficiently abstract, or contentless, to be applicable to any relevant aspect of any interpersonal relationship. Our categorization is as follows.

Attraction. We shall refer to orientations of a person, A, toward some other person, B, as instances of attraction. Person-to-person orientations are apt to be those that come first to mind in ordinary discussions of interpersonal relationships. Such phrases as "I'm rather fond of her," or "I refuse to have anything to do with him," suggest both sign and intensity of direct interpersonal orientations. It is doubtless natural to equate attraction with "liking," but we prefer to conceptualize attraction in somewhat broader terms. Thus respect, admiration, and dependence all refer to positive person-to-person orientations, and yet any of these may be associated with either positive or negative liking. In its most general form, therefore, attraction refers to any direct orientation (on the part of one person toward another) which may be described in terms of sign and intensity. By this general definition, any kind of orientation

[2] Each cognitively discriminated property of an object may be thought of as a sub-object of cathective orientations, in which case two persons' orientations to the same total object, though equivalent in sign and intensity, may represent resultants of different weightings of the same properties, or weightings of different properties, or some combination of both.

toward another person that involves psychological approach rather than avoidance, moving toward rather than against or away from, is one of positive attraction.

Attitude. Because orientations toward persons have distinctive consequences (potentially, at least), differing from those toward other objects, it is convenient to assign a distinctive label to the latter as well as to the former. Thus we shall refer to any orientation of a person, A, toward a nonperson object, X, as an attitude.[3]

Our formulation assumes that, under certain conditions, interpersonal relationships have to do with attitudes as well as with attractions. Pending a more formal statement of these conditions (on pp. 8–16), the justification for this assumption is simply that any two persons between whom a relationship of attraction exists live in a world of common objects, some of which are so important to them that both persons are bound to develop attitudes toward them. Since such pairs (or larger sets) of persons are, in many situations, affected by each other's behavior vis-à-vis the common objects, their relationship is necessarily affected by their attitudes toward them. The relationship between a husband and wife, for example, is pretty sure to be affected by the similarities and differences of their attitudes toward their joint bank account.[4]

Perceived orientation of others. If, as we have just argued, the attitude toward some object, X, on the part of another person, B, who is attractive to an individual, A, may have effects upon the relationship between A and B, then these effects are presumably mediated by some psychological processes of one or both persons. Psychologists commonly make the assumption that psychologically mediated responses to situations are more closely ordered to the responder's perceptions of that situation than to other persons'

[3] In principle, the word "person" should be followed by "or group of persons," but for the purposes of this monograph we shall follow the more restricted usage.

[4] It might equally well be added, "or by the similarities and differences of their attraction-orientations toward their children." Among the most important of common objects for almost any pair of persons, A and B, are other persons, orientations toward whom, we have insisted, should be referred to as attractions rather than as attitudes. While there are special reasons, as noted on p. 7, for distinguishing between these two forms of orientation, our basic point is that of orientations toward common objects; the system dynamics are the same, regardless of whether the common object of orientation is human or not.

(including the experimenter's) perceptions of it. Our inclusion of this third category of attitudes—that is, B's attitude toward X, as perceived by A—is based upon this assumption.

It is because of the omnipresence of orientations attributed to others, and because of the significance of their consequences, that we have insisted upon distinguishing between orientations of attraction and of attitude as applying to persons and to nonpersons, respectively. Person-objects, unlike nonhuman objects of orientation,[5] are *like* the orienting person in that both are capable of having orientations toward the same objects, and of knowing that this is the case. Hence attributions of orientations to persons, but not to other objects, become possible. By using a distinctive term for orientations toward objects regarded as having this capacity—that is, toward persons—this crucial distinction is more likely to be kept in mind.

SYSTEM PROPERTIES OF INTERPERSONAL ORIENTATIONS

We have referred to attraction as the direct component of interpersonal orientation, and by the same token attitudes (whether regarded as those of an individual or as those attributed by him to another person) are the indirect components. What the direct and the indirect orientations have in common is that both, hypothetically, have effects upon interpersonal relationships. We shall now hypothesize, further, that the two kinds of effects are interdependent and that therefore, in the sense to be defined, either of these two kinds of sets of orientations constitutes a system: (a) a set composed of A's attraction toward B, A's attitude toward X, and B's attitude toward X as perceived by A (an individual system); and (b) a set composed of both A's and B's attractions toward each other, both A's and B's attitudes toward the same object, X, and the attitudes toward X that are attributed both by A to B and by B to A (a two-person collective system). Fig. 2.1a presents a schematic diagram of an individual system of orientations (A rather than B being taken as the focal individual), and Fig. 2.1b that of a collective system (of two persons, in this instance).

[5] We omit consideration of the marginal case of animals, especially pets and domesticated animals. The distinction may be regarded as one of degree—though of very great degree, we believe—rather than as absolute.

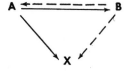

(a) Individual system
of Person A

(b) Collective system
of Persons A and B

Fig. 2.1. Schematic representation of systems of orientation. Arrows point from orienting person to person or object of orientation. Broken lines refer to orientations attributed by A to B (*a*) solid lines refer to own orientations of person from whom arrow stems. Broad bands refer to relationships between orientations connected by bands.

The General Nature of Systems

We shall define a system as any set of entities so related to one another that changes in certain states of any one of them (regardless of the source of that change) induce specifiable kinds of changes in one or more of the others. Since a system so defined is of little interest if such relationships of interdependency are only short-lived, we shall apply the term only when it can be shown that, under specified conditions, such interrelationships persist through time. And, since systems whose component entities are so related to one another tend to have (within observable limits) certain properties of their own (as distinct from the properties of the component entities), we shall further include the stipulation of relative stability of certain system properties. Finally, it must be assumed that stable properties at the system level can be maintained only by stable relationships among the constituent entities of the system. The system may therefore be *described* in terms of its own stable properties (and the limits within which they vary), and its stability may be *accounted* for in terms of relatively stable relationships among its constituent entities, or parts.

Individual Systems of Orientation

We now turn to a consideration of the internal dynamics of individual systems of orientation—that is, of the bases of stability and change in the relationships among the three categories of orientation on the part of a single person, A. We shall postpone until pages 20–22 the question of the direct relevance of our system-formulation for understanding the acquaintance process.

The requirements for system formation. A system of orientations potentially exists (by postulation) for an individual, A, if and only if all the following conditions are met.

1. A has an attitude, either positive or negative, toward some specifiable object, X, that he regards as of common relevance [6] to himself and to another person, B—that he assumes, in other words, to have some common impact upon both A and B.

2. A attributes an attitude, either positive or negative, to another person, B, regarding the same object, X.

3. A has some degree of attraction, positive or negative, toward B.

Since, typically, an individual has attitudes toward many objects and has some degree of attraction toward many other persons, at any given moment most of his systems of orientation are not actual, or effective, but only latent. A latent system becomes an activated one when the psychological processes corresponding to the three categories of orientation (attitude toward X, attraction toward B, perception of B's attitude toward X) are simultaneously occurring in A. Or, to use a convenient neologism, an activated system of orientation exists for A when he *co-orients* (that is, attends simultaneously) to B and to X in joint context, so that B is perceived in relation to X, and X in relation to B. For practical purposes it may be assumed that whenever A attributes to B an attitude toward an X toward which A himself also holds an attitude, A is co-orienting toward B and X, and an ABX system exists. Since A's attribution of an attitude toward X on the part of B evokes, for A, cues concerning both B and X, it is reasonable to assume that A's orientations toward both B and X will, in some degree at least, be activated simultaneously with the attribution.

Given a relatively constant environment of other persons and of common objects, latent systems of orientation tend to persist, simply by habit formation. That is, a given ABX system, once activated, tends to be re-evoked from time to time if cues from either B or X are repeatedly encountered, simply because an association between them has been learned. Thus either kind of cue, or both together (as when a familiar associate introduces a familiar topic of conversation), may activate a latent system.

As illustrated in Fig. 2.1a, the *components* of individual systems are a person's own orientations and the orientations that he attributes to another person. The *properties* of individual systems

[6] See p. 13 for further discussion of common relevance.

in which we shall be principally interested are relationships among these components, including the degree of similarity or discrepancy between own and other's perceived orientation to the same object.

Collective Systems of Orientation

A system of orientation may also be considered to exist on the part of a set of two or more persons. Groups, or collectivities, of persons have their properties, at their own level, that are no more and no less real than those of individuals, at their own level.

The potential basis for a collective system (for purposes of simplicity we shall consider only a two-person collectivity) is provided by the existence, on the part of A and of B, of activatable individual systems involving A, B, and the same X.[7] A collective system is activated during a given interval of time if and only if, during that interval, (1) both individual systems have been activated, and (2) each person, A and B, assumes that "the same" individual system has been activated both for himself and for the other. If, for example, during the same day A sees B kicking a dog and B sees A fondling the same dog, and if each of them assumes that the other has observed him in the act, then a collective system has been activated.

The usual precondition for the existence of a collective system is communication between A and B concerning X. As in the illustration just offered, communication need not be verbal; it need only be such as to result in the assumptions by *both* A and B that (1) some degree of attraction, positive or negative, exists on the part of each toward the other, and (2) each of them has an attitude, either positive or negative, toward the same X. Under certain conditions (especially close acquaintance), a person may correctly assume, without communication, that both of these conditions have been met by one or more other persons; in this case a collective system has been reactivated regardless of the absence of communication.

In practice we shall assume that (as illustrated in Fig. 2.1b)

[7] We are of course making assumptions of veridical perception; in other words, that the B of A's individual system corresponds in ascertainable ways to the actual person, B, whose individual system comprises A, and that the same is true of the A of B's individual system. Also, the X of both individual systems is "the same"; for present purposes, we need only define sameness in terms of assumptions by both A and B that both are co-orienting to a single entity.

the components of collective systems are exclusively the members' actual orientations—that is, their own orientations, and not those they attribute to others. A person's own orientations may be influenced by his perceptions of others' orientations (see "Dynamics of system stability and change," following), but the properties of collective systems in which we shall be interested are best described in terms of actual orientations "as they are," rather than in terms of the conditions which brought them about—especially the degree of actual similarity or discrepancy in A's and B's attitudes to the same object, and the degree of their mutual attraction to each other.

Dynamics of System Stability and Change

To say that systems of orientation tend to persist and to be reactivated does not mean, however, that they remain unchanged in all respects. Orientations change, particularly when their objects are still relatively unfamiliar and when new information about them may result in new evaluations. Our problem, as we have already indicated, is to find stability in *relationships* among orientations, in spite of changes in one or more of the orientations that are related.

Psychological strain and individual system stability. The key principle of individual system stability is one that involves relationships among all three categories of the ABX system. This principle postulates a psychological force upon A, varying in strength with intensity of positive A-to-B attraction (and with other parameters, noted later), toward maintaining a constant relationship between A-to-X attitude and perceived B-to-X attitude. This constant relationship is one of *minimal perceived discrepancy*—in other words, of maximal similarity—in attitude. In propositional form, the stronger A's attraction toward B the greater the strength of the force upon A to maintain minimal discrepancy between his own and B's attitude, as he perceives the latter, toward the same X; and, if positive attraction remains constant, the greater the perceived discrepancy in attitude the stronger the force to reduce it. We shall refer to this force as *strain*.

There are also, hypothetically, two other parameters of individual system strain. (1) *Importance* refers, conceptually, to the valence, positive or negative, of the attitude object, X, for A. Ideally, one would measure this variable in terms of the individual's degree of resistance to changing his attitude toward X; operationally, we have generally used as an index of importance the individual's expressed degree of favorability or unfavorability toward the attitude object.

(2) *Common relevance* refers to joint dependence of A and B (as perceived by A, in the case of individual systems) upon the object, X. If A considers an object of high common relevance to himself and B, then he perceives that their relationship to it is that of "common fate": the object is seen as having common consequences for both of them. For example, if one of two men on a raft in mid-ocean assumes that both of them regard the raft as essential to their survival, then for him the raft has high common relevance. At the other extreme, a person who likes very sweet coffee knows that a friend strongly prefers his coffee unsweetened; if each of them is free to sweeten his own cup or not, independently of what the other does, then there are no common consequences of sweetening it or not sweetening it, and the object "sweet coffee" will not be perceived as having common relevance. If, on the other hand, it is known that the common pot of coffee is sweetened before individual portions are served, then the same object will be perceived as having common relevance. Strain is more likely to be experienced under the latter than under the former conditions.

Thus the intensity of strain hypothetically varies, other things being equal, not only with the strength of A's attraction toward B but also with the importance and the common relevance that A attributes to X.

We find it useful to think of this postulated force as drivelike. That is, it tends to be activity-arousing and, following opportunity for learning, the kinds of activity that it arouses are those that tend to reduce the intensity of the drive. In view of its aversive character, we have come to refer to it as *strain*—or, more fully, the strain of perceived discrepancy with an attractive other person regarding a valued or disliked object.[8]

This state of strain, if drivelike, is a special case, we assume, of acquired drive, and it is not difficult to speculate plausibly as to the conditions under which it is learned. Indeed, the conditions

[8] The notion of strain (cf. Newcomb, 1953) is of course closely related to Heider's earlier one of balance (see p. 21) and Festinger's later one of dissonance (1957). It is equivalent to and perhaps less desirable than "imbalance," to which we have preferred it only because of its more obvious implications of intrapersonal, drivelike state.

of its acquisition are probably as fundamental as those of human socialization—a process to which the acquired drive of strain is probably instrumental. Human socialization necessarily includes the acquiring of many attitudes that are consensual with others' (especially adults') attitudes. To survive requires the acquiring of unfavorable attitudes (like those of adults) toward possibly drowning waters, or devouring beasts, or macerating machinery. To adapt comfortably to a stabilized family, community, or social order one must acquire the right attitudes (attitudes like those of one's associates who have already adapted comfortably to family, community, etc.) toward cabbages and kings and all else that is culturally approved or disapproved. Socialization, in short, includes the building in of danger signals when attitudinal discrepancies with trusted others are perceived. Some signals may, of course, prove to be false alarms, and with experience one learns to discriminate among them—a process that is also included in the socialization process. But there are few, presumably, in whom the acquired drive is ever totally extinguished, and for most of us it continues—under the stipulated conditions of strong attraction and intense attitude—to be a source of discomfort.

The hypothesized effects of strain are those of system change: strain tends to result in strain-reducing changes in one or more orientations or perceived orientations of others. Thus system stability varies inversely with intensity of strain. This assumption is central to the ensuing inquiry into the development of stable interpersonal relationships.

Balance and stability in collective systems. The key principle of collective system stability is analogous to that of individual systems. It postulates a force upon the collectivity the effects of which, under specified conditions, are toward minimal discrepancy in the attitudes of members of the collectivity. This force varies in strength with intensity of members' mutual attraction toward one another, with degree of discrepancy in members' attitudes, and with other parameters, as noted later. Just as, in the case of individual systems, the effects of the postulated force are toward minimal *perceived* discrepancy of attitude, so, in the case of collective systems, they are toward minimal *actual* discrepancy. The locus of impact of the postulated force is upon *relationships* between members' attitudes, not upon an individual member's attitude, singly. We shall refer to it as a force toward balance, or, more briefly, as *imbalance*.

Imbalance in collective systems also varies with the importance and the common relevance that is jointly attributed to the object by members of the collectivity. In two-person systems we assume that these levels of joint attribution are, minimally, equivalent to A's or to B's level of perceived importance or common relevance, whichever is lower. By the same token we assume that the limits of imbalance levels in two-person systems are determined by (though not necessarily commensurate with) A's and B's levels of strain. Imbalance in collective systems thus refers, as does strain in individual systems, both to system states that are unstable and to the postulated forces toward change resulting in greater stability.

New information and system change. Individuals' orientations toward different objects (including persons) differ from one another because properties are differentially attributed to them. One's attitude toward sugar stems from (or at any rate is justified by) its properties of sweetness or of caloric content, just as one's different orientations toward Presidents Eisenhower and Roosevelt are, in effect, orientations toward whatever sets of properties are attributed to them. Orientations are thus determined by the processes by which one acquires information about the properties of their objects. If new information—say about the properties of a food or of a political candidate—is acquired that is incongruent with information on which previous attitudes had been based, forces to change those orientations will arise. (Whether or not *actual* change ensues will depend, of course, upon whether such forces are countered by others.)

That it is continually possible to get new information about old things is the rule rather than the exception. Growth and decay are common facts; even things that objectively change little or not at all have new facets to show us; we ourselves, moreover, the observers, are never twice the same, so that new skills or new points of view may open avenues of information which only yesterday were closed to us. Thus we are constantly bombarded by influences which might change our orientations. Were these not countered by other forces, the history of conservatism would have to be drastically rewritten.

Sensitivity to the properties of objects tends, like sensitivity to strain, to be rewarded. The more accurately we assess them the more probably our motives with regard to them will be rewarded. Illusion, too, has its rewards of course, as does the blinding of oneself to new information, but both paths, if persistently pursued, are likely to end in *culs de sac*. For most individuals, in most situations, sufficient sensitivity to new information is maintained so that it can be considered a constant source of change in orientations.

And so we view single orientations in individual systems as being continually subject to change under the impact of new information. And change in single orientations—under the stipulated conditions of attraction, importance, and common relevance—tends to induce other changes within individual systems. Such changes in turn constitute modifications in the between-person relationships that are the components of collective systems. We shall refer to this kind of influence toward change as *reality* forces. And we view both individual and collective systems as also under constant influence to remain stable, in the sense that strain and imbalance, respectively, tend to remain minimal. We shall refer to such influences (essentially autistic in the case of individual systems) as *balance* forces. Thus change in the nature of system *content* (i.e., the properties of component orientations) is paralleled by stability in the system *properties* of strain and imbalance.

The problem posed by the simultaneous effects of these opposed forces inheres in the fact that system components (single orientations in individual systems, relationships among persons' orientations in collective systems) are subject to changes from two sources: directly, via new information about their objects; and, indirectly, via system-induced influences toward the minimization of strain and imbalance, with respect to which the effects are in the direction of stability.

Such, hypothetically, are the dynamics according to which new information, fed into existing systems of orientation relatively free from strain, is psychologically and/or communicatively processed in ways tending to maintain that state. The principles of information processing by systems already at relatively high levels of strain are essentially the same, the major difference being, presumably, that under these conditions there is more active search for new information which could, simultaneously, accurately represent the objects of orientation and serve to reduce system strain.

Alternative formulations exist in plenty, of course, for the phenomena of stability and change of orientations. This one is offered only because it is, in fact, the one according to which our data have been gathered, analyzed, and interpreted.

Modes of maintaining system stability. We have defined a system as a set of entities so related that a change in any one of them induces forces toward change in any of the others in ways that maximize the stability of certain relationships among them. We have also pointed to minimal states of individual strain and of collective imbalance as the principal condition of system stability. We must therefore consider the alternative ways in which changes in single orientations (in individual systems), or changes in the relationships between different persons' orientations (in collective systems), may so induce other within-system changes as to maintain minimal states of strain and imbalance.

Let us begin with an existing individual system that is stable, that is characterized by relatively little strain; let us assume that A's attraction toward B, his attitude toward a relevant X, and his perception of B's attitude toward X are all positive. If A now receives new information leading him to attribute to B a negative attitude toward X, strain is (by postulate) induced. It follows that any of the following changes can contribute to reducing the newly aroused strain: (1) a change in A's attitude toward X, such as to reduce the perceived discrepancy with B; (2) a discrepancy-reducing change in his perception of B's attitude; (3) a reduction in the importance assigned by A to his attitude toward X; (4) a reduction in the strength of A's positive attraction toward B; or (5) a reduction in the degree of perceived common relevance that A attributes to X for himself and B. These changes may come about via additional information about X or about B, commonly obtained through communication with B or with other persons, or simply by internal psychological processes (such as fantasy, memory loss or elaboration, or a shifting frame of reference). Regardless of the manner by which the changes come about, and regardless of which of them occurs, our adoption of the strain hypotheses implies the prediction that, given the initial change described in this illustration, one or more of these five kinds of changes may be expected to follow.

New information may first impinge upon any of the other orientations within an existing individual system, as well as upon A's perception of B-to-X, as in the preceding illustration. Regardless of the point of input of new information, its first consequence is toward change of the information-relevant orientation (assuming only that the information is noticeably incongruent with that previously available). If so, the further consequences are either that (1) the orientation to which the new information is immediately relevant is changed, in which case other system changes must follow if strain is not to be increased; or that (2) the new information is discredited, and thus immunity to system change is guaranteed.

The alternative modes by which balance is maintained within collective systems are not, of course, independent of those occurring within the individual systems of the members of the collectivity. Very often, in fact, the latter parallel direct communication between members, and in any case a change in any orientation of one member necessarily creates a change in the relationship between that orientation and the corresponding one of another member.

Assume that a collective system involving A, B, and a common X is in a state of balance: A's and B's mutual attraction is high, and they agree in taking a positive attitude toward a common X, which both consider important and relevant. If A's attitude toward X for some reason changes to a negative one, and the system thus becomes unbalanced, any of the following system changes will tend to reduce the imbalance: (1) a *rapprochement* between A's and B's attitudes resulting from changes by either or both; (2) a reduction in their mutual attraction toward each other: (3) a reduction in the common level of importance and/or of common relevance that they attribute to X. Such changes, like those in individual systems, may come about via communication or may result from intrapersonal, psychological processes in either A or B. In any case, the mechanisms by which the stability of collective systems tends to be maintained presuppose the operation of those by which individual systems tend to remain stable. And, in most if not all cases that are of more than trivial interest, they also presuppose enough communication, verbal or not, so that the orientations of any member of the collectivity are somehow adaptive to the corresponding orientations of other members.

Dynamic relationships between individual and collective systems. We have outlined the dynamics of individual and of collective systems in closely analogous ways, thus implying some dynamic interrelationships between the two kinds of systems. These relationships are best understood in the light of the fact that the individual system is a private version, on the part of a participant in a collective system, of that collective system. As in the case of other systems (molecules, for example) whose component entities are subsystems and whose properties are determined by interaction among those subsystems, the properties of collective systems—especially the property of balance—are determined by the relationships among individual systems as the latter are influenced by communicative interaction.

More specifically, our hypothetical model is as follows. Suppose a given two-person system is in imbalance; i.e., A's and B's mutual attraction to each other is positive, while A's attitude is positive and B's negative toward an object considered by each to be of importance and common relevance. Under these conditions, the attitudinal discrepancy is likely sooner or later to be discovered by one or both of them (assuming only the possibility of communication by which the discovery might be made), with resulting strain for one or both of them. It follows, hypothetically, that strain-reducing changes in one or more of the component orientations will be made by A or B, or both; most probably, either their discrepancy in attitude will be reduced by changes in A's or B's attitude, or the attraction of one or both of them toward the other will be reduced. Thus an imbalanced collective system has, via the interpersonal mechanism of communication and the intrapersonal mechanism of strain, led to changes in one or more of the associated individual systems. And these latter changes have, by definition, resulted in changes in the collective system.

The basic assumptions, in sum, are these: (1) If—under the stipulated conditions of attraction, importance, and relevance—a collective system is in fact imbalanced, then one or more of the members of the collectivity will discover the fact; this discovery will be followed by individual, strain-instigated changes on that member's part (and, assuming that they are observed by others, on their parts also) that tend to reduce collective imbalance. (2) If, under the stipulated conditions, an individual system is in strain that is not in fact justified by a corresponding state of collective imbalance, then that individual's strain-instigated behavior is likely to result in his discovery of his "error," with attendant reduction of strain.

The Interdependence of Attraction and Attitude

Our system-like formulation includes not only the assumption that attitude change is influenced by attraction but also the converse—that change in attraction is influenced by existing attitudes. The former proposition is scarcely news: it is well documented in the social-psychological literature—for example, in Homans (1950), Festinger, Schachter, and Back (1950), and Newcomb (1943, 1950)—and, moreover, "everybody knows it." The latter proposition is not so well documented, and probably less commonly assumed by the proverbial man in the street. Insofar, therefore, as the findings to be reported in Chapters 4–13 provide support for both propositions—and, in particular, insofar as they do so at the levels of both individual and collective systems—they may be interpreted as being consistent with our formulation in terms of systems composed of interdependent orientations.

SYSTEMS OF ORIENTATION AND THE ACQUAINTANCE PROCESS

In this chapter we have argued, in a rather general way, that the more obvious and direct aspects of interpersonal relationships (orientations of attraction) are so intimately interdependent with certain less direct ones (orientations of attitude) as to require a formulation in terms of system properties, for the understanding of our problem. But we have not yet indicated in any very definite way the special relevance of this formulation for our study of the acquaintance process.

Any formulation adequate for our purposes must, in the first place, take special account of the influx of new information that necessarily floods in upon persons in the early stages of acquaintance—information received from each other and, directly or indirectly, about each other. The formulation must cope with problems such as these: What kinds of information about each other are getting-acquainted persons most alert to? (The available stores of it are so plentiful that selections, presumably following some set of principles, must be made.) How are different items of information fitted together? (Our perceptions of persons, as well as of other objects, tend to be structured, not random; see Asch, 1951.) What does the receipt of new information about another person have to do with ways in which the receiver is thereby changed? (After all, persons do influence one another, and if no one were changed via the acquaintance process we should be little interested in it.) We have already indicated, by brief illustration at least, some ways in which our formulation can handle such problems.

The last of these problems introduces a second requirement for the kind of formulation that we need: it must take account of the facts of personal stability amidst constant influences to change. One aspect of this problem has been both propounded and illuminated, specifically within an interpersonal context, in Professor Fritz Heider's *Psychology of Interpersonal Relations* (1958). By way of summarizing his contribution, we take the liberty of quoting from a review of this book (Newcomb, 1958).

> The perception of persons, as of size, shape, and color, is mediate, not immediate. Since it is necessary to find stabilities in a world of ever-changing appearances, we "interpret" events in terms of the principle of *perceptual constancy*. Perception is directed toward invariant properties of and relations among things perceived, and in social perception these invariances correspond to psychological *dispositional properties*—e.g., wishes, intentions, beliefs—of other persons. Thus interpersonal perception requires the *attribution* to others of such dispositional properties. Central in all of these processes is the search for *personal causality* and its separation from impersonal causality. "Attribution of personal causality reduces the necessary conditions [of interpretation] essentially to one, the person with intention" (p. 102). The nature of these attributions varies, of course, not only with the interpersonal events observed but also with the properties of the perceiver, and foremost among these are *sentiments,* which are rather explicitly equated with person-object relationships of "liking" and "disliking." Sentiments towards objects (including persons) characterized by the *unit relation* (i.e., which "belong together") have system properties that are governed by the principle of the *balanced state,* in which there is "no pressure toward change, either in the cognitive organization or in the environment" (p. 176). Observed events are "always interpreted in terms of the relatively invariant contents of the world around us. These contents must be consistent with each other, and that means that we have definite ideas about fittingness, about consonance and dissonance" (p. 297). . . . Never before has it been argued so astutely that we "see" people, together with the things and events associated with

them, in terms of attributions which, because of their positive and negative evaluations, have a system-requiredness of balance.[9]

From Heider's contribution we select the following propositions (freely translated) as peculiarly appropriate to our purposes. (1) Individuals achieve perceptual constancy with regard to persons by attributing stable orientations to them. (2) Such attributed orientations are not capricious, but are governed by the principles of balance. The importance of these propositions for the study of acquaintance is that they point to a basis for psychological stability amidst the inrush of new information and its attendant consequences for changing orientations that inevitably accompany the process of making new acquaintances.

To these propositions, which we have already borrowed, almost intact, for our own formulation, we would add that *personal,* as well as perceptual, constancy must somehow be taken account of in a formulation adequate for our purposes. Perhaps the same point could be made in terms of perceptual constancy of the self; in any case the self, as a supremely valued object, is valued in considerable part for its constancy. Psychologically, it exists and is perceived not *in vacuo* but as figure against a ground of other valued objects, especially human ones, in which it may be said to be anchored. And so its constancy depends upon a constant anchoring in those objects; if they become devalued, so is the self devalued —a prospect likely to arouse psychological forces of considerable magnitude. We stress these matters not because they are inconsistent with the contributions of Heider or Festinger, for each of whom the emphasis appears to be on *cognitive* constancies, but rather because we believe that a self-and-value-oriented dynamics is more adequate than a "merely cognitive" one to account for the strength of the phenomena with which we are concerned.

The goodness of fit of our particular formulation for our particular problem hinges, we believe, upon its appropriateness for handling the phenomena of human processing of new information under those special conditions where new information bears directly upon the processor's stance vis-à-vis those sectors of his human and of his object world that are of most importance to him. For

[9] Reprinted by permission from *The American Journal of Sociology,* 1958, 23, 742–743.

better or for worse, the formulation has been devised for just such purposes.[10]

PROBLEMS INVESTIGATED IN THE LIGHT OF THIS FORMULATION

Following a description of our data, in the next chapter, the remainder of this monograph is devoted to a series of findings. Particularly in Part Two, these findings are designed to test predictions that are directly derived from hypotheses central to the preceding formulation. In very general form, these hypotheses are that individual systems tend to remain in balance at all times (Chapter 4), and that tendency toward balance in collective systems increases with acquaintance (Chapter 5).

The findings reported in Part Three are primarily exploratory, having to do with individual differences in sensitivity to strain and balance, and with personality variables associated with such differences. In Part Four we shall test certain predictions, derived from the preceding hypotheses, concerning the differentiation of high-attraction subgroups within populations, and concerning the structural relationships of subgroups to one another. In Part Five we present four studies, not primarily of hypothesis-testing nature, that are concerned especially with processes of change throughout the acquaintance period, and that we hope will illuminate the previously reported outcomes and further substantiate them.

[10] Our theoretical formulation has also been presented, in some respects more completely than in this chapter, in Newcomb (1953) and especially in Newcomb (1959).

Gathering Data

3

We have presented the outlines of a theoretical formulation for studying the acquaintance process. In the chapters following this one we shall present data by which some hypotheses and specific predictions derived from that formulation may be tested. Meanwhile, it is necessary to describe the research setting in which those data were obtained, the general procedures followed, and the specific instruments employed.

BACKGROUND AND SETTING

The Selection of Subjects

Certain limitations followed directly from the decision to conduct the research in a student house, and others from the nature of the research objectives. Two very general considerations, apart from the criterion of strangership, were of particular importance. (1) *Subject homogeneity:* from one point of view we would have liked to have seventeen identical twins (seventeen being the capacity of the house). The greater the similarity of the individual properties which the subjects brought with them, the greater the certainty with which later differentiation could be attributed to the experience of living in the house. (2) *Non-conspicuousness:* since we wished to observe "normal" processes of developing acquaintance, it was desirable to avoid both undue self-consciousness on the part of subjects, as they participated in the data-gathering process, and undue visibility of the project on the campus, which might affect various aspects of the getting-acquainted process in ways that our research procedures could not handle. These two considerations had, in some respects, opposed implications, and in any case more specific ground rules were needed.

There follows a list of all the criteria, other than that of strangership, upon which the selection of subjects was based, together with a brief rationale of each.

1. *Sex of subjects.* Since, with the exception of occasional part-time research assistants, all the research staff were men, and since there were obvious advantages in providing easy accessibility between research staff and the subjects, it was necessary to have men rather than women as subjects. Two research assistants lived in the basement of the student house throughout the period of study.

2. *Class status of subjects.* The initial plan was to select subjects from the incoming class of freshmen. The Dean of Students wisely advised us to select transfer students instead, on the grounds that freshmen are more frequently involved in "trouble"—either academic or disciplinary—than older students and that, however unjustifiably, the project might be held responsible by parents or others for any such problems. Hence all of our subjects were either sophomores or juniors, having had one or two years at other colleges or universities.

3. *Age of subjects.* Only with regard to veteran status did subjects' ages influence their selection, and only during the second year. The age-range could have been kept more homogeneous by excluding veterans altogether, but our requirement of selecting from our applicants those who were most certain to be strangers made it impossible to exclude them. Thus the first population, which was selected without regard to veteran status, included two veterans whose ages (24 and 25) averaged four or five years more than those of the others. During the second year, difficulties of matching the first population on a considerable number of variables made it necessary to include four rather than two veterans; two of these four, however, were no older than three or four of the nonveterans, whose ages averaged about 20 years, as in the first year.

Professional interests. All of both populations were enrolled either in the College of Literature, Science, and the Arts or in the College of Engineering. Many of them had not yet chosen a major field of study, on arriving, and in any case it would not have been possible to match the two populations on the basis of within-college majors. During Year I (1954–55), there were 10 Arts College students and 7 Engineering students; the comparable numbers in Year II were 9 and 8.

Country of birth. Since the research problem had been formulated as being in part a study of the consequences of communication, it was decided to include only those whose native tongue was English. Thus foreign students were automatically excluded.

Ethnic and religious background. In the interests of maximum homogeneity, both groups would have been chosen from a single ethnic-religious population. It soon became apparent, however, that both this criterion and that of strangership could be met only by selecting native-born, white Protestants. It was feared, however, that the advantages of obtaining homogeneity of this kind might well be outweighed by possible misgivings—both on the part of subjects themselves and by others—as to the investigators' reasons for "discrimination." Rightly or wrongly, therefore, it was decided to forego this degree of homogeneity, and thus obtain a reasonably "random" population of subjects. The only ethnic and religious criteria that were applied were to the effect that either two or more or none at all from any racial or religious category should be selected. The resulting distributions were as follows:

	Year I	Year II
Protestants	8	9
Catholics	4	4
Jews	5	4
Total	17	17

No applications were received from nonwhites, except for one Negro, who could not be accepted according to this criterion.

In sum, each of the two populations consisted of seventeen single men, native-born white Protestants, Catholics, and Jews; most of them were nineteen to twenty-one years of age, but two or three in each population were some four years older; roughly half were pursuing liberal arts courses, and half engineering courses. Each year, applications were considered in order of their receipt, and the men chosen represented the first possible combination of seventeen men who met our criteria. In addition, of course, the men themselves had their own criteria: they *wanted* to live in the house, either because of the "fraternity-like conditions" which had been described to them in our initial letter of inquiry, or because of the opportunity to save approximately $100 in room rent, or for both reasons.

House Arrangements

Characteristics of the house. Virtually our first problem, once the project had been decided upon, was to find a house that would be suitable by several criteria. As to *size,* we had early concluded that the range of fifteen to twenty was most desirable; too small a population could result in too little variance of response, and too little opportunity for subgroup formation, whereas a population of more than twenty would impose inordinate time demands in those many instances in which we would need detailed responses from each subject concerning each other subject.

We thought relative *independence* from other living groups to be, also, an important criterion. For this reason we did not take advantage of an opportunity to put our subjects into one wing of a University dormitory—an arrangement which would have resulted in their being dispersed among scores of other students for many purposes, including their meals. And so the availability of independent cooking and eating facilities became an added criterion.[1] We needed, too, a common living room which would invite informal camaraderie and also accommodate regular meetings of all House members.

We needed, also, quarters in which there would be semi-separate living space for two research assistants—partly because of sheer convenience, and partly because of the advantage of frequent opportunities for the research assistants to familiarize themselves with day-to-day events. Our quarters, further, should not be too far from the center of campus, and they should, if possible, contain at least some rooms large enough to accommodate two or more students, so that we might study the possible effects of the proximity of roommates to each other. And, finally, we needed quarters that could be rented at a figure that the project budget could afford.

Just such a house was in fact found, though not easily or quickly.

---

[1] As things turned out, there was one subject in each population (#15 in Year I and #37 in Year II) who for financial reasons found it necessary to work outside the House for his meals. Otherwise all subjects, both years, had their meals in the House dining room.

It accommodated seventeen men, nine on the second floor and eight on the third; on each floor there were one or more single, double, and triple rooms—three singles, four doubles, and two triples in all. On the ground floor there were a large living room, a dining room, kitchen and pantry, and a reception room. Two basement rooms accommodated two research assistants. Furnishings were comfortable and adequate but not elaborate.

Induction of new arrivals. All the men arrived, by request, at almost the same hour, eight days before the beginning of University classes, in time for new-student orientation and registration. Following a greeting by members of the research staff, each of them (in Year I) drew a number which served to determine both his room assignment and his roommates, if any. We explained, at the outset, that these were only initial assignments, and that they would be free at any time to make any changes that they could agree upon. (In neither year was any such change in fact made.) The procedure was exactly the same the second year, except that (for reasons described in Chapter 11) pre-arranged room assignments were posted.

At a meeting of all members on the third day, the following announcements were made, interspersed with a good deal of discussion.

1. Students would be subject to all general University regulations, specifically including those applying to fraternities. Although the Project Director would, in a sense, be held accountable for infractions, there would be no snooping and no punishments on his part; he would, if he felt that the good name of the House was being jeopardized, limit himself to warnings, private or before the House group, as he might see fit. (Except occasionally, on the score of cleanliness, no such warnings were in fact ever issued.)

2. Students were free, within these limits, to make their own House rules or to make none, though certain standards of cleanliness were required. They would be free to make such use as they pleased of the kitchen and dining facilities, or not to use them at all. (In each year is was soon decided to take advantage of the opportunity to purchase food supplies through the University at wholesale rates, to hire a cook, to share all expenses, and to do their own serving and dishwashing.)

3. Our time requirements (as they already knew, via previous correspondence) would never exceed five hours a week, and would

often be less. A weekly two-hour session, attended by all, was to be arranged at any time suitable to them; in addition, individual or small-group appointments would be made by each man, each week, with a member of the research staff. (These arrangements worked out, in fact, about as we had hoped; while there were occasional lapses by individuals in meeting their appointments, attendance was perfect at every one of thirty full-group meetings during the two years; no person was ever absent.)

4. The information that we needed from them would be openly gathered, and would be the same for all. It would consist mainly of responses to questionnaires, tests, and interviews. No observations of any kind would ever be recorded by staff members except in full view, and with subjects' full knowledge. (This promise was never violated, and post-project interviews with our subjects lent strong confidence in our belief that for the most part such misgivings as they might first have had were soon allayed.)

5. We stated that the purposes of our research (about which we correctly anticipated a good deal of curiosity) were those of understanding more about what goes on when strangers get acquainted with each other. We added that we could not divulge every detailed aspect of our purposes, lest such information influence their responses, but we also promised (1) either to answer their questions truthfully or to say frankly that we were not yet free to answer them; and (2) to give a complete, no-holds-barred reply to any and all questions *after* the project had been completed. (Such a session was in fact held, at the end of the second year's data-gathering. It was attended by nearly all the second set of subjects, for whom interest was still fresh, and by nearly half the first set. There were enough expressions of surprise, following our disclosures at this session, to reinforce our belief that subjects' responses had not been seriously affected by any consensualized guesses as to our specific research purposes.)

The regular weekly meetings. The weekly two-hour sessions were planned with various purposes in mind. Except for a few weeks at the very end of each semester (when the evening sessions were used exclusively for data-gathering), their invariable *general* purpose was to facilitate acquaintance, in the sense of providing planned opportunities for increasing each subject's store of information about other subjects. Toward this end four general sorts of procedures were employed.

1. House-relevant business was discussed, usually moderated by the House chairman, sometimes by a staff member. In either case our aim was never to interfere except for the purpose of stimulating further expression of opinion by subjects. Our objective was not to observe or measure the differential degrees of their participation, but rather so to arrange things that every subject would give all others the maximum possible amount of information about himself, in some sort of problem-oriented setting.

2. Presentations were made by invited speakers, usually on such controversial topics as politics or religion.[2] Our guests were asked to "stir things up" during the course of their remarks so that as many subjects as possible would be motivated to express themselves on the issue of the evening.

3. Occasional experiments were conducted—not only in the sense that pre- and post-measures of orientations were obtained (which was standard procedure) but in the further sense that specific manipulations, planned with predicted outcomes in mind, were introduced. The aim here was not just to stir things up, but to test specific predictions. One of these experiments is reported in Chapter 4. These experiments, too, were acquaintance-facilitating; in every instance they were designed to induce interaction by which subjects would give each other new information about each other.

4. Acquaintance-facilitating devices of various other sorts were also introduced, especially in the early weeks. These included games in which partners were systematically rotated, and pre-arranged role-taking activities.

In each year such a meeting was held during fifteen of the sixteen weeks of data-gathering, which ended just before the beginning of the final examinations.

Staff members' roles. Most staff members (usually numbering six or seven) attended evening meetings. The two research assistants who were in residence took their meals in their own quarters, but spent a good deal of time in the common rooms on the ground

[2] We wish once more to thank Professors Samuel Eldersveld, Roger Heyns, Elton McNeil, Leslie White, Representative George Sallade, Father Chris Keeler, Doctors Leslie Beach, Leonard Lansky, and Herbert Saltzstein, and Messrs. Eugene Abravanel and Fritz Mosher for their helpfulness and skill in arousing the active participation of House members in their appearances at one or more of the evening meetings.

floor of the House. None of us entered the second or third floors, where the men's rooms were, except following a plainly audible request to enter. Staff members were occasionally invited to have a meal with the men. Each of the resident staff members was likely to have some dealings—perhaps casual, perhaps in connection with matters of housekeeping, or often in connection with data-gathering —with most of the men every day. The rest of us, in general, visited the House at least two or three times each week.

We attempted to maintain a stance of friendly objectivity. We carefully avoided expressing any opinion that might bear upon any of the attitude responses that were at any time to be obtained.[3] We refused to discuss any House member, in personal terms, in the presence of any other. To occasional complaints brought by one House member concerning another (generally regarding noise, or cleanliness) we routinely replied that, within the limits permitted by University regulations, these were problems for House members to handle, either formally or informally.

Nature of the Data

In view of the general formulation described in Chapter 2, our basic data had to do with our threefold category of orientations. We shall first describe these and then go on to others.

Meanwhile we must note that in several instances our second year's instruments differed markedly from comparable ones used the first year. Such changes represent, without exception, a deliberate change based upon the conviction—which in turn was based upon a year's experience (both with administering the instruments and with analyzing responses to them)—that a significant improvement was possible. In each such instance we were faced, anew, with the dilemma we have already mentioned: to sacrifice exact replication or to sacrifice known improvability. In almost every case we chose the former alternative, and hence we must often describe separately our first and second years' instruments.

[3] We took a certain satisfaction in the discovery, during the meeting following the end of the second year's data-gathering at which we "told all," that in at least some areas we had been fairly successful in keeping our silence. To the question, for example, "What are you guys' political preferences?", asked during this meeting, we replied by asking them to guess. A considerable majority guessed that all or most of us were Republicans—a highly inaccurate estimate.

Measures of Attraction

General liking, year I. Our basic concern was to obtain an index of general, undifferentiated, personal attraction on the part of each subject toward every other one. Our first procedure—necessarily decided upon before the arrival of our subjects, and unchangeable throughout the first year—involved both ranking of all other *S*s and dividing them into three categories. Instructions for the first set of responses (on the third day) were given to each subject in the course of an individual interview, during which assurances of confidentiality were given, and the use of code numbers explained. The first week's instructions were as follows:

> Here is a stack of 17 cards, on each of which appears the name (on one side) and the code number (on the other) of one man in the House. First, remove your own card, and then shuffle the cards. Next, sort them into three piles, labeled "Prefer," "Do Not Prefer," and "Undecided." In the first pile put all the cards of the group members that you *like;* in the third pile the cards of those that you *dislike* or have *negative feelings* about; in the middle pile those that you feel *neutral* or *undecided* about, or don't know well enough to put in either of the other piles. Then take the cards in each pile, separately, and rank order them in terms of *how much you like each man* (even if, in the case of the middle pile, it's only a guess). Finally, look over the cards to make sure that they are arranged in the way that you really want them. Leave them with the code numbers showing, not the names, so that I can copy them.

During later weeks, when subjects had become familiar with the procedure, they simplified it by inserting into prepared blanks (numbered 1–16) the code numbers of all other *S*s in rank order of preference, and drawing lines to mark off the three categories.

Responses were made by all *S*s once or more each week except for Weeks 3, 4, and 10.

General attraction, year II. Our second year's procedure was such as to yield identical results in terms of rank orders of expressed attraction toward all other *S*s, but differed from that of the first year in these ways. (1) Instructions were phrased in terms of general "favorableness of feeling" rather than of "liking." This change seemed to bring our operations into closer correspondence with our conceptual definitions; also, it promised to have the advantage of permitting responses to be influenced by any kind of interpersonal feelings (for example, admiration as well as merely personal liking) which were in fact operative. (2) Absolute ratings from which ranks could be derived were obtained, as illustrated below. Additional information, with no loss, was thus obtained, making it possible, in particular, to detect instances of large differences between adjacent ranks, which had previously been obscured. (In fact, however, such large differences rarely appeared.) (3) The neutral category, which turned out to be of little value, was abandoned as such, in terms of the favorable-unfavorable continuum shown below. Instructions, throughout the second year, were as follows.

This questionnaire deals with how you feel toward other men living in the House. First, look at this scale:

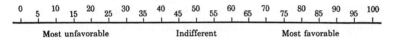

In using this scale, you would assign a value of 100 to a person that you feel *as favorable as possible* toward; a value of 0 to any one that you feel as *unfavorable as possible* toward; and a score of 50 to a man toward whom you feel *completely indifferent,* neither favorable nor unfavorable. These are only illustrations, of course; you may not want to use any of these particular values, and you probably will want to use some numbers not divisible by 5—like 36 or 79. . . . At the left of the page you will find a column of the code numbers of all the men in the house, with a blank following each code number. First, insert an X after your own code number, and then insert in each blank whatever number, from 0 to 100, represents the *degree to which you feel favorable or unfavorable* toward the person for whom the code number stands; use the list of names and code numbers, to make sure that you have the right number for the right man.[4] *One further point:* Do NOT assign the same number to any two men; if any two seem to be the same to you, separate them by one point.

Ratings were made by all *S*s during each of the 16 weeks, except for Week 9.

Usage of general-attraction responses, both years. For most

[4] During the first three weeks of Year II, photographs of every subject, together with his name, were also supplied to respondents, in order to insure recognition in every case.

purposes (and henceforth unless otherwise noted) the A-to-B rank order of attraction provided the basic datum for analyses involving the attraction variable. This usage had two considerable advantages: (1) it provided comparability for the responses made by the two populations; and (2) it circumvented the disadvantage, in the second year's data, that subjects differed quite considerably in the range of the 100-point scale that they used. To have used raw ratings would have introduced a good deal of inter-subject non-comparability.

Reported clique membership, both years. Given continued opportunity for acquaintance, and for inter-subject observation, behavioral consequences of varying degrees of attraction are to be expected, and they should be reportable by others. In particular, varying degrees of reciprocated attraction on the part of two or more persons should correspond, roughly at least, to the amounts of time that they are observed to spend together. By way of obtaining an independent measure of attraction, we therefore decided to take advantage of the fact that our subjects were constant observers of each other. In each of the two years, all Ss responded, in writing, to the following written instructions, during at least three (early, middle, and late) weeks.

> Divide the 17 men in the House into groups, as you think they divide themselves into groups. Make any number of groups that you want; put as many men in any group as you want. If you think a particular man belongs in two or more groups, put him in both or all of them.

Since we shall be interested, for the most part, in person-to-person relationships rather than in attractiveness as a property of individuals, these responses were tabulated in matrix fashion. The number of respondents (excluding self-mentions) who assign any pair of persons to the same group may be taken as an index of the attractiveness of those persons to each other—but not, of course, of the degree of attraction by either, alone, toward the other. (When any respondent included the same pair in two overlapping groups, only a single frequency was counted for that respondent, so that no pair could receive a count greater than 15.) The validity of the index rests upon the common-sense assumptions that observable association is voluntary on the part of both members of a pair, and that voluntary association is equally observable on the part of all pairs.

Attraction responses as related to reported clique membership. As noted in Chapter 5, we have developed a procedure for combining the ranks of attraction that the members of any pair of Ss assign to each other, to indicate the level of attraction between them *as a property of the pair*. Henceforth we shall in fact make use of the index thus derived, rather than the index based upon group reports just described, in our analyses of pair attraction as related to other variables. We shall stop to justify this procedure (before presenting the analyses, in subsequent chapters) by showing that the two rather different indices of pair attraction are closely related, particularly on later acquaintance, when the group reports follow ample opportunity for Ss' observation of one another.

Table 3.1 shows that the same pairs of Ss tend to be identified by both indices as being at about the same level of pair attraction— significantly so, even after only two weeks of acquaintance, in the second population. And the prediction that pairs *very high* (in about the top quarter) in attraction according to the index of combined ranks will be high according to the group-report index —a prediction of special importance for our theory—is well supported; the χ^2 values for the four distributions in Table 3.1 range from 12.54 (Year I, Week 2) to 71.84 (Year II, Week 14), with 1 df, if attraction pair scores are dichotomized between 64 and 65.

Henceforth, therefore, we shall use the index based upon combined ranks, since on early acquaintance the group-report index is based upon too limited observation to be dependable, and since on late acquaintance the two indices yield essentially the same results.

Attribution of favorable and unfavorable traits, Year II. During each of five scattered weeks in the second year, Ss responded to sets of adjectives selected from the Gough list (1955) by checking each adjective deemed applicable to each of the other Ss. The check-lists used for this purpose at Weeks 2 and 14 included 180 adjectives, of which only 60 were used during the intervening weeks. Equal numbers of favorable and unfavorable adjectives (as reported by Gough) were included in both the longer and the shorter list. (See Appendix II for further details.) A count of the number of favorable or of unfavorable adjectives checked as apply-

Table 3.1. FREQUENCIES WITH WHICH EACH PAIR OF Ss IS MENTIONED BY REMAINING 15 Ss AS BELONGING IN THE SAME SUBGROUP, AT FOUR LEVELS OF ATTRACTION FOR THE SAME PAIRS, AS MEASURED BY PAIR MEMBERS' OWN ATTRACTION RESPONSES

Attraction pair score [a]	N of mentions, Year I					N of mentions, Year II				
	0–1	2–3	4–7	≧8	Total	0–1	2–3	4–7	≧8	Total
Week 2										
1–20 (high)	4	7	2	6	19	0	3	7	9	19
21–64	6	6	5	1	18	3	6	6	4	19
65–128	12	12	6	1	31	10	11	6	1	28
129–256 (low)	34	31	3	0	68	41	21	8	0	70
TOTAL	56	56	16	8	136	54	41	27	14	136
	$\chi^2 = 3.67; p < .06$ [b]					$\chi^2 = 19.83; p < .001$ [b]				
Week 14										
1–20 (high)	3	5	5	8	21	0	2	10	6	18
21–64	12	5	1	0	18	4	5	13	0	22
65–128	18	10	3	2	33	12	10	3	0	25
129–256 (low)	55	8	1	0	64	54	17	0	0	71
TOTAL	88	28	10	10	136	70	34	26	6	136
	$\chi^2 = 22.17; p < .001$ [b]					$\chi^2 = 34.08; p < .001$ [b]				

[a] See pp. 72–74 for description of these scores.
[b] Distributions are dichotomized as nearly equally as possible, and χ^2 is computed with 1 df. See Appendices IV and V concerning the use of χ^2 and an N of 136 for significance tests.

ing to any individual—either by a single respondent or by all others, summed—may be considered an index of that person's attractiveness, in terms of his personal characteristics, relative to others'. In the language of Chapter 2, it is a cognitive rather than a directly cathective index.

Measures of Attitude

In preparing our instruments for obtaining attitude responses, our most serious problems had to do with the selection (in advance, for the most part) of attitude objects. The specific subproblems confronting us were these. (1) Diversity rather than uniformity of response to any single item was required, since analysis presupposes variance. (2) Attitudes of importance rather than of indifference to respondents should be measured, since (hypothetically) system forces are not otherwise brought into play (see p. 12). (3) A wide range of content should be sampled, if we were to catch in our net a sufficient number of attitude objects that would be of importance to all Ss. (4) The form (and the simplicity) of the response should be such that respondents could estimate others' responses, as well as making their own, without undue difficulty or cost in time.

There follow descriptions of the major instruments [5] which were used.

Families of specific issues, Year I. The criteria we have described led us to decide, before the arrival of the first-year subjects, upon seven general areas within each of which responses to five specific kinds of issues would be obtained repeatedly during the data-gathering period. Decisions regarding both the general areas and the specific issues followed conversations with students, faculty, and University officials whom we considered knowledgeable about the local scene, as well as a perusal of various published studies of student attitudes. The seven general areas were as follows:

> House policies
> University practices
> Public affairs (domestic and international)
> Racial and ethnic relations
> Religion
> Sex and family
> Interpersonal relationships

It was further decided to present, under each of the 35 specific issues, five alternative positions; the resulting 175 statements are reproduced in Appendix I. Ss responded to each of the 35 issues both by rank-ordering the five alternatives in terms of acceptability, and by indicating one or more alternatives regarded as acceptable. Some of the sets of five alternatives relevant to each specific issue were rationally scaled (e.g., all-most-many-few-no), and there were

[5] The following list does not include all of those that were in fact used to obtain data, but it does include all of those yielding data which have been analyzed. Others (in the main improvised for on-the-spot use) either seemed, by inspection, to be of questionable usefulness or were sufficiently similar to those here reported as not to seem likely to add to our information; hence responses to them have not been analyzed.

virtually no "errors" in ranking these sets of alternatives. Other sets, however, were not so scaled, and in a few cases there was little uniformity in the dimensionality reflected by individual rank-orderings (see Coombs, 1952). We decided to include some sets of statements not subject to rational scaling because (1) with respect to a few of the 35 issues we felt that any single dimensionality would be too limited to arouse very high levels of concern among all of our subjects; and (2) we were less interested in our subjects' "absolute" positions with regard to any issue than in person-to-person similarities and discrepancies in attitude. The procedures by which we computed indices for the latter, with respect to each of the 35 issues, are described on pages 77–78; and the indices of person-to-person agreement concerning the total list of 35 issues are described in Appendix III.

Wide-ranging specific attitudes, Year II. Preliminary analysis (between January and August of 1955) of our first year's data was in some respects disappointing. In particular, we became convinced that our range of attitude content, as imposed by the scheme of seven families on specific issues, had been unnecessarily restricted. We concluded, in the first place, that we had needlessly sacrificed one of our most important criteria, according to which as many as possible of the attitude objects should be of high importance to all subjects. There was pretty convincing evidence that for some of our first-year Ss virtually none of the issues that we had selected were of very great importance. The range appeared to be too limited.

Our first means of attempting to improve things involved the dropping of the scheme of families of issues. We substituted for it 85 specific items, representing much greater diversity than the seven families of issues, and deliberately assembled to represent as wide a range as possible. The list included such diverse items as these: believing in a life after death; getting high grades; not having to conform to the opinions of others; having parties as a House, on week-ends; being in a school which does not require military training; mathematics as a major; D. D. Eisenhower as President; being in the same house or dormitory with Negro students; playing card games; listening to classical music. (The full list, together with instructions, is reproduced in Appendix I.)

We might have taken, as indices of discrepancy (either perceived or actual), simply the arithmetic difference between the two responses to be compared. In fact, we developed an index not based upon the assumption of equal intervals between adjacent response values, and which was weighted by the extremeness—corresponding, roughly at least, to the variable of "importance" (as described on p. 12) of response. (See Appendix III for full details.) Our reason for this weighting was simply that the testing of our hypotheses required it.

The total battery of 85 items was responded to only twice, at Week −1 (by mail, before the subjects arrived in Ann Arbor) and at Week 15. At repeated intervals, subjects responded to one or more of the items during the intervening weeks, at times determined by events considered likely to have effects upon specified attitudes—in particular, events in connection with the weekly evening meetings.

General values, Year II. Our second means of attempting to obtain attitude responses more closely in keeping with our own criteria stemmed from our conclusion, following preliminary analyses, that our first year's items had been too exclusively specific ones (as well as too restricted in range). After all, we reasoned, *post hoc,* there was little reason to anticipate that *any* single, specific item would meet all our criteria, and surely little probability that many of them would do so. The most promising solution to the problem of too great specificity lay, we thought, in that particular species of attitude that has come to be known as a *value,* which may be thought of as a widely generalized attitude, applicable to many specific situations and objects. And so we devised two instruments which, we hoped, would in some degree remedy the shortcoming.

The first of these consisted of the following ten items, assembled from various sources, of rather general, goal-like nature.

a. being successful in financial arrangements
b. being well liked by other persons
c. being successful in your family life (wife, children)
d. being successful in your chosen occupation
e. being intellectually capable and increasing your knowledge
f. living in accordance with religious principles
g. being able to help other persons in this world
h. being a normal, well adjusted person
i. working cooperatively with people
j. doing a thorough and careful job

Instructions were to "rank the ten goals in the order of their importance to you." Responses to these items were made twice, in Weeks 0 and 13, but estimates of others' ranks were not obtained. The Spearman rank-order coefficient of correlation was used as an index of similarity.

The well-known list of six values suggested by Spranger (1928) also seemed to us a promising source of the kind of information that we needed. We considered the use of the Allport-Vernon-Lindzey *Study of Values* (1951), but decided upon an alternative procedure that would simplify the task of obtaining from each respondent estimates of the value positions of all other subjects.[6] This procedure, as shown in the instructions reproduced below, consisted of obtaining a rank-ordering, by each *S*, of the importance of the six values to himself and also his estimates of how each other *S* would respond to the same task.

> Below are listed six important areas, or interests, in life. People differ in the emphasis or degree of importance that they attribute to each of these interests.
>
> Rank order the following interests in terms of *their importance to you*. Insert "1" in the blank before whichever one of the six is most important to you, "2" before the next most important one, and so on down to "6" for the one that is least important to you.
>
> ——*Theoretical:* Interested primarily in empirical, critical or rational matters—observing and reasoning, ordering and systematizing, discovering truths.
> ——*Economic:* Interested primarily in that which is useful and practical, especially the practical affairs of the business world —judge things by their tangible utility.
> ——*Aesthetic:* Interested primarily in beauty, in form and harmony for its own sake—an artistic interpretation of life.
> ——*Social:* Interested primarily in other human beings—human relationships and love are very important.
> ——*Political:* Interested primarily in power and influence—leadership and competition are key-words descriptive of such an interest.

[6] The AVL *Study of Values* was in fact administered to all *S*s, but only for the purpose of comparing the test scores with rank-order responses, as described above. The test booklets, however, were lost or inadvertently destroyed after they had been completed. This was the only instance in which any data were lost.

———*Religious:* Interested primarily in the satisfaction and meaning to be derived from religious experiences—interested in relating oneself to the unity of the universe as a whole.

Attributions of Orientations to Others

Such responses, for reasons described in Chapter 2, were essential for testing hypotheses derived from our formulation, and with rare exceptions Ss's own attitude responses were always accompanied by estimates of all others' responses. There follow brief descriptions of the procedures by which this kind of data was obtained.

General liking, Year I. Our initial intention had been to obtain estimates (beginning after a reasonable period of acquaintance) from each S of every other S's degree of attraction toward the remaining 16 Ss—a total of 256 estimates—at frequent intervals. The difficulties of the task proved considerable; there were problems of insufficient acquaintance in the earliest weeks, problems of time demands, and problems of distaste for the task on the part of respondents. A series of compromises was therefore made (some of them ill advised), with the result that the following estimates were in fact obtained.

Week 1: rank orders attributed by each S to his two best-liked, his two least-liked, and two intermediate choices regarding the 16 other Ss

Week 5: the total set of 256 estimates, rank-ordered by each S as attributed to each of the other 16 Ss regarding all others

Weeks 6, 8, 10: rank orders attributed by each S to each other S, with the limitation that if the estimatee was judged to rank the estimator at 5, for example, only the first five of the estimatee's ranks needed to be indicated, etc.

Week 14: the total set of 256 estimates, but in terms of a three-category system (favorable, neutral, unfavorable) rather than in terms of ranks attributed to each estimatee

These estimates, as already implied, specifically included judgments of attraction toward the estimator himself.

General attraction, Year II. We decided upon a new set of compromises for obtaining estimates in Year II. First, each rating (on the 100-point scale) of attraction toward another S was accompanied, routinely, by an estimate of that S's reciprocated rating of the estimator, on the same scale. These estimates differed from the respondent's own ratings only in that he was not forbidden to assign the same rating to more than one person—a procedure that resulted in some ties when ranks of perceived attraction toward the estimator were computed. It was necessary to use ranks rather than raw ratings as indices of perceived reciprocation of attraction, because respondents differed a good deal in the ranges of the 100-point scale that they made use of. For certain purposes, however, simple discrepancies between an S's rating of attraction toward another S and his rating of reciprocation from that S could be used, on the assumption that the respondent was making use of the same kind of scale, subjectively, in making both kinds of response.

Second, we made a radical innovation for obtaining estimates of attraction by a second person toward a third (estimated B-to-C attraction), via a sampling procedure. Beginning with Week 2, each S made 12 preselected B-to-C estimates, as determined by a random drawing from the total population of the 120 pairs, excluding the estimator himself, in the population; the 12 estimates included both the B-to-C and the C-to-B attractions on the part of six pairs. For each S, as estimator, three different samples were drawn, in such manner that each of all 136 pairs was included in at least 2 of the 51 set of pairs (17 Ss $\times$ 3 samples). Responses were made in successive weeks to the three samples, and then the same cycle was repeated in the next three weeks, and so on for four full cycles. Estimates were made not only in terms of ratings on the 100-point scale but also in terms of quartiles—that is to say, A estimated that B's attraction toward C was in the highest, second, third, or lowest quarter of B's attractions toward all Ss.

Estimates of others' attitudes, both years. Except as otherwise noted in connection with reports of findings in later chapters, instructions for estimating others' attitudes were always of the general form, "Now indicate your best judgment of how each of the other men in the House would respond" to the same item, or set of items.

Personality Variables

Our basic propositions do not include personality variables, as distinct from attitudinal ones. We were aware, nevertheless, that individuals almost certainly differ in several ways relevant to the operation of individual systems of orientation. Our subjects might well differ, for example, with respect to thresholds for tolerating strain, or in characteristic manner of attempting to minimize it. Quite apart from these considerations, moreover, the more or less persisting personal properties that our subjects brought to the research setting were surely among the crucial determinants of the kinds of interpersonal relationships that developed among them. We were thus in the position of needing measures of personality variables not for hypothesis-testing but rather for exploratory purposes.

With the advantages of hindsight, we believe that our personality data should have been more complete, and more systematically obtained, in spite of our understandable reluctance to take time from an overcrowded schedule of data-gathering to obtain information the possible uses for which we could only guess at. Were we to repeat the research, we should feel much more confident about several ways in which such data could be used, in hypothesis-testing fashion (see Chap. 7). To this extent, at least, certain gains have accrued from our purely exploratory use of personality measures.

There follow brief statements about the kinds of personality data that we did obtain.

1. *Authoritarianism* (the 30-item F-scale). All Ss in both populations responded to this instrument, which was scored in the standard manner (Adorno *et al.*, 1950). It was administered only once each year, at Week 7.

2. *Conformity* (a set of 27 items from the Minnesota Multiphasic Inventory). Each S's score was the number of items answered in the conforming direction, under forced-choice, true-false instructions.

3. *Projection* (a set of 18 items from the MMPI). Score was the number of items answered in the projective direction, as above. (These two sets of items were interspersed in a single list, which was responded to in Week 10 of each year.)

4. *Need Achievement* (from coded responses to four Thematic Apperception Test pictures; see Atkinson, 1958). Score was the number of themes in each S's story that were coded as indicating n Ach.

5. *Need Affiliation* (from coded responses to the same two pictures). Score was the number of themes in each S's stories that were

coded as indicating *n* Aff.[7] Responses were obtained in Week 10 of each year.

In addition to these standard instruments, we also obtained personality-relevant information from adjective check-lists (see p. 35) and from certain response tendencies revealed in attitude and attraction responses (see Chap. 6).[8]

Other Data

We also obtained many other sorts of data, of secondary importance for purposes of hypothesis-testing but such, we anticipated, as to be of supplementary value. Most of the categories of data not referred to above have never been analyzed,[9] and other categories will be referred to later in more or less incidental fashion. There follows a list of these other categories, most of which are not again referred to in this monograph.

1. *Sociometric approaches to attraction variables.* At irregular intervals we included such questions as these: With whom would you most like to study for an examination? to participate in a bull session? to work in the kitchen? to talk over a personal problem? Who would make the best House leaders?

2. *Respect,* as an object-specific form of attraction not necessarily related to personal liking. We used such questions as these: How sound and reasonable do you feel that each of the other men's arguments would be about ————? How competent do you feel that each of the other men is to assess the various aspects of this issue as a basis for arriving at a reasonable judgment about it?

3. *Common relevance* of a specified attitude object (see p. 13). Such questions were sometimes phrased in terms of "each of the other men," individually, and sometimes in terms of "other men,"

[7] Dr. William Morrison kindly scored the story-responses to the TAT pictures.

[8] Our most serious lapse, the result of a misunderstanding among members of the research staff, was our failure to obtain responses to the Strong *Vocational Interest Blank* in either year. Its appropriateness for our purpose seems obvious, and the relatively few vocation-relevant items included in our 85-item inventory of Year II are not an adequate substitute. In addition, we might have made good use of the masculinity-femininity scores derived from responses to this instrument.

[9] We hope later to publish separate articles reporting further analyses. This alternative seems to us preferable to a further delay in publishing our findings concerning the central hypotheses of the study.

in general. An example of the latter type is this: To what extent would your relationship to other men be affected by their feelings and attitudes toward the topic of ———?

4. *Frequency of communication*—sometimes regarding a specified topic, sometimes "in general," regardless of content.

5. *Personal familiarity.* We used, at times, a five-point "scale of acquaintance" ("I feel I know him extremely-very-pretty well, a little, hardly at all"); and at times a score representing the number of correct answers to these six questions about each of the other individuals: What is his former college? Does he smoke, and if so what brand? What is his middle name? What kind of job did he have last summer? What type of job does his father have? Does he have a steady girl, and if so what is her first name?

6. *Extra-House reference groups.* Questions of two kinds were occasionally asked. The first concerned content: How would parents, members of various religious, political, or other groups "typically" reply to an item already answered by the respondent? The second had to do with the degree of influence imputed; e.g., How competent do you think each of the groups or persons mentioned would be in coming to decisions about ———?

7. *Certainty of estimates.* Occasionally in Year I and quite regularly in Year II, each estimate of another S's attitude response was accompanied by a rating of the estimator's certainty (very-fairly-only a little-not at all certain of this estimate).

8. *The House members as a group.* Ss were queried in various ways, during both years, as to their attraction toward the group as a whole. For example: "How would you feel about living with the other House members for another semester?" "From the point of view of congeniality of the men in this House, how fortunate do you feel that you have been in the selection of these men?" Occasionally, also, we asked Ss to attribute both modal attitude responses and modal attraction responses to the entire group.

9. *Cognitive aspects of attitudes.* Because (as suggested on pp. 5–6), we recognized the possibility that agreement or disagreement on certain aspects of an attitude object might be just as significantly involved in systems of orientation as agreement or disagreement in over-all evaluations of those objects, from time to time we introduced a set of cognitive items relevant to each of ten attitude objects about which Ss made repeated responses. Ss both rated (on the six-point scale) and ranked ("for relative importance for your

over-all point of view about the topic") each of six cognitive items relevant to each of the ten issues. The questionnaire was introduced by the comment that "Most things about which people have attitudes are many-sided; there are many angles, or aspects, or ways of looking at the same thing. With regard to each of the topics below, several of these various sides, or aspects, are noted." For example, with regard to the topic, "Having sexual relationships before marriage," the following cognitive items were presented:

> the possibility of pregnancy
> religious teachings on the subject
> the enjoyment of intimacy with some one you are fond of
> the possibility of "entangling alliances" afterwards
> possible effects on a later marriage with some one else
> healthy expression of biological urges

10. *Miscellaneous attitude objects.* On several occasions, in each year, we took advantage of immediate and unanticipated events to obtain attitude responses and estimates of others' responses. Representative events of this kind were a misunderstanding about the cook's wages, and a suddenly announced "health inspection" by city authorities.

11. *Relationships with research staff.* In addition to the two research assistants in residence and the project director, there were at different times either three or four other assistants with whom subjects became reasonably well acquainted, especially via interviews and consultations about completing questionnaires. Certain questions were therefore asked about Ss' feelings about all staff members. Code numbers were used; the data were gathered by a faculty member who happened to live next door to the House; [10] and Ss were promised that the sealed envelopes containing their responses would not be opened before the final termination of the research project.

Such were the kinds of data that we obtained, and the conditions under which we obtained them. Certain further details, especially those involving the processing of raw data and those describing analytic procedures, will be added at appropriate moments as we present our findings in the next few chapters.

[10] Professor Stephen B. Withey, to whom we are most grateful for this help.

The remaining chapters of this monograph are devoted primarily to reports of our research findings. Because we have occasionally propounded somewhat unusual questions, we have taken pains, as each set of data is presented, to describe explicitly both the nature of those data and our procedures in analyzing them. If the latter have sometimes been unconventional, we have at least tried to be conservative in assessing the significance of our findings. In our frequent use of χ^2 analyses, we have without exception made corrections for continuity when there is but one degree of freedom, and all p values are reported in terms of two-tailed tests, even when explicitly stated predictions are being tested. Otherwise—excepted as noted in the immediate contexts of our several analyses—we believe that our analytic procedures have been standard ones.

PART TWO

System
Balance

In Chapters 2 and 3, which deal with individual and with two-person systems, respectively, we present the results of testing some predictions directly derived from our hypotheses concerning system balance. Before turning, in subsequent chapters, to the consideration of certain preconditions, consequences, and associated conditions of system balance, it seems wise to indicate the degree to which our data provide support for our most basic hypotheses, at varying stages of our subjects' acquaintance with each other.

Since we have argued that intrapersonal tendencies toward balance constitute an essential mechanism for the maintenance of multiperson balance, we shall begin with questions about the prevalence of balanced individual systems. And since our hypotheses concerning balance in collective systems can be adequately tested, for present purposes, by considering only two-person systems, we shall defer till later the consideration of larger collective systems.

Individual Systems _____4

The *general hypothesis* with reference to which the data in this chapter have been selected is derived from our formulation, in Chapter 2, concerning the properties of balanced individual systems: the stronger a given A-to-B positive attraction, the lesser the perceived discrepancy on A's part between his own and B's attitudes toward X. And since the forces toward individual balance are presumed not to vary with the intake of new information, but rather to determine, in constant ways, the processing of new information, we shall also test a prediction from this presumption: tendencies toward individual balance will not change from early to late acquaintance. Other, more specific predictions derived from this presumption, and from the general hypothesis, will be stated in the immediate context within which they are tested by a given body of data.

For reasons described on pages 54–56 we shall, in the latter part of the chapter (as well as in subsequent chapters), treat individual House members as objects of common orientation to pairs of persons not including those particular members; that is, for certain purposes a person will be treated as an X in Figure 2.1. In this chapter, therefore, we shall distinguish between House-member objects and nonperson objects, with regard to which individual systems are hypothetically balanced.

NONPERSON OBJECTS OF ATTITUDES

An essential datum for testing predictions derived from the general hypothesis of this chapter is an estimate by one *S* of another

S's attitude toward some object of the first *S*'s attitude. Many such estimates were obtained from both populations, but with an important difference which resulted in restricted usefulness of the first year's data. The specific objects of attitude responses and estimates, during Year I, were so selected as to be representative of seven different areas (see Appendix I) believed to be of importance to undergraduate males in their university, and about which considerable variance in attitude response was anticipated. Though both of these anticipations were more or less correct, the selection of attitude objects suffered in one respect. Nearly every one of the 35 items proved to be of adequate importance to one or more *S*s, but hardly any of the items were of sufficient importance to *all* subjects to meet the requirements of testing predictions derived from the present hypothesis.

That is, predictions of a relationship between attraction and perceived agreement are based upon the assumption of strain, which hypothetically varies as a function not only of degree of attraction but also as a function of object-valence (importance). Since any single object toward which we obtained attitude responses was of strong valence for only a few *S*s, and since each *S* was strongly attracted to only a few other *S*s, in a 2 × 2 × 2 table the number of entries in the cell labeled "high attraction, high valence of X, high estimated agreement" becomes exceedingly small—and not susceptible to tests of significance. For present purposes, therefore, the first-year estimates of agreement have not been employed. (See, however, Chapter 6, where they are used for other purposes.)

Analysis of the first-year data did not proceed far enough and fast enough so that the needed kinds of data could be obtained from the first population. Just too late we realized that what was needed was certain *general* objects of attitudes—objects so inclusive and so inescapable that no one could be indifferent to them, but with regard to which there would still be response variance. And then, to make assurance doubly sure, in the second round, we decided to obtain rank-orderings of these generalized attitude objects, the assumption being that any subject's first rank (in order of importance to him) could safely be taken as an object of strong valence.[1]

---

[1] Although we had obtained rank-orders of degree of importance among the seven "families of issues" during the first year, it proved impossible

During the second year, therefore, subjects rank-ordered two sets of "general values" (see pp. 39–41); in each case instructions were: "Rank order the following interests in terms of *their importance to you.*" It was only with regard to the set of six values proposed by Spranger (1928), however, that estimates of others' rank-orderings were made, each of them being defined in terms of brief statements, as shown on p. 40. The following findings, therefore, are based upon subjects' estimates of others' rank-orderings of these six values.

Indices of estimated agreement regarding the Spranger Values were rank-order correlations (*rho*) between the rankings of the estimator and those attributed to the person being estimated. In these terms, the prediction put to the test was this: correlations representing estimated agreement with highly attractive others will be significantly higher than those with less attractive others.

Tables 4.1 and 4.2 support this prediction. Since different subjects by no means use the same part of the total range in estimating agreement with others. Table 4.2 tests the prediction by relating all *S*s' *ranks* of agreement with all other *S*s to the same estimators' ranks of attraction toward the same 16 *S*s. Thus the prediction is supported by both relative and absolute indices of estimated agreement—somewhat more strongly by the former index.

Still other types of analysis provide support. (1) If individual rank-order correlations (*rho*) are calculated between rank of estimated agreement with and rank of attraction given to all other *S*s, 15 of the 17 coefficients are positive both at Week 2 and Week 14; the probabilities with which 15 or more of 17 coefficients would be positive are <.001.

(2) As an inclusive index of the relationship between tendency-to-be-liked and tendency-to-be-perceived-as-agreed-with, a rank-order coefficient was calculated between popularity status of the 17 *S*s (mean of attraction ranks received) and perceived agreement status (mean of all other *S*s' estimates of agreement with each *S*). Since for nearly all *S*s there is a slight positive correlation between these two variables, a pooling of the same variables (i.e., responses concerning each *S* by all other *S*s) might be expected to accentuate the relationship. This variant of the prediction being tested in this

---

to obtain a single attitude index for an entire "family," and hence impossible to obtain a single estimate of others' attitudes to the entire "family."

Table 4.1. NUMBERS OF INDIVIDUAL ESTIMATES AT THREE LEVELS OF AGREEMENT ABOUT SPRANGER VALUES, CLASSIFIED BY THREE DEGREES OF ESTIMATOR'S ATTRACTION (YEAR II)

Rhos *of estimated agreement*	Attraction ranks assigned by estimator							
	Week 2				Week 14			
	1–4	*5–12*	*13–16*	*Total*	*1–4*	*5–12*	*13–16*	*Total*
$\geq .60$	31	39	20	90	28	63	14	105
.00–.59	17	59	18	94	25	44	31	100
< .00	20	38	30	88	15	29	23	67
TOTAL	68	136	68	272	68	136	68	272

$$\chi^2 = 14.35 \qquad\qquad \chi^2 = 12.01$$
$$p < .01 \ (4 \ df) \qquad p < .02 \ (4 \ df)$$

Table 4.2. NUMBERS OF INDIVIDUAL RANKINGS OF OTHER 16 *S*s IN ESTIMATED AGREEMENT ON SPRANGER VALUES, AS RELATED TO SAME ESTIMATORS' RANKING OF ATTRACTION TOWARD SAME *S*s (YEAR II)

Attraction ranks assigned	Ranks of estimated agreement							
	Week 2				Week 14			
	1–4	*5–12*	*13–16*	*Total*	*1–4*	*5–12*	*13–16*	*Total*
1–8	45	70	21	136	46	62	28	136
9–16	23	66	47	136	22	74	40	136
TOTAL	68	136	68	272	68	136	68	272

$$\chi^2 = 17.19 \qquad\qquad \chi^2 = 11.63$$
$$p < .001 \ (2 \ df) \qquad p < .005 \ (2 \ df)$$

section is supported by *rho* values of .73 and .67 at Weeks 2 and 14, respectively—both significant at beyond .01.

Thus, using the most appropriate set of available data (estimates of others' orderings of Spranger Values in Year II), the prediction that agreement is estimated to be closer with highly attractive than with less attractive others is supported by various tests. And, as predicted, the magnitude of the relationship between attraction and estimated agreement is approximately the same on early and on late acquaintance.

Other House Members as Objects of Orientation

Various lines of evidence led us to conclude—before we had even begun to analyze our first year's data—that in our research setting House members, considered as common objects of orientation, were the objects that most clearly met the conditions under which our hypothetical predictions should find support. This conclusion rests upon the following grounds.

First, for purposes of measurement and of statistical testing, it is necessary to obtain responses of orientation toward *common* objects—those objects toward which all *S*s have orientations and concerning which there is interperson variance. With one prominent exception, there are few common objects which meet both this requirement and the additional one that orientations be rather readily susceptible to change. This prominent exception is other House members, orientations toward whom were nonexistent at the outset and fluid in the early weeks. In these ways, House members provided the most nearly ideal kinds of common objects.

Second, as became evident to us in the earliest weeks of the first year's data gathering, the research setting was such as almost to guarantee that person-orientation would dominate task-orientation. There were no common tasks except the promptly routinized ones of serving meals (prepared by a hired cook), washing dishes, and preserving a modicum of cleanliness in the "public" parts of the House. With regard to these there was little intensity of feeling, and comparatively little attitude variance. With regard to "the House" as an object of attitude there was, similarly, neither much intensity nor much variance in attitude, in view of the common knowledge that House membership would last for only one semester.[2] Hence intramural sports and other possible activities were hardly engaged in at all, as House enterprises, though certain individuals and small groups did engage in them.

Rather intense interest in each other was, however, almost preordained by the following circumstances. The opportunity to live

[2] During Year II, but not Year I, it was known that those who so chose might continue to live in the House for a second semester, on payment of standard fees for room rent, but it was commonly (and correctly) assumed that not all members would avail themselves of the privilege.

in this House (under what had been described to them as "fraternity-like conditions") was—apart from academic experiences, which for many members involved anticipatory ambiguity and insecurity—the one certain thing that, as newly arrived in a strange community, our subjects had to look forward to. All of them arrived simultaneously (a week earlier than other students, except freshmen and other transfer students), without other acquaintances in this community, in a place to which they had been individually invited and where they were greeted by name. They all arrived "in the same boat" as transfer students, each with a story to tell, presumably, about his reasons for transferring, and each with some misgivings as to his own marginality in a new community in which peers-to-be were already acquainted. Under these conditions, the most obvious candidates for friendship were to be found within the House. Furthermore, it very soon became evident that the only real House problems to be solved were the problems of getting along with each other. This they were forced to do because they were presented with a completely outfitted set of facilities, and told to "run it as you please, within the limits of regulations applying to fraternities in this University." Perhaps, furthermore, their common status as "guinea pigs in an experiment" concerned with "getting to know each other" tended to result in turning their interests, centripetally, toward each other. Small wonder, then, that person-orientation was dominant in this research setting.

It does not necessarily follow, however, from our conviction that person-objects are the most suitable ones for testing our hypotheses, that a third person, C, can be substituted for a nonperson object, X, in our theoretical formulation, or in our analyses, concerning ABX systems. The fact is, of course, that under conditions of mutual acquaintance and interaction a person, C, though he may be treated for research purposes as a common object to a given A and B, is also the locus of co-orientation with that A and that B with respect to various objects. In our research setting this was particularly the case; and if House members are to be treated as common objects to pairs of other House members, then every individual must be treated alternately as A, as B, and as C if complete analyses are to be made. Persons treated as common objects, in short, are unlike nonperson objects in that they reciprocate the very orientations (on the part of A and B) that constitute the systems under analysis, as nonperson objects do not.

We must therefore consider in what ways and to what extent we are confounding our own theoretical assumptions by treating House members as common objects of orientation to pairs of other House members. We shall argue, quite simply, that our decision so to treat them is justified as an instance of the universal scientific practice of abstracting single properties from complex, multipropertied entities for the purpose of testing specific and limited hypotheses. We do not assume, naturally, that person-object C has no influence upon person-subject A—especially when that same person, C, who at one moment is treated as common object to A is at the next moment treated as a B who is influencing that same A. What we do assume, hypothetically, in treating a person as common object to A and B, is that A's orientations toward C and his attribution of B's orientations toward C are influenced by (among other things) his perception of his own relationship to B. This is the only proposition that is being tested in considering C as common object to A and to B in the former's individual system.[3] We assume that it is not necessary, in testing a prediction of covariation between two variables, to take into account all other parameters of either variable. . . . For such reasons, and only in such ways, we justify our treatment, in the present section, of House members as common objects to pairs of other House members.

Attraction and Perceived Agreement about Other House Members

If House members are as important to each other as we have suggested—that is, if a member's valence for another member tends to be strong, compared to that for other objects—then we can derive, directly from our general formulation, the prediction that the higher A's attraction to B the greater the likelihood that A will attribute to B agreement with himself in attraction toward the remaining House members.

[3] We make essentially the same assumptions in Chapter 5, where persons are treated as common objects in collective systems. In this case the proposition that is being tested is that A's and B's mutual attraction toward each other varies with the degree of similarity in their actual orientations toward C. And in this case also, for the sake of testing a limited prediction derived from the general theory, we momentarily ignore, without denying, the contribution made by a third person, C, to the relationships between A and B—a contribution made by virtue of the fact that that third person has the same properties as do A and B, and that his relationships to A and to B are in principle undistinguishable from those between A and B.

This prediction must be tested in different ways for the two populations, since (as more fully explained on pp. 41–42) in Year II estimates of others' attraction responses were made for only a small sample of all the 240 attraction relationships among Ss other than the estimator (240 because for each estimator there were 16 other Ss, for each of whom he could have estimated attraction responses toward the remaining 15 Ss). In describing each year's findings, however, the symbol "A" will be used to refer to the estimator. For statistical purposes, responses by all 17 Ss, each considered as A—both their own and their estimates of others' attraction ranks—will be pooled.

In *Year I*, Ss were asked to estimate others' attraction responses *in ranked form* only at Weeks 1 and 5;[4] in Tables 4.3 and 4.4

Table 4.3. NUMBERS OF ESTIMATES AT THREE LEVELS OF PERCEIVED AGREEMENT ABOUT ATTRACTIVENESS OF OTHER HOUSE MEMBERS, AT THREE LEVELS OF ESTIMATORS' ATTRACTION TOWARD ESTIMATEES (YEAR I)

Rank of attraction	Agreement rho, Week 1				Agreement rho, Week 5			
	$\geq .70$	.30–.69	$\leq .29$	Total	$\geq .70$	.30–.69	$\leq .29$	Total
1, 2 (high)	23	9	2	34	18	15	1	34
8, 9	9	18	7	34	9	15	10	34
15, 16 (low)	4	9	21	34	1	13	20	34
TOTAL	36	36	30	102	28	43	31	102

$$\chi^2 = 40.06 \qquad\qquad \chi^2 = 33.17$$
$$p < .001 \text{ (4 df)} \qquad p < .001 \text{ (4 df)}$$

the relationship between three levels of A's attraction toward B and A's perceived agreement with B in rank-ordering the attractiveness of the remaining 15 Ss (in terms of Spearman *rhos*) is shown.

---

[4] At Week 1 each S made estimates of the attraction ranks of only those individuals whom he himself ranked at 1, 2, 8, 9, 15, and 16. At Week 5 each S estimated the attraction ranks of all 16 other Ss. At later times estimates were made for all other Ss, but only in terms of positive, neutral, and negative attraction. This procedure was much less time-consuming than the ranking procedure, but it yielded less information. Since, however, the plus-neutral-minus procedure was also used at Weeks 1 and 5, comparisons can be made between early and late responses.

Table 4.4 shows analogous relationships at Weeks 1, 5, and 14, but in terms of frequencies of A's estimates of others' attraction, at three levels (favorable, neutral, unfavorable) toward A's first four choices. (Comparisons with Week 14 can be made only in terms of the category system of response made at that time; see footnote 4, page 57.)

Table 4.4. NUMBERS OF ESTIMATES IN THREE CATEGORIES OF ESTIMATED B-TO-C ATTRACTION, AT THREE LEVELS OF A-TO-B ATTRACTION, WHEN A-TO-C ATTRACTION IS HIGH (RANKS 1–4) (YEAR I)

Actual A-to-B attraction rank	Estimated B-to-C attraction [a] at											
	Week 1				Week 5				Week 14			
	+	0	−	Total	+	0	−	Total	+	0	−	Total
1, 2 (high)	94	8	0	102 [b]	88	14	0	102 [b]	83	17	2	102 [b]
8, 9	116	20	0	136	107	27	2	136	105	30	1	136
15, 16 (low)	74	54	8	136	76	51	9	136	65	56	15	136
TOTAL	284	82	8	374	271	92	11	374	253	103	18	374

$\chi^2 = 55.81$ [c] $\qquad$ $\chi^2 = 31.13$ [c] $\qquad$ $\chi^2 = 38.94$ [c]

$p < .001$ (2 df) $\qquad$ $p < .001$ (2 df) $\qquad$ $p < .001$ (2 df)

[a] Instructions for making estimates were as follows: "plus = like more than dislike; zero = neutral or undecided; minus = dislike more than like."

[b] Totals in the "high" category of attraction are smaller than in the other categories because A's Rank-1 and Rank-2 choices, as B, are included in A's high-attraction category of C, and hence are not estimated as being attracted toward themselves.

[c] In computing χ^2, the "0" and "−" categories were combined.

Tables 4.3 and 4.4 together show that the tendency to perceive others as agreeing with oneself in attraction to other House members increases with the attraction of the estimator toward the person whose responses are estimated; and consistently so on early, intermediate, and late acquaintance. The predicted relationship is highly significant at all times. When A-to-C attraction is high (as in Table 4.4) it is, moreover, a universal tendency: only one subject (#29), at Week 1 only, fails to estimate closer agreement with high-attraction estimatees than with other estimatees.

During *Year II* only a 5 percent sample of all possible estimates was obtained in any single week (12 estimates by each *S,* of the

240 that he might have made); the sample was selected by a random-number procedure. Each estimator assigned, for each B-to-C response, a value on the 100-point scale ranging from maximally favorable to maximally unfavorable attraction (see pp. 33, 42). Because of the random assortment of individuals assigned (both as B and as C) to each estimator, and because no B and no C appeared more than once on any estimator's list, this procedure introduced certain problems of noncomparability. There might, for example, appear on one estimator's list several individuals highly attractive to him, or none at all, either as sources or as recipients of estimated attraction, or both. Both the specific prediction to be tested from these data, therefore, and the analytic procedures for testing it, were necessarily somewhat different from those employed in the case of the Year-I data.

The following prediction, analogous to but not identical with that tested from the Year-I data, was therefore derived from the general hypothesis of this chapter: A's estimates of B's attraction to C will be more closely in agreement with A's own attraction toward C, in estimating responses of a B who is relatively attractive to A himself, than in estimating responses of a less attractive B. The procedures adopted for testing this procedure were as follows.

1. "High attraction" on the part of A (the estimator) toward B was operationalized as those of A's highest four actual ranks of attraction which were included in A's list of B-persons (sources of estimated attraction).

2. The 12 recipients of A's B-to-C attraction estimates were ranked from 1 to 12, in the order of their appearance in A's ranking of his own attraction preferences among the other 16 Ss.

3. The assumption was made that in estimating ratings, on the 100-point scale, by the 12 B-persons, A would use the same frame of reference (the same part of the 100-point scale for the same level of attraction) as he used in making his own attraction ratings. Therefore the 12 rating-estimates made by each A were rank-ordered, with the assumption that these ranks could be directly compared with the 12 ranks described in the preceding step.

4. Discrepancies (simple arithmetic differences) between A's actual and B's estimated ranks of attraction toward the same C were then computed—separately for those in the sample of 12 that were included in A's actual first 4 ranks and for those included in A's last 12 ranks. Since the sample pairs were selected,

in advance, by random-number procedures, it might happen that for any given A any number, from 1 to 4, of his first four attraction choices would be included. The actually obtained frequencies ranged from 1 to 4.

5. Frequency distributions of rank discrepancies (which could range from 0 to 11) were then compared, as between all estimates by every A which represented ratings attributed to his attraction ranks 1–4 and all estimates representing ratings attributed to his attraction ranks 5–16. The relative numbers of discrepancies were, of course, about 1 to 3, since attraction ranks 1–4 represent one-fourth of all ranks from 1–16.[5]

Table 4.5. FREQUENCIES OF FOUR DEGREES OF ESTIMATED DISCREPANCY BETWEEN ESTIMATOR'S OWN AND OTHERS' ATTRACTION TOWARD THE SAME Ss, AT TWO LEVELS OF ESTIMATOR'S ATTRACTION (YEAR II)

Estimated A-B dis-crepancy, in ranks [a]	A's rank of attraction toward B, at times noted								
	Week 2			Week 3			Week 12		
	1–4	5–16	Total	1–4	5–16	Total	1–4	5–16	Total
0	8	0	8	6	7	13	6	4	10
0.5–3.0	32	70	102	28	65	93	30	68	98
3.5–8.0	9	75	84	17	65	82	13	70	83
8.5–11.0	0	10	10	0	16	16	0	13	13
TOTAL	49	155	204	51	153	204	49	155	204
	$\chi^2 = 17.54$ [b] $p < .001$ (1 df)			$\chi^2 = 6.73$ [b] $p < .01$ (1 df)			$\chi^2 = 9.95$ [b] $p < .005$ (1 df)		

[a] Half-point discrepancies result from ties in ranks.
[b] Estimated discrepancies are dichotomized at 0–3.0 vs. 3.5–11.0.

In Table 4.5 appear the results of applying this procedure. At all three times, subjects attribute to most attractive others significantly more agreement (i.e., smaller discrepancies in ranks)

[5] This somewhat cumbersome procedure is more suitable for testing the present prediction than any correlational analysis that we could devise, since a complete set of ratings was available only for A; any given B or C appeared but once in A's estimates at any one week.

with themselves about other House members than they attribute to less-liked others—in support of the prediction.

The Perception of "Perfect Triads"

If we make the further assumption that an individual House member is as important to himself as to others, and that his orientations toward himself tend to be favorable, it follows from our general hypothesis that he will attribute favorable orientations toward himself to those toward whom he is most strongly attracted. And it follows from this, and from the preceding prediction (supported by Tables 4.3 and 4.4), that an individual should tend to perceive all six of the attraction orientations involving himself and any two of his own high-attraction choices as being at high levels of attraction. That is, if A's attraction toward B and toward C is high, then he should perceive B's and C's attraction toward himself (A) and toward each other, as being high. Such a set of orientations we shall refer to as a perceived perfect triad.

Table 4.6. FREQUENCIES OF ATTRACTION RANKS ATTRIBUTED BY ALL Ss TO THEIR OWN HIGHEST TWO ATTRACTION CHOICES, BY THREE CATEGORIES OF RECIPIENTS OF ESTIMATED ATTRACTION (YEAR I)

Estimated attraction ranks	Estimated responses by B and C, Week 1				Estimated responses by B and C, Week 5			
	To each other	To A	To other 14 Ss [a]	Total	To each other	To A	To other 14 Ss [a]	Total
1– 4	22	24	90	136	22	26	88	136
5– 8	9	6	121	136	11	7	118	136
9–12	3	4	129	136	1	1	134	136
13–16	0	0	136	136	0	0	136	136
TOTAL	34	34	476	544	34	34	476	544

$$\chi^2 = 47.20 \ ^b \qquad\qquad \chi^2 = 66.60 \ ^b$$
$$p < .001 \ (1 \ df) \qquad\qquad p < .001 \ (1 \ df)$$

[a] For comparisons with column headed "To other 14 Ss," frequencies in that column should be divided by 14.

[b] In computing χ^2, attraction ranks are dichotomized at 1–8 vs. 9–16, and the first two columns in each half of the table are combined.

Tests of both of these predictions appear in Tables 4.6 and 4.7. It is clear, in Table 4.6, that the distributions of estimates of B's and C's attraction toward each other and to A (the estimator) do not differ significantly (each p value $>.1$) and hence it is permissible to combine them for purposes of testing our prediction. It is also clear that Table 4.6 provides strong support for both predictions in the preceding paragraph (for the first of these predictions, compare the frequencies in the column headed "to A" with those in the column headed "to other 14 Ss"; the second is tested by the χ^2 values appearing in Table 4.6).

Since the estimates of ranks assigned by B and C to each other and to A (the estimator) are all those and only those that are involved in the triads composed by each S together with his highest two attraction choices, it may be concluded from these findings that at these times the tendency to perceive "perfect triads" is very strong indeed.

Table 4.7, in which estimates made at Weeks 1 and 5 of Year I are presented in plus-neutral-minus terms, compares these relatively early estimates with those made at Week 14 (see footnote 4, p. 57). At none of these three periods are the distributions of responses "to each other" and "to A" significantly different. At all three times, on the other hand, differences between the first two columns, combined, and the third column are significant at $<.001$. Thus the findings in Table 4.6 (by more precise methods) for earlier weeks are closely paralleled by those resulting from the cruder procedures employed on final acquaintance.

Does the tendency to perceive "perfect triads" increase or decrease with time? As far as perceiving one's own preferred choices as reciprocated is concerned, there is no consistent or significant change between Weeks 1 and 14. As for estimates of B-to-C attraction (B and C representing the subject's first two choices), there is no evidence of significant change between Weeks 1 and 5, by either method of response, though the trend is toward fewer Rank-1 estimates between B and C at the later time. Between Weeks 1 and 14, however, by the cruder, three-degree method of response, this trend is significant. At the earliest time all 34 of the "to each other" estimates are "favorable," whereas at the latest time only 26 of the 34 are "favorable." By exact test the p value of this difference is .002.

Insofar as this trend may be accepted as a dependable one, then the autistic component contributing to the perception of "perfect triads" becomes somewhat less strong with acquaintance, pre-

Table 4.7. Frequencies of Three Categories of Attraction Attributed by All Ss to Their Highest Two Attraction Choices, by Three Categories of Recipients of Estimated Attraction (Year I)

Estimate of attraction	Week 1				Week 5				Week 14			
	To each other	To A	To other 14 Ss [a]	Total	To each other	To A	To other 14 Ss [a]	Total	To each other	To A	To other 14 Ss [a]	Total
Favorable	34	31	270	335	32	34	265	331	26	32	274	332
Neutral	0	3	166	169	2	0	166	168	8	2	133	143
Unfavorable	0	0	40	40	0	0	45	45	0	0	69	69
TOTAL	34	34	476	544	34	34	476	544	34	34	476	544

$\chi^2 = 36.29$ [b] $\chi^2 = 40.98$ [b] $\chi^2 = 18.09$ [b]

$p < .001$ (1 df) $p < .001$ (1 df) $p < .001$ (1 df)

[a] For comparisons with column headed "To other 14 Ss," frequencies in that column should be divided by 14.
[b] In computing χ^2, "favorable" category was compared with the "neutral" and "unfavorable" categories, combined; and the first two columns are in each case combined and compared with the third column.

sumably being increasingly influenced by reality forces. Nevertheless, even this component (perceived B-to-C attraction) still remains a significantly [6] strong one at the end of four months of acquaintance.

From Tables 4.6 and 4.7, together, we conclude that our prediction of a significant tendency to perceive "perfect triads" at all times is well supported.

CHANGE IN AGREEMENT FOLLOWING A MANIPULATED CHANGE IN ATTRACTION: AN EXPERIMENT [7]

Changes in attraction and in perceived agreement, as so far reported, have been those that occurred "naturally"—that is, in a situation involving no manipulation other than that involved in providing a particular kind of setting—and they have been gradual changes, in no case involving intervals of less than a week. The changes predicted in the following experiment, however, would presumably occur within a very brief period of time, following deliberate manipulation.

We planned to manipulate attraction toward a person who would take so clear a stand on a certain issue that our subjects would all perceive his attitude in the same manner. The prediction was that they would agree with him more closely when attraction toward him was high than when it was not. If so (assuming only that they correctly perceived his position), the experimental findings would be in support of the hypothesized tendency for individual systems to remain in balance, in spite of changes in single orientations.

Procedures

Since the experiment was to take place, in Year I, after several weeks of acquaintance (Week 8, which was the ninth week), it was necessary that the object of attraction be a stranger. Ideally, also, he would be a person possessing greater than ordinary skills,

[6] Comparing the "to each other" distribution at Week 14 (see Table 4.6) with the expected distribution, as it appears in the "Total" column, the χ^2 value is 5.52, and $p < .02$ with 1 df.

[7] A more condensed report of this experiment has been published by H. A. Burdick and A. J. Burnes (1958).

so that he might succeed in arousing attraction toward himself at one level and then in changing the level rather radically.[8] As a topic regarding which we hoped to induce attitude change, we selected "the individual's own responsibility for acts of juvenile delinquency." The successive steps in our procedure were as follows.

1. Ss were informed, in advance, that at the next evening meeting a professor of psychology would speak on two topics: juvenile delinquency during the first hour, and during the second, standards of propriety in the attire of college men (an item concerning which was included in the long attitude inventory to which they had previously responded).

2. Ss were asked to read, before the meeting, "The case of Johnny Sandron" (see Burdick, 1956).

3. Just prior to the arrival of the speaker (E), Ss responded to a set of attitude items concerning whether the boy, personally, or his environment should be considered responsible for a crime that he had committed. They also indicated their opinions concerning the proper dress for college man on campus. Ss recorded their first and second choices among a set of five alternatives.

4. E was introduced, with the announcement that during the first hour he would speak about juvenile delinquency, a problem with which he had thorough professional familiarity. E spoke affably and convincingly about the case report that the Ss had recently read, arguing forcibly that the environment should be considered totally responsible for the boy's crime. At the end of the hour Ss again responded to the two sets of attitude items, and also to a five-step scale of liking for the speaker.

5. It was then announced that (as had sometimes occurred in earlier meetings) there would be a brief intermission. During this period the speaker and the Project Director (who, as on some previous occasions, was acting as moderator) engaged in conversation just outside the meeting room—a conversation during which their voices became increasingly audible, and showed increasing irritation.

6. When the meeting reconvened, the moderator announced that our speaker preferred—in fact, very strongly preferred—not

[8] Professor Elton McNeil, of the Psychology Department at the University of Michigan, succeeded with uncanny skill at this difficult task, and we are very greatly indebted to him.

to discuss the topic that had been announced for the second hour. The moderator expressed his personal regret that such a change was necessary, but said that he had reluctantly agreed, since E felt very strongly about another topic that he did want to discuss and since, after all, he was a guest and entitled to every reasonable courtesy.

7. E spent the remaining hour in a gradually mounting tirade against the Ss for their docility and submissiveness—as illustrated by their behavior during the preceding hour, when confronted by an older person labeled as an authority—finally rising to a crescendo of abuse. He discussed neither juvenile delinquency nor college attire, but simply attempted (by pre-arrangement, of course) to make himself personally disliked.

8. At the height of this attack the moderator interrupted, mumbling something about the lateness of the hour, and offering perfunctory thanks. E and the moderator immediately left the house, engaging in audible and angry dispute as they left.

9. Ss were asked (by a research assistant, as usual) to respond again to the same attitude items, with an explanation by him to the effect that he thought it wiser to continue with the original plans for answering the questions, even though the evening's schedule had gone awry.[9]

The manipulation had been planned so as to create positive attraction toward the visiting speaker (a total stranger) and then to reduce the level of Ss' attraction toward him. These objectives were reasonably well attained: at the end of the first hour 14 of the 17 Ss reported either that they "liked him very much" (5 Ss) or that they "liked him" (9 Ss); of the remainder, 2 reported neither like nor dislike, and 1 reported that he "disliked him." Liking for him was significantly less ($p < .01$) one hour later, 14 of

[9] Not unnaturally, there were occasional questions as to whether the affair had been "rigged." Having anticipated such questions, we reminded the questioners of our earlier promise to "tell all" when the project had been completed, and added such comments as "If we're *that* good as actors, we're in the wrong business; we should be in the theatre game." On the part of a few Ss, suspicions probably remained, and for this reason we never repeated this kind of experiment; we could not afford to sacrifice our subjects' confidence for the sake of a few incidental experiments. About 15 months later, the deception was fully explained, together with our assurance that it had been the only incident of its kind, in either year. At the time of this final explanation, two or three Ss maintained that they had suspected it all along; most of the others expressed surprise.

the 17 Ss having checked a lesser level of liking at the later time.

Our predictions had been (1) that, following the first hour's presentation, there would be changes in attitude in the direction favored by the speaker; and (2) that, following the second hour, there would be changes in the opposite direction. As to the first of these, only 8 Ss had changed, by the end of the first hour, from their original attitude positions, but all of these eight changes were in the predicted direction.[10] Based upon cumulative binomial probabilities, the p value of 8 out of 8 changes all being in the same direction is .004, and the probability that in none of 17 cases would there be a change contrary to the predicted direction is $<.001$. As to the second prediction, at the end of the experiment only 6 Ss had changed their responses from the position taken at the end of the first hour; of these six, five changes were in the predicted direction; the corresponding p value is .109.

Responses may also be analyzed in individual terms. If the 7 Ss whose attraction toward the speaker declined most during the second hour (three or more points on a five-point scale) are compared with the remaining 10 in respect to attitude change during the same interval, results are as shown in Table 4.8. As required by our hypothesis, those whose liking for E declined most tended also to be those whose attitudes changed in the direction contrary to that which he had advocated.

Table 4.8. NUMBER OF Ss WHOSE ATTITUDES CHANGED IN RELATION TO THOSE ADVOCATED BY E DURING SECOND HOUR OF EXPERIMENT, CLASSIFIED BY DEGREE OF DECLINE IN LIKING FOR E

Decline in liking	Attitude change		Total
	Away from E's position	None, or toward E	
$\geq$3 points	4	3	7
$\leq$2 points	1	9	10
TOTAL	5	12	17

$p = .030$ (exact test)

[10] There was no S whose initial response was so extremely "anti-environment" that change away from the speaker's position was impossible. There were, however, 3 Ss whose initial responses were maximally "pro-environment," so that change toward the speaker's position was possible for only 14 Ss. None of these 3, incidentally, changed his initial position at either subsequent time.

And so we conclude that, in spite of the small frequencies of attitude change, it is possible to find support for our hypothesis about the interdependence of changing attraction and changing agreement by experimental means as well as by observations under "natural" conditions.

A Test of an Alternative Hypothesis Concerning the Relationship between Attraction and Perceived Agreement

Considerable evidence has now been presented in support of the hypothesis that attraction and perceived agreement tend to be associated. It has not, however, been demonstrated that this state of affairs necessarily follows from the postulated mechanism of strain reduction. An alternative possibility—that culturally stereotyped notions exist to the effect that such relationships tend in fact to occur—might account for the findings without assuming that strain was actually experienced. If so, then our respondents' estimates of others' orientations may have been determined by these stereotypes, rather than by individual mechanisms of strain prediction. That is, it is possible that respondents might have felt equally "comfortable" about making estimates of agreement bearing no relationship to attraction, but were only relying upon a reasonably safe rule of thumb in making estimates that were related to attraction. Insofar as this occurs, it would tend to invalidate all estimates, from the point of view of the postulate of strain.

A test of this possibility is available, though it is somewhat indirect. If the estimates were based merely upon culturally determined rules of thumb, then estimates of agreement on the part of pairs *excluding the estimator* (estimates in which his own personal involvement is minimal) should show as close a relationship to estimates of attraction on the part of the same pairs as would appear in self-involved estimates. Psychological forces toward strain-reduction, we reason, should be stronger when they impinge directly upon an estimator of others' attitudes than when they do not. At any rate the cultural stereotype, if it is operating at all, should influence relationships between estimated attraction and estimated agreement even when the self is not directly involved.

From this point of view of the central hypothesis of this chapter, therefore, the prediction is as follows: A's estimates of B-C agreement will not be significantly related to A's estimates of B-C attraction.

This prediction is well supported, as shown in Table 4.9. The data involve the six B-C pairs whose members' attraction to each other was estimated by each S, both in terms of ratings on the

Table 4.9. A's Estimates of B-to-C Attraction as Related to Estimates of Agreement by Same B and C on Spranger Values (Year II)

Rho *of* agreement	*Week 2* attraction			*Week 14* [a] attraction		
	High	*Low*	*Total*	*High*	*Low*	*Total*
High	54	48	102	46	52	98
Low	58	44	102	50	56	106
Total	112	92	204	96	108	204
		$\chi^2 = 0.18$			$\chi^2 = .00$	

[a] The samples for these two weeks were identical: the same Ss estimated the same B-to-C relationships after a three-month interval.

100-point scale and in terms of quartiles (the latter being used in the present analysis), as related to estimates of each others' ordering of Spranger Values. During the same week, all Ss also made estimates of every other S's rankings of Spranger Values, and from these responses *rhos* were calculated representing each S's degree of perceived agreement on the part of all pairs not involving himself. For present purposes, only those *rhos* are used which refer to the same pairs whose attraction to each other was also estimated. If, for each of the seventeen estimators, both degree of perceived agreement and degree of pair attraction are ranked for the six pairs estimated, the resulting individual *rhos* at both weeks are positive in eight of the seventeen cases, and negative in nine—in support of the null prediction.

These findings are particularly revealing in view of the fact that (as has been shown) respondents' own attraction toward others is rather closely related to perceived agreement with them with regard to Spranger Values. Together, these findings suggest that the hypothesized strain mechanism may be operating as subjects make their own responses, but is not recognized by them as affecting the relationship between attraction and agreement on the part of others.

Summary: Individual Systems

The general hypothesis of the chapter is that the stronger an individual's attraction to another person, the greater the likelihood that he will perceive agreement with that other person concerning objects important and relevant to him. Tests of several specific predictions, derived from this hypothesis and formulated in terms of available data, provided support for them at significant levels. Predictions concerning individual balance with respect to nonperson objects of common orientation could be tested with only one of the two populations. Analogous predictions concerning House members, considered as common objects, were supported at higher levels of confidence than those concerning nonperson objects, as we anticipated in view of the generally person-oriented setting in which the research was conducted. Comparisons of tendencies toward individual balance at different stages of acquaintance indicate that those tendencies are relatively constant at all times. A test of an alternative hypothesis, not requiring the assumption of individual strain, yielded negative results; thus it is plausible to interpret the obtained findings as consistent with the postulated mechanism of strain-reduction.

Two-person Collective Systems   **5**

This chapter deals with actual agreement (rather than with perceived agreement, as in Chapter 4) in relation to mutual attraction (rather than to A's attraction only); as outlined in Chapter 2, these are the two kinds of components in collective systems.

The predictions to be tested rest upon the assumption that the research setting provided ample opportunity for House members to become familiar with each others' orientations if they cared to obtain the relevant information. If this be assumed, and if attraction is indeed determined in some part by perceived agreement about important and relevant objects, then it should follow that, following but not before adequate opportunity for becoming familiar with each others' attitudes, actual agreement should be a significant predictor of mutual attraction. Thus the *general hypothesis* of this chapter is that, as a function of increasing acquaintance, actual agreement by pairs of persons is increasingly associated with degree of positive attraction of those persons toward each other. As in the preceding chapter, specific predictions will be introduced in terms of the data by which they are to be tested.

Before proceeding to specific predictions, however, two implicit aspects of our general hypothesis should be made more explicit. First, we have deliberately stated the relationship between agreement and mutual attraction in terms of covariation rather than in terms of dependent and independent variables. This kind of *inter*dependency is inherent in our system-like approach. It happens that our subjects showed little change in attitudes toward objects other than House members; in principle, however, we assume that a change in either kind of variable will induce a change in the other, under the stipulated conditions. Second, the general hypothesis of this chapter (unlike that of Chapter 4) is stated in terms of changes presumed to occur with increasing opportunity for acquaintance. There was little actual change in agreement about nonperson objects and much change in agreement about House members, from early to late acquaintance, and there were many changes in mutual attraction.[1] The fact is, of course, that our research setting was specifically designed to make possible the study of such changes.

OTHER HOUSE MEMBERS AS COMMON OBJECTS

The following predictions are directly derived from our general hypothesis: (1) pairs of subjects most closely agreeing about the attractiveness of others will be most strongly attracted to each other; and (2) this predicted relationship between agreement and mutual attraction will become closer with increasing acquaintance.

Procedures

The index of *agreement* for any pair of Ss is the rank-order correlation (*rho*) between the attraction ranks assigned by the 2 Ss to the other 15 House members. Each S's 16 ranked attraction responses were therefore reranked 16 times, each time pairing him with a different S with whose ranking of the remaining 15 Ss his own ranking of the same 15 Ss could be correlated. Indices were thus computed for each of the 136 pairs, each pair requiring 2 new rerankings of the original attraction responses made by the 2 pair members.[2] The more nearly the members of any pair rank the remaining 15 Ss in the same order, the closer their agreement.

As an index of *pair attraction,* some method is required of combining the attraction ranks that each member of the pair expresses for the other. The simplest procedure would be to sum the ranks, but this would be unsatisfactory both for theoretical

---

[1] We shall in general observe changes by comparing relationships between early and late agreement and early and late attraction, rather than making direct use of change-scores as a variable; the latter alternative would introduce questionable assumptions concerning the metrics that we have employed.

[2] See Appendix V for a discussion of the problem of the significance of correlations between this index of agreement and the index (described later) of pair attraction.

and for operational reasons. First, it seemed desirable not to equate a pair of more or less mutual—that is, similar—ranks (say 6 and 8) with another pair of distinctly nonmutual ranks (say 1 and 13) adding to the same total. Perhaps because of sheer uncertainty as to the meaning of combined nonmutual responses, we felt safer in assigning less "favorable" values to them than to more nearly mutual ones summing to the same value. Second, the method of summing ranks could result in a maximum of 31 different pair scores (from 2 to 32), which among 136 pairs would necessarily result in many tied scores. What was needed, in short, was a procedure that would result in finer discriminations among combined scores, and at the same time be based upon a defensible rationale in ordering them. The procedure adopted was simply to sum the *squares* of the ranks. Thus the pair score of the combined ranks 6 and 8 is $36 + 64$, or 100, and for the combined ranks 1 and 13 it is $1 + 169$, or 170. This procedure is such that level of pair attraction is reduced by disparity of reciprocally assigned ranks: if either member of a pair receives a strongly negative response, the pair score cannot be very low (and attraction level cannot be high), regardless of how strongly positive the response received by the other.

We decided upon this procedure for ordering levels of mutual attraction because it seemed to us more consistent with our way of conceptualizing a collective system than any other. The components of a two-person system, by definition, are pairs of orientations (from each person toward the other, and from each toward the common object); its level of balance is determined by within-pair relationships of these orientations; and these relationships (A-to-B vis-à-vis B-to-A, and A-to-X vis-à-vis B-to-X) are consequences of communicative interaction between persons A and B. It is this last consideration that determines the present issue. Since we have conceptualized mutual attraction as an interactional product (rather than a summation computed from A's and from B's scores of attraction toward each other), our index of mutual-attraction level must take account of the conditions under which the interactional product presumably emerges. In our research setting, these conditions were such that each subject (considered as A) necessarily acquired some notions of the level of attraction accorded him by each other subject (considered as B). This being the case, it seems to us to follow that mutual attraction, as an interactional product, is more likely to approach the lower than the higher of the two individual attraction levels between A and B: the higher of them is a level that is desired by only one of them, whereas the lower is the maximum level that is common to both of them.

The scores that result from this procedure represent a defensible order—from highest possible to lowest possible—of degrees of reciprocal attraction, but they do not provide a metric. The scores are irregularly distributed between 2 and 512, sometimes with large gaps between adjacent scores [3] and sometimes with identical scores that result from different combinations of reciprocally assigned ranks. These scores were therefore transmuted into a 256-point rank-order scale, according to procedures described in Appendix IX. The basic rationale of this transmutation is as follows: (1) any rank assigned by an A to a B has an equal probability of being reciprocated by any rank, from 1 to 16, by B to A; (2) each of the possible 256 combinations in a 16×16 matrix, representing the equally probable combinations of ranks exchanged, can be placed in an order determined by the sums-of-squared-ranks procedure; (3) all possible combinations, thus ordered, can be renumbered from 1 to 256; each value on the scale is thus determined by the number of combinations higher in the order (e.g., the combination 1–1 is first, and appears only once in the matrix, and thus receives the rank-order value of 1, and the combination of 16–16 follows 255 others, and so receives the value of 256); (4) the resulting values, having the properties of an ordinal scale, are less misleading than the raw values of sums of squares.

Findings

As a background for the analysis of two-person systems, we shall start with the prediction that on late but not on early acquaintance there will be, for each population as a whole, a significant correlation between pair-scores of attraction (level of mutual attraction) and pair agreement regarding the 15 Ss not included in each pair. Table 5.1 provides support for this pre-

---

[3] For example, the five sums of squared ranks representing highest attraction are 2, 5, 8, 10, and 13, while the five lowest are 512, 481, 452, 450, and 425. Around the middle of the continuum they are rather closely clustered together—for example, 178, 180, 181, 185.

Table 5.1. PRODUCT-MOMENT COEFFICIENTS BETWEEN MUTUAL PAIR ATTRACTION AND ACTUAL AGREEMENT [a]

Week	Year I	Year II
0 [b]	.13	.16
1	.18	.20
2	.43	.28
3	—[c]	.44
4	—[c]	.39
5	.48	.35
6	.42	.36
7	.54	.40
8	.55	.44
9	.59	—[c]
10	—[c]	.48
11	.52	.44
12	.50	.36
13	.48	.42
14	.41	.60
15	.50	.56

[a] In this table (from Nordlie, 1958, p. 65), $N = 136$ for each coefficient.
[b] Week 0, actually the first week, was so labeled because it presupposed no acquaintance.
[c] Attraction responses were not made at these times.

diction. In both years the earliest correlations are near zero, and the final ones in the neighborhood of .5; using a one-tailed test of significance, the coefficients at Week 15 are significant at the .02 level in Year I, and at the .01 level in Year II, with 15 df.

The significance of this increasing trend of the correlations over time was tested by correlating the rank order of the weekly coefficients with the number of weeks of acquaintance, for both years combined. A *rho* of .79 results; with 14 df this is significant well beyond the .01 level. That the trend is characteristic of nearly all individuals is indicated by the fact that in Year I all but 3 of the 17 individual correlations increased from early to late acquaintance, and in Year II all but 4. The probabilities that as many as these individual changes will occur in the predicted direction are about .01 for Year II, and well beyond that for Year I.

An analogous prediction, which takes into account our theoretical assumption that forces toward balance are particularly strong when attraction is highest, is this: following adequate opportunity for Ss to become familiar with each others' orientations, pair agreement about other House members will be closer at very high than at lesser levels of mutual attraction. This prediction is well supported in Table 5.2.

Table 5.2. NUMBERS OF PAIRS AT THREE LEVELS OF MUTUAL ATTRACTION AND AT TWO LEVELS OF AGREEMENT AS TO ATTRACTIVENESS OF OTHER HOUSE MEMBERS (WEEK 15)

Attraction level	Year-I agreement level			Year-II agreement level		
	$\geqq .22$	$\leqq .21$	Total	$\geqq .49$	$\leqq .48$	Total
Highest fourth	26	9	35	30	4	34
Second fourth	16	17	33	20	14	34
Lower half	25	43	68	18	50	68
TOTAL	67	69	136	68	68	136

$$\chi^2 = 10.87\ ^a \qquad\qquad \chi^2 = 24.51\ ^a$$
$$p < .001\ (1\ df) \qquad\qquad p < .001\ (1\ df)$$

[a] Since the prediction being tested specifies very high agreement, χ^2 is computed by dichotomizing between highest and second quarters of the distribution, with respect to attraction.

By various tests, then, there is good support for the prediction that, as a function of increasing **acquaintance, pair agreement** about the attractiveness of other House members becomes increasingly associated with mutual pair attraction, and significantly so on final acquaintance.

INVENTORY OF SPECIFIC TOPICS, AS "OBJECTS" OF AGREEMENT

Nature of the Data

There is no reason to suppose that degree of agreement about any *single* and specific attitude object would provide an adequate basis for predicting to attraction relationships among *all* members of either population. There are so many possible objects of importance that it seems unlikely that degree of agreement about any one of them, of specific nature, would in itself account for very much variance in attraction throughout the entire population. Under certain conditions, of course, populations do become subdivided on the basis of critical issues, but in the present research setting there was no reason to anticipate the arousal of specific issues both controversial and of crucial import. No such issues did, in fact, arise; and if they had, they could have been studied only *ex post facto* since they were not anticipated.

With regard to specific issues, the following strategy was therefore planned. (1) While predictions could not be made from single attitudes of specific nature, the *number* of specific objects about which agreement or disagreement exists could be taken as an index. Such an index, of course, would totally ignore the content of attitude items. (2) Since, by hypothesis, attraction is predictable from agreement weighted by importance (and not necessarily from agreement alone), the frequencies of agreement and disagreement from which such an index is computed should include only responses indicating greater than minimal importance. (3) Since the desired index was one that would be distinctive of each pair of persons, the qualification of importance should apply to *both* of the members of any pair.

The general formula therefore took the following form, for each pair of persons:

$$\frac{N \text{ of disagreeing responses of importance to both pair members}}{N \text{ of disagreeing responses of importance to both members}}$$

Degree of agreement was then expressed (as described in Appendix III) in terms of the improbability with which any obtained combination of Ns is to be expected, given the total population's distribution of responses. As here reported, high p values represent high agreement. That is, a p value of .99 indicates an expected probability of at least 99 in 100 that in this population the ratio of agreements to disagreements (given the absolute number of items involved) will be less than that actually obtained—which is to say that the obtained ratio is improbably high.

The specific attitude items from responses to which the agreement indices are computed were quite different for the two populations studied, as shown in Appendix I. The reason for this discrepancy is simply that we were not wise enough to "do it right the first time." Our initial pretesting paid careful attention to the criteria of relevance to the kinds of populations to be studied, and of "controversiality" (response variance), but not to the criterion of range of issues. Only following analysis of the first year's data (as explained on pp. 38–39) did it become clear that, for our purposes, it was more important to have a wide range of attitude objects than to have more limited sets of interrelated items. As shown in Appendix I, the items selected for Year I were limited to seven "families" of issues, each of which was subdivided into five more specific issues; thus there were thirty-five more or less specific issues, in only seven content areas. The second year's inventory of attitude items was deliberately as miscellaneous as we could make it. While there is some common content between them, the two inventories must be regarded as quite different. Our decision to sacrifice exact replication for the sake of getting better data was difficult; the reader may judge, by comparing findings subsequently reported for the two populations, whether it was a wise one.

Before presenting the findings concerning the predictive power of agreement for attraction, we shall stop to note the distributions of index values at different times, for each of the two years; they appear in Table 5.3. These distributions show that responses to

Table 5.3. DISTRIBUTIONS OF INDEX VALUES OF PAIR AGREEMENT ON INVENTORIES OF SPECIFIC ITEMS, AT TIMES NOTED

Agreement index	Week 0		Week 13		Expected frequencies
	Year I	Year II	Year I	Year II	
$\geq .99$	11	7	12	6	1.4
.90–.98	27	15	28	8	12.2
.80–.89	15	24	18	27	13.6
.20–.79	53	63	46	39	81.6
.10–.19	9	9	7	16	13.6
.00–.09	13	16	17	28	12.2
$< .00$	8	2	8	12	1.4
TOTAL	136	136	136	136	136.0

$$\chi^2 = 4.81 \,^a \qquad \chi^2 = 14.02 \,^a$$
$$p < .05 \;(1 \text{ df}) \qquad p < .001 \;(1 \text{ df})$$

[a] Agreement indices dichotomized between .89 and .90. This point was chosen, *post hoc,* not to test a prediction but, in purely exploratory fashion, to discover whether there might be important differences between the two instruments. As it turns out, this nonpredicted finding is of special relevance to the next prediction to be tested.

the two years' inventories were rather different. In particular, frequencies of very high agreement are significantly higher in Year I (perhaps because that year's inventory dealt exclusively with familiar issues toward which populations like ours had relatively homogeneous attitudes).

Findings

We view the relationship between agreement and mutual attraction as one of interdependence, as we have previously indicated: changes in either can induce changes in the other. But, as shown in Table 5.4, our populations showed little change in attitudes

Table 5.4. FREQUENCIES OF VARYING DEGREES OF EARLY AND LATE AGREEMENT CONCERNING INVENTORIES OF SPECIFIC ITEMS, ON THE PART OF THE SAME PAIRS OF Ss

| Agreement level, Week 0 [b] | Year I | | | | Year II | | | |
| | Agreement level, Week 13 | | | | Agreement level, Week 13 | | | |
	High [a]	Middle [a]	Low [a]	Total	High [a]	Middle [a]	Low [a]	Total
High [a]	25	11	2	38	22	13	4	39
Middle [a]	12	43	13	68	15	30	14	59
Low [a]	4	10	16	30	0	15	23	38
TOTAL	41	64	31	136	37	58	41	136

$$\chi^2 = 47.75 \qquad\qquad \chi^2 = 43.16$$
$$p < .001 \ (4 \ df) \qquad p < .001 \ (4 \ df)$$

[a] For Year I the ranges of index values for the three categories of agreement are .00–.19, .20–.89, and .90–.99; for Year II they are .00–.29, .30–.69, and .70–.99 (low, middle, and high, respectively).
[b] Actually before arriving at the University, in Year II.

toward nonperson objects. Hence our analysis of changing relationships, with increasing acquaintance, is necessarily limited to the treatment of agreement as the independent and mutual attraction as the dependent variable.

Table 5.4 shows the relationship between early and late agreement on the part of the same pairs, which is highly "reliable." (It is necessary to measure change in this way, rather than by correlating early and late scores by the same individuals, because there is no score on the total inventory of items.) In Year I only 6 of 136 pairs, and in Year II only 4 of 136, change from the highest to the lowest quarters (approximately) of agreement, or vice versa.

Thus our first prediction concerning attraction as related to agreement about these miscellaneous issues is that, on later but not on earliest acquaintance, very high attraction will occur more frequently on the part of pairs whose agreement is very high than on the part of other pairs. In view of the fact that very few pairs show much change in agreement, this is equivalent to a prediction that close *pre*-acquaintance agreement (as well as post-acquaintance agreement) will predict to high *post*-acquaintance attraction. Tables 5.5 and 5.6 show that both parts of the prediction are well supported. Table 5.7 shows that, also as expected, pre-acquaintance agreement does not predict to *early* attraction.

Table 5.5. NUMBERS OF PAIRS OF Ss AT VARIOUS LEVELS OF ATTRACTION, AT VERY HIGH AND AT LESSER LEVELS OF EARLY AGREEMENT ABOUT SPECIFIC TOPICS

Week 15 *pair scores* *of attraction*	*Agreement,* *Year I, Week 0*			*Agreement,* *Year II, Week 1*		
	$p \geqq .97$ (*High*)	$p \leqq .96$ (*Not high*)	*Total*	$p \geqq .90$ (*High*)	$p \leqq .89$ (*Not high*)	*Total*
1–64 (high)	13	31	44	12	26	38
65–128	1	21	22	2	28	30
129–192	4	27	31	3	27	30
193–256 (low)	3	36	39	5	33	38
TOTAL	21	115	136	22	114	136

$$\chi^2 = 8.36\,^a \qquad\qquad \chi^2 = 7.70\,^a$$
$$p\ <.005\ (1\ df) \qquad p\ <.01\ (1\ df)$$

Final attraction, both *years combined*	*Early agreement, both years combined*		
	High	*Not high*	*Total*
1– 64 (high)	25	57	82
65–256 (not high)	18	172	190
TOTAL	43	229	272

$$\chi^2 = 18.86 \quad p < .001\ (1\ df)$$

^{a} χ^2 is computed, here as in the following tables, by dichotomizing pair scores of attraction between 64 and 65, rather than at the midpoint of the distribution, since our prediction is stated in terms of very high agreement.

Table 5.6. NUMBERS OF PAIRS OF Ss AT VERY HIGH AND AT LESSER LEVELS OF ATTRACTION AND OF AGREEMENT ABOUT SPECIFIC TOPICS, ON LATE ACQUAINTANCE

| Week 15 pair scores of attraction | Agreement, Year I, Week 13 | | | Agreement, Year II, Week 13 | | |
	$p \geqq .98$ (High)	$p \leqq .97$ (Not high)	Total	$p \geqq .85$ (High)	$p \leqq .84$ (Not high)	Total
1– 64 (high)	14	30	44	12	26	38
65–256 (not high)	9	83	92	7	91	98
TOTAL	23	113	136	19	117	136

$$\chi^2 = 8.78 \qquad\qquad \chi^2 = 11.68$$
$$p < .005 \ (1 \ df) \qquad p < .001 \ (1 \ df)$$

Table 5.7. NUMBERS OF Ss AT VERY HIGH AND AT LESSER LEVELS OF ATTRACTION AND OF AGREEMENT ABOUT SPECIFIC TOPICS, ON EARLIEST ACQUAINTANCE

| Week 0 pair scores of attraction | Agreement, Year I, Week 0 | | | Agreement, Year II, Week 1 | | |
	$p \geqq .97$ (High)	$p \leqq .96$ (Not high)	Total	$p \geqq .90$ (High)	$p \leqq .89$ (Not high)	Total
1– 64 (high)	6	35	41	7	24	31
65–256 (not high)	15	80	95	15	90	105
TOTAL	21	115	136	22	114	136

$$\chi^2 = \text{approximately } 0.0 \qquad \chi^2 = 0.69$$

We regard the set of findings that appear in Tables 5.5, 5.6, and 5.7 as being among our more important ones, and for two somewhat different kinds of reasons. First, the fact that agreement predicts to final but not to early attraction is crucial to our whole theoretical position: if the relationship had been significant on early acquaintance, the finding would have been incomprehensible, since the influencing of attraction by agreement presupposes opportunity for Ss to discover each others' attitudes. Hence it is a plausible interpretation that changes in high attraction followed the discovery of close agreement.

Second, the predictability of final attraction from pre-acquaintance agreement [4] makes it possible to disentangle the hypothetically interdependent effects of the two variables upon each other, since we know that pre-acquaintance agreement could not have been influenced by existing attraction. It has been demonstrated in previous investigations that under a wide range of conditions agreement is influenced by attraction; hence the present demonstration that the reverse process may also occur (presumably coincidentally) reinforces our initial belief that the phenomena are interdependent, and best conceptualized in system-like terms.

VALUES AS OBJECTS OF GENERALIZED ATTITUDES

Procedures

Obvious as it seems with the advantages of hindsight, it did not become clear to us till after the first year's data had been gathered that only rather highly generalized attitudes could be counted on as important and relevant for *all* subjects. Nor could it be assumed that any single one, even among such values, would meet these requirements. Since we were not primarily interested in placing individual Ss on any attitude continuum, but rather in noting degrees of agreement among them, they were asked to rank-order the sets of values, and the index of agreement became a rank-order correlation between Ss' ranks. The predictions tested by these responses are identical with those in the preceding section.

During Year II, two sets of values were thus responded to, each of them both at early and at late weeks. The first was the set of six values as described by Spranger (1928): theoretical, economic, aesthetic, social, political, and religious (see p. 40 for exact instructions). The stability of these rank-orderings is indicated by the following facts: (1) correlations between Week-2 and Week-14 responses were significant at the .01 level (*rhos* between .71 and 1.00) for 14 of the 17 Ss, at the .05 level (*rho* $= .49$) for 1 S, and negative for only 1 S (*rho* $= -.14$); (2) the same values were ranked first at both times by 11 of the 17 Ss, and 4 of the remaining Ss merely exchanged places between their first and second ranks at the two times. These responses were made only at Weeks 2 and 14, and in view of the many instruments responded to

[4] Literally pre-acquaintance in Year II, when responses were returned by mail some weeks before arriving at the University; and effectively so in Year I, when responses were made about 48 hours after arriving at the House.

during the three-month interval it is not at all likely that the Week-14 responses were influenced by attempts to duplicate the earlier ones.

The second set of values, also rank-ordered by each S both early and late (Weeks 0 and 13), was a list of long-range goals that we had reason to believe were meaningful to male college students in this University. The items (henceforth referred to as the "Ten Values") appear exactly as worded, together with verbatim instructions, on pp. 39–40; they may be briefly labeled as follows:

1. financial success
2. being liked
3. success in family life
4. being intellectually capable
5. living by religious principles
6. helping others
7. being normal, well adjusted
8. cooperating with others
9. doing a thorough job
10. occupational success.

Findings

Table 5.8 shows results very similar to those for agreement concerning the inventories of specific issues. (Because changes in

Table 5.8. NUMBERS OF PAIRS OF Ss AT VERY HIGH AND AT LESSER LEVELS OF ATTRACTION AND OF AGREEMENT CONCERNING SPRANGER VALUES, AT TIMES NOTED (YEAR II)

Week 2 rho of agreement	Pair attraction, Week 2			Pair attraction, Week 14		
	≤ 64 (High)	≥ 65 (Not high)	Total	≤ 64 (High)	≥ 65 (Not high)	Total
$\geq .65$ (high)	10	13	23	14	9	23
.00–.64	13	41	54	13	41	54
< .00 (low)	20	39	59	14	45	59
TOTAL	43	93	136	41	95	136

$$\chi^2 = 1.17 \, ^a \qquad\qquad \chi^2 = 10.84 \, ^a$$
$$p \; < .50 \; (1 \; df) \qquad\qquad p \; < .001 \; (1 \; df)$$

[a] Agreement *rhos* are dichotomized between .64 and .65.

Spranger-Value responses are so slight, the relationship of *final* agreement to final attraction is almost identical with that between early agreement and final attraction; hence the former distribution is not presented in Table 5.8.) With regard to both "objects," close early agreement predicts to high attraction on late but not on early acquaintance. With respect to the Ten Values, as in the case of Spranger Values, individuals' correlations between early and late rank-orderings were high (15 of the 17 significant beyond the .05 level, and all 17 positive); hence, in Table 5.9, we make

Table 5.9. NUMBERS OF PAIRS OF *Ss* AT VERY HIGH AND AT LESSER LEVELS OF ATTRACTION AND OF AGREEMENT CONCERNING TEN VALUES (YEAR II)

Week 0 rho *of agreement*	*Pair attraction, Week 0*			*Pair attraction, Week 13*		
	$\leqq 64$ (*High*)	$\geqq 65$ (*Not high*)	*Total*	$\leqq 64$ (*High*)	$\geqq 65$ (*Not high*)	*Total*
$\geqq .57$ (high)	7	14	21	11	10	21
.38–.56	9	18	27	9	18	27
$\leqq .37$ (low)	25	63	88	20	68	88
TOTAL	41	95	136	40	96	136

$$\chi^2 = \text{approximately } 0.0 \; ^a \qquad \chi^2 = 5.08 \; ^a$$
$$p < .025 \; (1 \text{ df})$$

[a] Agreement *rhos* dichotomized between .56 and .57.

use only of the early agreement responses. This table shows, again, that early agreement predicts significantly to late but not to early attraction.

SUMMARY: PAIR AGREEMENT AND MUTUAL ATTRACTION

We have found that the association between high pair attraction and high pair agreement about the attractiveness of other House members, which on early acquaintance was very slight, becomes significant on late acquaintance, in both populations. We have also found, in both populations, that close pre-acquaintance agreement in responding to inventories of specific topics predicts significantly, on late but not on early acquaintance, to high pair attraction. And in Year II, when Ss rank-ordered two sets of values, early or pre-acquaintance agreement at high levels also predicted significantly to late but not to early attraction at high levels. This total set of findings, in support of our predictions, suggests (1) that agreement concerning attitudes which change very little during the acquaintance process becomes a significant determinant of attraction preferences; and (2) that high-attraction preferences (with regard to which pre-acquaintance orientations are nonexistent) change, from early to late acquaintance, in such manner that agreement concerning other House members also becomes a significant determinant of high pair attraction. Both of these processes, occurring during the trial-and-error process of developing stable relationships of high mutual attraction, are consistent with our hypotheses concerning tendencies toward system balance.

Objective Variables

We could not, of course, obtain information from our subjects concerning all of the attitudes which might contribute to system formation. Insofar as our objectives were to apply tests of general propositions to entire populations, it was necessary to limit ourselves to a very few attitudes that were presumably of population-wide importance and relevance. At the same time, we assumed that the members of most if not all high-attraction pairs, or larger sets of persons, would hold similar attitudes not included among those that we happened to measure. Our selection of a very few of these was for purposes of illustrative testing of our hypotheses, and not for purposes of complete explanation of all sources of attraction. In short, we assumed that any high-attraction set of persons could be viewed as a set of overlapping systems in which the same persons held similar attitudes toward many objects of importance and relevance to them. Figure 5.1 illustrates this assumption, in schematic form.

Even though we obtained only a very few comparable attitude responses from our Ss, certain information was available to us from which attitudes could be inferred. In particular, we knew something about our subjects' residential and religious backgrounds, their ages, their College affiliations within the University, and their room assignments in the House. These kinds of information may be regarded as quasi-demographic variables.

Our assumptions were simply that Ss similar in these objective respects (with the exception of room assignments) are likely, in

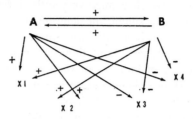

Fig. 5.1. Schematic diagram of overlapping systems of high-attraction persons. *Plus* indicates favorable and *minus* unfavorable attitudes.

a probabalistic sense, to have similar attitudes; that if so, they are likely to discover this fact; and if so, their attraction toward each other is likely to increase.

The Variables

The rationale for employing each of these variables, together with our procedures for obtaining indices of them, was as follows.

1. *Age.* The age range in each population was 18–25, on first arriving at the House. The first population included two, and the second four, military service veterans. The attainment of one's twenty-first birthday is an important event among males in a community where laws concerning the serving and selling of alcoholic beverages to minors are enforced; there is apt to be a distinction between those who can and those who cannot enjoy the rewards of legal majority. Hence we dichotomized our Ss as either 21 years of age (of whom there were five in the first population and seven in the second) or not.

2. *College Enrollment.* Ten Ss in the first population, and 9 in the second, were enrolled in the College of Literature, Science, and the Arts. The remainder, in both years, were in the College of Engineering. It is reasonable to assume that students in either college are likely to share certain attitudes and interests that are less characteristic of students in the other college.

3. *Religious Preference.* In each population there were either

4 or 5 *S*s who indicated Jewish preference or affiliation, 4 of Roman Catholic, and 8 or 9 of Protestant preference or affiliation.[5]

4. *Urban-rural Background.* About a third of our 34 *S*s' homes were in small towns in Michigan, and all but one of them had previously attended out-state (and for the most part small) colleges or junior colleges. Nearly a quarter of them had similar backgrounds in other, near-by states. Thus 9 *S*s in the first population and 10 in the second were classified as of rural residential background. The remainder [6] were either from cities of a million or larger or from smaller cities in thickly populated areas near the Atlantic seaboard; most of these had attended large universities or nationally known colleges. These *S*s were classified as urban, or more properly nonrural. We were not sure exactly what kinds of attitudes, if any, were likely to distinguish subjects in the two categories—perhaps a complex of attitudes that might be labeled "sophistication."

5. *Room Assignment.* In both years, subjects were arbitrarily given room assignments, which necessarily determined roommateship also. Nine men lived on the second and eight on the third floor of the House. There were one triple room, two doubles, and either one or two single rooms on each floor. Thus there were ten pairs of roommates, each year. We reasoned that proximity, as determined by residence on the same floor—and, *a fortiori,* in the same room—would speed up processes of acquaintance; thus there would be earlier opportunity for the discovery of common interests and attitudes (whatever they might be) among floormates. We also allowed for the possibility, particularly on the part of roommates, of sharing confidential intimacies of a nature that would necessarily not be known to us. The presumed contribution of this variable, unlike that of the preceding four, is by way of post-acquaintance influence.

Thus, with regard to each of these five variables, every pair of *S*s was noted as either similar or dissimilar. It was neither possible nor necessary that the exact content of the attitudinal similarities likely to be associated with these quasi-demographic similarities be known to us. Our prediction, therefore, was simply that pairs of *S*s

[5] One subject who replied "none" to this question was classified as Protestant because of his known family background.

[6] With one exception: one subject in the second population could not be classified unambiguously, and was excluded from analyses of this variable.

similar in one or more of these variables were more likely to become highly attracted to one another than dissimilar pairs. Unless otherwise noted, we considered all pairs whose combined ranks of attraction to each other were in the highest one-sixth of all pair scores (as nearly as possible, allowing for ties) to be high-attraction pairs.

Findings

Year I. At Week 0 (after about four days of acquaintance), similarity with regard to no one of the five variables significantly distinguished between high-attraction and other pairs. However, with regard to college of enrollment, floor assignment, and urban-rural residence, differences are significant at or about the .10 level; moreover, any combination of two of the three variables distinguishes at about the .05 level between the high-attraction and other pairs. Six of the fifteen pairs (40 percent) alike in all three variables were among the highest sixth in attraction, as compared with only 14 percent of the remaining pairs.

One week later (Week 1), the variable that most clearly distinguished high-attraction from other pairs was none of these, but similarity of religious preference was almost significantly distinctive of the high-attraction pairs ($\chi^2 = 3.60$; 3.8 is significant at the .05 level, with 1 df). College of enrollment is no longer distinctive at all, and similarity in floor assignment and in urban-rural background only slightly so.

At Week 2 only urban-rural background is at all distinctive of the high-attraction pairs; 25 percent of them, as compared with 12 percent of the other pairs, are similar in this respect. But this variable tends to be associated, for the high-attraction pairs, with college of enrollment, age, and floor assignment—especially the first of these; the combination of similarity in college of enrollment and in residential background distinguishes significantly between high-attraction pairs (of whom 37.5 percent are similar in both respects) and other pairs (of whom 10 percent are similar in both ways).

On final acquaintance (at Week 15), only similarity of urban-rural residence (treated as a single variable) distinguishes between high-attraction and other pairs at a level of significance approximating .05. But in combination with similarity of age it discriminates very clearly. Thirteen of the 34 pairs (38 percent) of *S*s alike in both respects are among the highest sixth in attraction, as compared with 1 of 102 (or 1 percent)—a highly significant difference.

Since—particularly after ample time for acquaintance—involvement in high-attraction pairs is not equally distributed among all Ss, we may ask whether the popular Ss, who slightly overchoose each other, differ in respect to these variables from the least popular ones. The evidence is clear that they do not. (1) The 5 older Ss hardly differ at all in mean popularity from the 12 others, though the older ones (who rank from 4 to 14 in popularity at Week 15) tend not to be extreme. (2) All 4 of the most popular Ss and 3 of the 4 least popular ones are enrolled in Arts rather than in Engineering. (3) The 4 most popular Ss include all three religious preferences, 2 of them being Protestant, as might be expected, since this is the largest group; the 4 least popular include 2 Protestants and 2 Jews, which is hardly surprising, since the Catholics are least numerous. (4) Both the 4 most popular and the 4 least popular are equally divided between the two floors. (5) Both the 4 most popular and the 4 least popular are equally divided between Ss of urban and of rural background; in mean rank of popularity, however, these labeled "rural" are slightly preferred, their mean rank being 8.0 as compared with 10.1 for the others.

Hence we may conclude that at Week 15 the significant tendency for high-attraction pairs to resemble each other in age and in residential background is not an artifactual consequence of any association between these variables and general popularity status. Rather, it is a differentiated, person-to-person phenomenon.

Year II. In none of the first three weeks was similarity in any one of the variables significantly associated with high attraction. At each of these weeks, however, similarity in two of the variables was associated with high attraction at a significance level of about .1. No combinations of these variables improved this significance level. At Week 0 these variables were college of enrollment and floor assignment; at Weeks 1 and 2 they were age and floor assignment. By Week 15, however, three of the variables showed relationships at or about the .05 level of significance; college enrollment, floor assignment, and residential background.

The interpretation of this last finding is confounded, however, by the fact that each of these three variables is associated with popularity. Subjects enrolled in the Arts College, who lived on the second floor, and whose backgrounds were urban received significantly more high-attraction choices than those in the opposed categories. But the individuals in none of these three categories received high-attraction choices significantly more often from each other than from members of the contrasting category.

This combination of findings raises the question whether it is similarity with respect to college enrollment, floor assignment, and urban background that tends to result in high attraction, or whether it is a case of popular Ss being attracted to each other, or some combination of both, or whether other factors are responsible for the association between popularity and similarity. One additional set of facts is relevant: it is not necessarily similarity as such, with regard to these variables, that results in high attraction, but (except for floor assignment) similarity with respect to a specific one of the two categories of each variable. That is, similarity in being enrolled in the *Arts* College, and in *urban* background contributes to high attraction, but similarity in being enrolled in the Engineering College and in rural background does not. With respect to both variables, the differences are significant, as shown in Table 5.10.

Table 5.10. NUMBERS OF PAIRS WHO ARE ALIKE IN EACH OF TWO CATEGORIES OF TWO "OBJECTIVE" VARIABLES, ACCORDING TO TWO LEVELS OF ATTRACTION (YEAR II, WEEK 15)

Attraction level	College enrollment		Residential background	
	Arts	Engineering	Urban	Rural
Very high	13	3	6	4
Other pairs	23	25	9	41
TOTAL	36	28	15	45

$$\chi^2 = 4.14$$
$$p < .05 \text{ (1 df)} \qquad p = .010 \text{ (exact test)}$$

Furthermore, Arts College students do not receive significantly more high-attraction choices from each other than from Engineering students; they receive relatively many from both groups. Exactly the same thing is true of urban subjects, who are almost as attractive to rural subjects as to each other. With regard to popularity status, however, the reverse is true. The most popular

*S*s at Week 15 are significantly more often in high-attraction pairs with each other than with other *S*s, as shown in Table 5.11.[7]

Table 5.11. NUMBERS OF HIGH-ATTRACTION AND OF OTHER PAIRS IN WHICH MOST POPULAR SUBJECTS ARE INVOLVED (YEAR II, WEEK 15)

Level of pair attraction	Four most popular *S*s		Eight most popular *S*s	
	With each other	*With remaining *S*s*	*With each other*	*With remaining *S*s*
Highest quarter [a]	5	17	16	18
Other	1	35	12	54
TOTAL	6	52	28	72

			$\chi^2 = 7.96$
	p = .023 (exact test)		*p* < .005 (1 df)

[a] Highest quarter of expected, not obtained, frequencies.

Hence, we must conclude either (1) that popular *S*s are attracted to each others' popularity; or (2) that they are attracted by certain characteristics in each other (beyond college of enrollment and residence background) that they tend not to find in other *S*s and which "happen" to be associated with popularity. The first of these possibilities is not implausible (even though popular *S*s are not particularly attracted to each other in Year I); since popular individuals are in a position to reciprocate many high-attraction choices, they might elect to choose those high in the pecking order of popularity. The second alternative seems to us more probable, however. We have elsewhere shown that the more popular *S*s tend to be similar in ordering Spranger Values, and tend to be low *F*-scorers. Thus it seems probable that it is the *attitudes* that tend—though not necessarily—to be associated with urban background, and with enrollment in the Arts College, and not the *objective facts* of enrollment or residential background that lead to reciprocal

[7] The comparable tables for Week 15 of Year I show no significant relationships. Among the 4 most popular *S*s the comparable distribution to that shown in Table 5.11 is $\begin{smallmatrix} 2 & 21 \\ 4 & 31 \end{smallmatrix}$, and among the 8 most popular it is $\begin{smallmatrix} 13 & 21 \\ 15 & 51 \end{smallmatrix}$; the χ^2 value of the latter distribution is 1.99, significant at <.25 with 1 df.

attraction among those holding such "typically" urban and Arts-College attitudes. Thus we find, among the 4 most popular Ss, 2 of urban background, both of whom do hold such attitudes; and 2 of rural background, one of whom does and one of whom does not hold those attitudes. All of the three attraction relationships between this one among the 4 Ss whose attitudes are not "typically" urban are less close with the other 3 individuals than are the three pair relationships among those three who are both popular and urban in attitude.

Why is it that one set of attitudes rather than another tends to go with popularity? Perhaps the apparent sophistication of the urbanite is part of the answer, but we are convinced that sheer chance had a good deal to do with it. That is, the personality traits that tend to make male student-peers widely attractive to others are not necessarily associated with such a set of attitudes, and no such association was in fact found in the first population. Our selective procedures turned up one population in which characteristics making for popularity were associated with attitudes that might be labeled "intellectual-nonauthoritarian," and one population in which comparable personal attributes were not associated with those attitudes. It could happen in either way—and in fact happened in each way. (See Chapter 13 for further evidence on this point.)

Comparison of Populations

The differences between the two populations are consistent, finally, with the interpretation that a significant and influential number of individuals in the second population, but not in the first, were characterized by sensitivity to attitudes, on the part of their peers, that were both important to themselves and not readily observable. Their attraction choices, furthermore, were influenced thereby. Relative to this population, the attraction choices among the more influential members of the first population tended to be determined by the more readily observable characteristics of their peers.

Number of Objective Variables in Common

If sheer numbers of the five variables with respect to which pairs are similar are counted, without regard to the content of the variables, pairs may be categorized as having from 0 to 5 of them in common. We assume (1) that pairs alike in these "objective" respects are more apt to have similar attitudes than those different in the same respects; and (2) that the wider the range of similar attitudes on the part of pairs of Ss, the greater the probability that high attraction will develop on their part. Hence we predict higher attraction on the part of pairs alike in many than on the part of those alike in few of these five variables.

A second prediction is based upon two other considerations. As we have already noted, the "expected" attitudes are not invariably associated with these objective characteristics; according to our hypotheses, attraction is determined by perceived and not necessarily by actual similarity of attitudes. Further, it is more likely that others' attitudes will be inferred from objective characteristics on early than on late acquaintance, since acquaintance makes it possible to distinguish between fact and expectancy. We therefore predict that the relationship between range of objectively similar characteristics and attraction will decrease with acquaintance.

We have computed the necessary relationships for testing these predictions for both populations, at Weeks 0, 1, 2, 5, and 15. The relevant data appear in Table 5.12 for Weeks 0 and 15; at the intervening weeks the cell frequencies are intermediate (with few and trifling exceptions). None of the four distributions shown in

Table 5.12. NUMBERS OF PAIRS ALIKE WITH RESPECT TO VARIOUS NUMBERS OF FIVE OBJECTIVE VARIABLES, AT TWO LEVELS OF PAIR ATTRACTION

Attraction level	Year I Number of variables			Total	Year II Number of variables			Total
	0 or 1	2 or 3	4 or 5		0 or 1	2 or 3	4 or 5	
Week 0								
Higher half	11	48	13	72	16	32	11	59
Lower half	16	42	6	64	18	40	3	61
TOTAL	27	90	19	136	34	72	14	120
Week 15								
Higher half	9	43	12	64	12	39	5	56
Lower half	18	47	7	72	22	33	9	64
TOTAL	27	90	19	136	34	72	14	120

this table is statistically significant, though the relationship is in the predicted direction at Week 0 in each population, and if the Year-I and Year-II tables for Week 0 are combined, the relationship is significant: $x^2 = 8.68$, and $p < .02$ with 2 df. So far, then, our prediction is reasonably well supported. At no other time do the combined distributions for both years show a significant relationship. At Week 15, it is only in Year I that the predicted relationship appears at all, and to about the same extent as at Week 0 (and all intervening times). At no time in Year I, however, is p less than .10.

In sum, the predicted relationship appears, nonsignificantly and without change, at all times in Year I; and in Year II it appears nonsignificantly at Week 0 and eventually disappears entirely.

The two populations thus appear to be somewhat different, and the data in Table 5.13 show that this is indeed the case. In Year I, there is at all times an increase in level of attraction paralleling

Table 5.13. Percentages of Pair Relationships that Are in the Upper Half [a] of the Distribution of Attraction, at Three Levels of Similarity in Objective Variables

	Year I Number of variables			Year II [b] Number of variables		
Week	0 or 1	2 or 3	4 or 5	0 or 1	2 or 3	4 or 5
0	40.7	53.3	68.4	47.0	44.4	78.6
1	44.4	48.9	68.4	50.0	50.0	57.1
2	40.7	51.1	57.9	38.2	52.8	50.0
15	33.3	47.8	63.1	35.3	54.1	35.7

[a] That is, of the expected, not necessarily of the obtained distributions.
[b] Excluding one subject, whose status on one of the variables is indeterminate. The Year-II percentages have been recomputed, including this subject also, once assigning him to the urban and once to the nonurban category; the above percentages are hardly changed at all as a result.

increase in the number of variables with respect to which pair members are alike; and there are only slight week-to-week changes. In Year II, however, only at Week 0 does an increase in attraction parallel an increase in the number of similar variables; and there is a steady decline, with increasing acquaintance, in the proportion of pairs with maximum similarity in variables who are high-attraction pairs. The most important change in Year II involves the category of similarity in four or five variables; of the 14 (of 120) pairs who have this degree of similarity, the numbers in the upper half of attraction are 11, 8, 7, and 5 at Weeks 0, 1, 2, and 15, respectively. The change from Weeks 0 to 15 is indicated by the distribution $\begin{smallmatrix} 11 & 5 \\ 3 & 9 \end{smallmatrix}$, the χ^2 value of which is 3.64, significant at approximately the .05 level (3.8 being the required value).

There is, however, one set of conditions under which the predicted relationship between pair attraction and number of objective variables in which pair members are alike appears consistently in both populations. If we contrast 0–1 with 4–5 variables and apply a sign test for all weeks in which the attraction data were obtained, results are as follows: In Year I the difference is in the predicted direction in 13 of 13 weeks, and in Year II in 14 of 15 weeks. Only by this criterion does the predicted relationship appear consistently in both years.

Summary

We conclude that, on earliest acquaintance, the number of objective variables about which pairs are similar is related to their attraction level, as predicted. In one population but not in the other, this relationship declines steadily with acquaintance. This finding is consistent with the interpretation—which is also suggested by other findings (see pp. 88–92)—that in the first population attraction was more determined by individuals' readily observable characteristics than in the second.[8]

Summary: Two-person Collective Systems

The relationship between pair members' attraction toward each other and their degree of agreement about the attractiveness of the remaining fifteen House members increases with acquaintance (in both populations), as predicted, and becomes significant in the final weeks of acquaintance. A similar prediction concerning pair attraction and pair agreement in responding both to batteries of miscellaneous attitude items and to lists of values is also supported: degree of pre-acquaintance agreement predicts significantly

[8] A more detailed analysis of attraction relationships among roommates and floormates appears in Chapter 11.

to pair attraction on late but not on early acquaintance. This latter finding would not have been possible except for the fact that pre-acquaintance attitudes hardly changed at all. Since pre-acquaintance agreement could not have been influenced by post-acquaintance attraction, it is clear that early and unstable orientations toward persons were influenced by pre-existing and stable orientations, especially those of value-like nature.

We also found that pair similarity with regard to certain objective, quasi-demographic variables predicted to early pair attraction—and also, in one population, to later attraction. The total set of findings is consistent with the interpretation that the predictive power of pair similarity of these kinds inheres in the common orientations that are likely to be associated with similarity of environment, or that are assumed to be associated with them.

Thus several quite diverse sets of data all provide support for the general hypothesis that, following but not before adequate opportunity for pair members to become familiar with each others' attitudes, pair attraction is predictable from actual agreement. Attraction preferences change in balance-promoting ways as individuals acquire further information about one anothers' orientations.

PART THREE

Individual Differences

Individual systems of orientation are characterized by certain psychological processes, and it would be somewhat surprising if these processes operated in identical form in all individuals. It is even possible that they do not operate at all in certain persons. And since, according to our formulation, the maintaining of balance in collective systems is dependent upon individual tendencies toward achieving or maintaining balance, such individual differences—insofar as they exist—will have their effects upon collective systems, also.

We shall therefore be especially interested in the question of individual differences in sensitivity to strain. And since we have viewed strain as a consequence of the opposition between autistic forces toward balance and forces toward realistic assessment of things, we shall particularly want to note whether individuals differ in susceptibility to each of these kinds of forces. This is the problem of Chapter 6. And in Chapter 7 we shall inquire whether such individual differences as have been reported in Chapter 6 are associated with certain other personality variables.

So far, our findings have been described exclusively in statistical terms, involving total populations of persons or pairs. If it should turn out that such support as we have so far found for our predictions is contributed by only a fraction of our Ss—that is by those who are sensitive to strain while the remainder are not, or only by those distinguished by certain personality characteristics—then we could generalize, from our findings, only to persons who resemble those particular kinds of subjects. Part Three is concerned, in this sense, with the generalizability of the basic findings presented in Part Two.

Strain-related Variables: _____ 6

Accuracy and Balance

It is by the assessment of estimates of others' orientations that sensitivity to forces of balance and of reality may be detected. Our analysis of individual differences, in this chapter, will therefore be based upon subjects' estimates, in both populations, both of others' attraction toward House members and of others' attitudes toward various common objects.

ESTIMATES OF OTHERS' ATTRACTIONS TOWARD HOUSE MEMBERS: YEAR I

Accuracy of Estimates

Our subjects had no information about each other before meeting; moreover, no general information about the American scene, or about the campus culture, could contribute to their success in differentiating among different Ss' rank-ordering of the other House members in attractiveness. Insofar as Ss are accurate in estimating one another's rank-ordering of the remaining Ss, therefore, it may be assumed that their accuracy has been acquired through familiarity with those Ss whose responses they have estimated.[1]

[1] There is also the possibility that, instead of being familiar in any direct way with estimatees' actual attraction preferences, estimators were familiar only with House-wide stereotypes of popularity statuses. It is altogether unlikely, however, that this latter possibility contributed in any significant way to the findings reported below, since the indices of general agreement among all 17 Ss (cf. Kendall's formula for W, 1948) are .23 and .17 at Weeks 1 and 5, respectively; and since the median *rhos* of actual agreement for the sets of pairs described below are .21 and .19 at the same times.

The universality of tendencies toward accuracy. The attraction responses at Weeks 1 and 5 of Year I are appropriate for testing the hypothesis that all Ss show some tendency toward accuracy. In the first of the following analyses we have used only the rank-orderings attributed by each S to his first 2 and last 2 attraction ranks—68 of them in all, at each of these times. (Only for Weeks 1 and 5 are comparable data of this kind available.) Our index of accuracy is the rank-order correlation (*rho*) between these attributed rank-orderings and the actual ones made by the estimatees. The basic data appear in Table 6.1.

Table 6.1. NUMBERS OF Ss WHOSE INDICES OF ACCURACY (*rhos*), IN ESTIMATING OTHERS' RANK-ORDERING OF HOUSE MEMBERS' ATTRACTIVENESS, ARE AT LEVELS INDICATED (YEAR I)

| | Attraction rank given by estimator to estimatee | | | | | | | |
| | 1 | | 2 | | 15 | | 16 | |
Accuracy rho	Week 1	Week 5	Week 1	Week 5	Week 1	Week 5	Week 1	Week 5
$\geqq .75$	0	4	3	1	1	0	0	1
.50–.74	4	9	4	4	5	4	6	5
.25–.49	10	3	5	8	6	7	3	6
.00–.24	2	1	3	4	2	2	7	3
$< .00$	1	0	2	0	3	4	1	2
TOTAL	17	17	17	17	17	17	17	17

Among these 136 *rhos,* only 13 are negative, though the initial probabilities of either sign are equal. Thus the general tendency toward making accurate estimates is very clear (p is far beyond .001). In individual terms, the 13 negative *rhos* are distributed among 10 Ss, of whom 3 have 2 each (#15, 16, 28).

There are two conditions, relevant to the data in Table 6.1, that might be expected to affect the accuracy of estimates: length of acquaintance and level of attraction toward the estimatee. More accuracy is to be expected after 38 than after 10 days of acquaintance, and toward very high- than toward very low-attraction estimatees—because of the greater amount of time presumably spent with the former, with consequently greater opportunity for acquiring information about them. In the second and fourth columns of frequencies in Table 6.1 both of these conditions are maximized, and in neither of these columns is there a single instance of a negative correlation. The condition of attraction can be further maximized by considering only Rank-1 choices (column 2), since the difference in accuracy between Rank-1 and Rank-2 choices at Week 5 is significant ($\chi^2 = 5.78$, and $p < .02$ with 1 df). Under these optimal conditions, only 4 of the 17 individual *rhos* are less than .54, significant at approximately the .05 level with 13 df. These 4 individuals are #16, 27, 28, and 29, of whom 2 (#16 and 28) are mentioned above as showing 2 negative *rhos* each.

Another possible index of accuracy is improvement between Weeks 1 and 5. Its satisfactoriness is impaired, however, by the fact that there were many instances of rather sharp change in attraction level between these two times, and changes in attraction (as we have already noted) are likely to be accompanied by changes in frequency of association and by consequent change in opportunity to acquire information. We have therefore compared accuracy *rhos* for Weeks 1 and 5 only in those 17 instances in which the same estimator assigned the same estimatees either Rank 1 or Rank 2 on both occasions. In only four of the 17 comparisons are the later estimates less accurate—in the cases of #15, 17, 21, and 27. Of these individuals, both #15 and 27 have been mentioned as relatively inaccurate by one criterion but not by another. Subject #26 (relatively low by both previous criteria) was not among those for whom a comparison between Weeks 1 and 5 could be made.

In summary, there is no individual—not even #28, all four of whose accuracy *rhos* at Week 5 are positive, and whose two positive *rhos* at Week 1 are larger than his two negative ones; nor #16, three of whose accuracy *rhos* at both weeks are positive, whose positive *rhos* at both times are larger than his negative ones, and who improves between Weeks 1 and 5—who shows complete immunity to considerations of reality in estimating other *S*s' degrees of attraction toward other House members.

Ordering individuals with respect to accuracy. Individual accuracy *rhos* (as described above) provide a possible basis for rank-ordering. Unfortunately, however (from the point of view of discovering a reliable index), individuals tend not to maintain very stable positions between Weeks 1 and 5. The highest correlation obtainable is a *rho* of +.60 between *S*s' accuracy *rhos* at Weeks 1 and 5, in respect to their Rank-1 choices (who are not necessarily the same individuals at these two times). Since this coefficient is significant at the .01 level, with 15 df, we may use the two sets of coefficients as a basis for rank-ordering our *S*s in respect to accuracy of estimating the person to whom each is most strongly attracted at the time of making the estimate. Each *S*'s position is determined by the mean of his two accuracy *rhos* (at Week 1 and at Week 5) with respect to his Rank-1 choice. The order is as shown in Table 6.2.

Table 6.2. INDIVIDUAL MEANS OF ACCURACY *rhos* IN ESTIMATING THEIR RANK-1 CHOICES REGARDING ATTRACTION TO OTHER HOUSE MEMBERS AT WEEKS 1 AND 5, TOGETHER WITH INDIVIDUAL RANKS (YEAR I)

Subject	Mean rho	Rank
15	.76	1
24	.71	2
17	.70	3
14	.69	4
22	.62	5
18	.61	6
21	.56	7
19	.53	8
23	.52	9
26	.51	10
30	.50	11
20	.43	12
29	.35	13.5
25	.35	13.5
27	.33	15
28	.13	16
16	.10	17

Balance: Perceived Agreement Associated with High Attraction

In Chapter 2 we described forces toward balance as autistic, in the sense that they represent personal, psychological tendencies, irrespective of external reality. Forces toward balance and toward reality are not necessarily opposed, since in the case of actually perfect agreement the demands of both kinds of forces would be met by accurate estimates. But in most instances actual discrepancy is sufficient to introduce some conflict, since both demands cannot be fully met.

The universality of tendencies toward balance. The Week-1 and Week-5 data that we have just analyzed from the point of view of accuracy may also be examined for tendencies toward balance. Insofar as all *S*s tend to perceive closer agreement with their high- than with their low-attraction choices, we may conclude that there is a universal tendency toward balance. The basic data appear in Table 6.3 (analogous to Table 6.1), in which the index

Table 6.3. NUMBERS OF SUBJECTS ESTIMATING AGREEMENT AT VARIOUS LEVELS WITH HIGHEST- AND LOWEST-ATTRACTION OTHERS REGARDING HOUSE MEMBERS (YEAR I)

Rho *of* estimated agreement	Estimator's rank of attraction							
	1		*2*		*15*		*16*	
	Week 1	*Week 5*	*Week 1*	*Week 5*	*Week 1*	*Week 5*	*Week 1*	*Week 5*
≧.75	7	8	8	8	2	0	0	0
.50–.74	9	7	6	6	3	4	4	6
.25–.49	1	2	2	3	4	3	2	2
.00–.24	0	0	1	0	6	5	4	1
<.00	0	0	0	0	2	5	7	8
TOTAL	17	17	17	17	17	17	17	17

of perceived agreement is the correlation (*rho*) between *S*'s attribution to another *S* of a rank-ordering of attraction toward the remaining 15 *S*s and his own rank-ordering of attraction toward the same 15 *S*s.

The general tendency toward balance is clear enough in Table 6.3: at either time, alone, there is significantly more perceived agreement at Ranks 1–2 than at Ranks 15–16, at levels well beyond .001.[2] Since there are no significant differences between Ranks

---

[2] The actual χ^2 values are 24.05 at Week 1 and 19.48 at Week 5, with 1 df.

1 and 2, or between 15 and 16, they may be combined for purposes of making this test.

From the point of view of the universality of susceptibility to balance (that is, its occurrence in all Ss), we may note the following. (1) At neither time is any S's *rho* of estimated agreement with either his first or his second choice negative, whereas at Rank 15 there are 2 and 5 negative *rhos* at Weeks 1 and 5, respectively, and at Rank 16 nearly half of them are negative. (2) At Week 1 and at attraction Rank 1 (where probabilities of autism are greatest), only one S's *rho* is less than .50 (#29). (3) The 9 (out of 68) *rhos* at Ranks 1–2 for both times that are less than .50 are contributed by only 5 Ss, as estimators; but only 1 of these 5 (#29) contributes one or more *rhos* below .50 at both times, and only 1 other S (#30) contributes more than a single equally low *rho* (at both Ranks 1 and 2, Week 5). (4) Only 3 Ss (#20, 23, 29) contribute at Week 1 any reversals of the expected order of magnitude of *rhos* (i.e., both of those at Ranks 1 and 2 are expected to be higher than either at Ranks 15 and 16). Of these 3 Ss, however, only #29 contributes more than one reversal (the possibilities being 0, 1, or 2). At Week 5, only Ss #28 and 29 contribute any reversals (one each).

Assembling these "exceptions," according to the preceding criteria, it is apparent that only #29 is relatively conspicuous for lack of balance. No other subject provides an exception by more than a single criterion.

Ordering individuals with respect to balance. The individual's discrepancy between perceived agreement with his attraction Ranks 1–2 and his Ranks 15–16 would provide a good index of his state of balance, providing it offered reasonable stability over time. The fact is, however, that individual degrees of perceived agreement at attraction Ranks 15–16 are not at all stable. As a matter of fact, individual *rhos* of perceived agreement at Rank 15 do not correlate well with those at Rank 16 (particularly at Week 5, when the coefficient is only .32), so that they cannot well be pooled. At both times, however, degree of perceived agreement at Rank 1 correlates rather well with that at Rank 2 (*rho* = .70 and .60 at Weeks 5 and 1, respectively), so that pooling at these two ranks is a reasonable procedure. Thus pooled, the correlation between perceived agreement at Week 1 with that at Week 5 is .785; with 15 df, this is significant at less than .01.

In order to establish a rank order of individuals we therefore used, for each *S,* the median of his four *rhos* for Weeks 1 and 5 at Ranks 1 and 2, with results as shown in Table 6.4. Not sur-

Table 6.4. INDIVIDUAL MEDIANS OF *rhos* INDICATING DEGREES OF ESTIMATED AGREEMENT WITH THEIR FIRST TWO ATTRAC-TION CHOICES REGARDING OTHER HOUSE MEMBERS AT WEEKS 1 AND 5, TOGETHER WITH INDIVIDUAL RANKS (YEAR I)

Subject	Median rho	Rank
18	.83	1
27	.80	2
21	.77	3
19	.74	4
14	.62	5
22	.58	6
17	.56	7
16	.55	8
24	.41	9
25	.40	10
23	.38	11
15	.22	12
26	.21	13
28	.14	14
30	.05	15
20	−.07	16
29	−.21	17

prisingly, *S* #29 emerges with Rank 17, and a median *rho* that is negative. The *rhos* of two other *S*s (#30 and 20) also approach zero. In both of the latter cases, however, *rhos* of perceived agree-ment are higher for Ranks 1 and 2 than for Ranks 15 and 16 (con-sistently for #30, and, for #20, by large differences with the ex-ception of one of his four *rhos* at Ranks 1–2). Since these latter facts are not taken into consideration by the index appearing in Table 6.4, we may conclude that only in the case of #29 is there clear evidence of indifference to balance, with respect to other House members.

Relationships between Accuracy and Balance

The rank orders that appear in Tables 6.2 and 6.4 are not significantly correlated, the coefficient being +.30. From the point of view of understanding the relationships in which we are interested —and not for purpose of hypothesis testing—it is legitimate to consider the fact that discrepancies by 2 Ss (#15, 27) reduce considerably what would otherwise be the significant coefficient of .59 ($N = 15$). Thus, for the great majority of the subjects in this population, sensitivity to reality and to psychological balance tend to go together.

Summary: Year-I Estimates Concerning House Members

Individuals differ in the accuracy of their estimates and also in perceived agreement with high-attraction others (balance) about their differential attraction toward House members. In a crude way, subjects may be rank-ordered with respect to these differences. All subjects show, by various criteria, at least some tendency to be accurate in their estimates, and with one probable exception all show at least some tendency toward perceived balance.

ESTIMATES OF OTHERS' ATTITUDES TOWARD VARIOUS SPECIFIC ISSUES: YEAR I

As we have previously indicated, our procedures for obtaining estimates of others' attitudes in Year I suffered from serious defects. Because, first, the attitude objects were limited to specific ones, there were very few of them of sufficient importance and relevance to all subjects so that, according to our theoretical formulation, system strain would be dependably induced on the part of all subjects. A second defect was probably more serious: because responses were made to items containing five alternatives, the more extreme among which were rarely chosen—especially in estimating others' responses—most of the estimates yielded little variance, especially in respect to accuracy, most of them being reasonably accurate when specific issues were of importance to most Ss. Hence comparability among Ss, as to accuracy or balance concerning any single attitude object, was sacrificed. For these reasons our analyses of individual differences in tendencies toward accuracy and balance in this population have been rather unrewarding.

The following analyses are based upon responses to the following instructions: "Now indicate which of the five alternatives each of the other men would choose as his Rank 1."

Accuracy of Estimates

In view of these limitations, we have, in order to maximize the range among subjects, used the following procedure for obtaining indices of accuracy in estimating others' attitudes toward specific issues. After selecting, for each item, an arbitrary range beyond which estimates would be considered in error, each S's estimate of every other S's response was labeled as either right or wrong; the estimator's score of accuracy then became the number of right estimates, out of a total of 16. Even this procedure resulted in limited ranges of accuracy, as can be noted in the distributions on the following pages.

Attitudes toward sex practices. This issue, above all others, received high ratings of importance to the Ss. The distribution of responses to the question "How important is this matter to you? I.e., how much do you care about it?" was as follows (Week 12).

1	not at all
1	very little
5	somewhat
5	pretty much
5	very much

The distribution of actual responses to the several alternatives was as follows:

N	Code	Statement
7	A	Sexual activity for either men or women before marriage, and extramarital sexual activity after marriage, are wrong.
2	B	Some sexual freedom for men but not for women should be permitted before marriage, but not after marriage for either.
6	C	Freedom in sexual activity for both men and women should be permitted before marriage but not afterward.

0	D	Both sexes should be allowed sexual freedom before marriage, and some extramarital sexual activity after marriage is OK for men but not for women.
2	E	Both sexes should be allowed sexual freedom both before and after marriage, provided both partners agree on the arrangement.

Individual frequencies of errors ranged from one to seven. Following the presentation of comparable data for two other issues, we shall note the degree to which there are individual consistencies in accuracy in estimating others' responses to all three issues.

Attitude toward living in the house. Subjects rated this issue as a reasonably important one to them. Their responses to the question about its importance were as follows (Week 9).

0	not at all
1	very little
5	somewhat
8	pretty much
3	very much

The alternatives to be ranked, together with the numbers of Ss making a Rank-1 response to each, were as follows.

"If you had the choice to make over again, do you think you would volunteer for this project?"

10	would definitely volunteer
5	would probably volunteer
1	neutral: would have mixed feelings, and would have a hard time deciding
1	would probably not volunteer
0	would definitely not volunteer

Using the same procedures previously described, individual errors ranged from four to eight.

Attitudes toward making friends. The alternatives to be ranked, together with the numbers of Ss making a Rank-1 response to each, were as follows.

3	Be self-sufficient and don't form close ties with any one; one doesn't get hurt that way.
6	Form close ties with only a few people who are really understanding and can be trusted.

3 Become close friends with any one you trust; a lot of people can be trusted but a lot cannot.

3 Try to become close friends with all the people you know; most people will be loyal friends if they know they are trusted.

2 Let people know you trust them and want to be close friends with them; they will respond in kind.

The Ss' degree of concern with the issue was almost as high as for the two preceding issues, as indicated by the following distribution of responses:

1 not at all
2 very little
4 somewhat
7 pretty much
3 very much

Accuracy concerning all three issues. In spite of the large number of tied scores of accuracy,[3] an individual's rank position indicates roughly his relative success in making accurate estimates of others' attitudes. If each S's ranks with regard to all three issues are averaged, a reasonably wide dispersion results, as shown in Table 6.5.

Because of the crudeness of the procedures used in these analyses, there is no good way of assessing the indices in any absolute sense; it can only be said that even the least accurate estimator (#22) was slightly more accurate than he would have been by chance (25 actual vs. 29 expected errors). With the possible exceptions of Ss #22 and 24, it cannot be said, however, that any individual's estimates showed no concern for accuracy.

Pending a fuller discussion on pages 111–112, we may also stop to note that the two most inaccurate estimators regarding these three issues (#22 and 24) are not conspicuously inaccurate estimators of others' differential attraction to House members. There is some evidence for individual consistency of accuracy in estimating attraction, and also in estimating attitudes, but so far none for consistency in regard to both.

---

[3] With regard to one issue (sex activities) 7 Ss were tied with two errors; with regard to each of the other two issues there was an instance of ties involving 5 Ss. Typically, there were two or three Ss at each error frequency for each issue.

Table 6.5. INDIVIDUAL MEANS OF RANK POSITIONS OF ACCU-
RACY IN ESTIMATING OTHERS' ATTITUDES ON THREE ISSUES
(YEAR I)

Subject	Mean of 3 ranks [a]	Rank of mean ranks
30	4.7	1.5
19	4.7	1.5
21	5.0	3
27	5.2	4
15	6.7	5
18	7.0	6
29	9.0	7.5
16	9.0	7.5
23	9.3	9.5
14	9.3	9.5
20	9.7	11
28	10.7	12.5
17	10.7	12.5
26	11.2	14
25	11.3	15
24	15.0	16
22	15.7	17

[a] Maximum possible rank is 16.

Tendencies toward Balance

With respect to the same three issues (sex, House membership, and making friends), all estimates were classified, in the same manner as in categorizing them for accuracy, as either in agreement or in disagreement with the estimator's own response. With regard to each of the three issues, the number of each S's agreeing and disagreeing estimates was separately counted for his attraction Ranks 1–4 and Ranks 5–16. These numbers were then reduced to percentages (of 4 and of 12), and the difference in these percentages taken as the index of tendency to perceive agreement with most attractive others (positive differences being considered high and negative differences low). Individual rank orders of the means of each S's three ranks of tendency toward balance [4] are as shown in Table 6.6.

Table 6.6. INDIVIDUAL MEANS OF RANK POSITIONS IN TENDENCY TOWARD BALANCE IN ESTIMATING OTHERS' ATTITUDES ON THREE ISSUES (YEAR I)

Subject	Mean of 3 ranks [a]	Rank of mean ranks
27	5.3	1
23	6.2	2
30	6.5	3
22	6.7	4
26	7.0	5
20	7.2	6
21	8.2	7
25	8.7	8
14	9.0	9
16	9.7	10.5
15	9.7	10.5
24	9.8	12.5
17	9.8	12.5
29	10.0	14
18	10.7	15
19	13.2	16
28	13.5	17

[a] Maximum possible rank is 16.

The great majority of the Ss, with respect to each of the three issues, have positive differences—there is a clear tendency, for the population as a whole, to perceive most agreement with high-attraction others. Our present concern, however, is with individual differences, and the finding is that all but 2 Ss (#19 and 28) show the predicted relationship between attraction and perceived

[4] Means of ranks are used instead of means of percentage differences because occasional extreme scores would otherwise introduce distortions into means based upon only three values.

agreement in at least two of the three attitudes. Subject #28 shows the predicted relationship in none of the three cases (one negative and two zero differences), while #19 has one positive, one zero, and one negative difference.

The three rank orders of tendency to associate perceived agreement with attraction show intercorrelations that are close to zero, from which fact we may conclude either that the indices are so unreliable as to be meaningless, or that the variable that they are intended to measure is specific to specific attitudes. But the fact that, for the population as a whole, the general tendencies are entirely consistent with those obtained by more exact methods (especially as reported in Chapter 4) suggests that some confidence may be placed in findings of extreme individual deviations that are revealed by the present procedure. Hence we are reasonably safe in concluding that only Ss #19 and 28 (whose sums-of-difference scores differ quite conspicuously from all others) fail to show the predicted relationship.

Relationships between Accuracy and Balance

The correlation between tendency toward balance, as thus indexed, and accuracy (Table 6.5) is exactly .00. In view of the fact, however, that there are two very extreme discrepancies in ranks on the two issues (#19 and 22), it may again be concluded that there is, on the part of a great majority of subjects, a nonsignificant tendency for sensitivity to reality and to psychological balance to go together—exactly as in the case of estimates of others' rank-ordering of House members in attraction. The individual exceptions with respect to balance are not the same individuals who were exceptions with regard to accuracy, and so we have no grounds for concluding that any individuals are consistently excluded from this generalization.

In any case, it is a generalization neither for nor against which we have any theoretical basis, and in view of the shaky grounds on which it is based we regard it as a very tentative one indeed.

Summary: Year-I Estimates Concerning Various Issues

In spite of the inadequacies of our data for purposes of assessing individual differences, our indices of the latter have some degree of validity, judging from the fact that they show the same trends for the total population that are shown by other and more dependable methods. It seems clear that not more than two subjects (#19 and 28) seem not to be affected by influences toward balance, with respect to these particular issues. It is probable, also, that we are justified in concluding that individuals do differ, both in accuracy and in tendencies toward balance, in making estimates of others' attitudes toward these issues.

ACCURACY AND BALANCE REGARDING DIFFERENT OBJECTS OF ORIENTATION: YEAR I

House members, as objects of orientation, differ in many ways from the specific attitude objects described on pages 106–8. If, therefore, we had found consistent individual differences with respect to accuracy and balance, regardless of the nature of the objects of orientation, we could put considerable confidence in the findings. But our failure to find consistent individual differences does not mean, of course, that they could not have been found by other means.

With respect to each kind of object of orientation, we have found one or two Ss who are very low in indices of accuracy and one or two others low in balance. The Ss who are low in accuracy with respect to the three specific issues and those most indifferent to balance with respect to the three issues are not particularly inaccurate or indifferent with respect to House members. Further, the correlations between the two indices of balance and between the two indices of accuracy both approximate zero.

SUMMARY: YEAR I

Insofar as our data permit any inferences at all, we therefore conclude (1) that all of our Year-I subjects were probably, in some degree and in some manner, influenced by forces both toward accuracy and toward balance; and (2) that individual differences in these respects are specific to the particular objects concerning which others' orientations are estimated. If these conclusions are justified, it follows that all members of this population were in some degree subject to strain, as we have previously defined the term, but differentially so.

ESTIMATES OF OTHERS' RANKINGS
OF SPRANGER VALUES: YEAR II

As previously noted, at Weeks 2 and 14 all subjects ranked statements describing Spranger's six values (theoretical, economic, aesthetic, social, political, religious) in order of "their importance to you," and also estimated each other S's rank-ordering of the same values (pp. 40–41). The analyses in this section are all based upon these estimates.[5]

Accuracy

Of various possible indices, the simplest is the mean, for each S, of the 16 *rhos* each of which represents the correlation between an estimatee's actual rank-ordering of the values and the order attributed to him by that S. The validity of this index is somewhat impaired by our Ss' presumed familiarity with what are common and uncommon responses by male undergraduates in contemporary American culture, and its utility in differentiating among the 17 estimators rests on the assumption of common familiarity on the part of *all* of them with such stereotypes. And, like any average, it may be unduly influenced by a very few extreme scores. We shall refer to this as an *absolute* index, since it is independent of the estimator's success in rank-ordering estimatees in the correct order of their agreement with him, indicating only his absolute degree of success.

A *relative* index, not subject to the above limitations, measures accuracy in terms of the relationship between each estimator's

---

[5] For the sake of completeness we ought also to include, in the section on accuracy of estimates, findings concerning estimates of others' preferences among House members. As elsewhere explained (pp. 41–42), however, Year-II estimates were obtained with respect to only a 5 percent sample, for each estimator, of all pairs of Ss excluding himself. This was a costly mistake in planning; the responses proved useless for purposes of obtaining individual indices of accuracy, though not for certain other purposes. The estimates revealed no individual consistency in accuracy: even in three consecutive weeks of late acquaintance, week-to-week correlations of accuracy for the 17 Ss hovered around zero. Inasmuch as the more complete but otherwise comparable data from Year I showed consistencies that could not have resulted from merely random responses, we must conclude that the shortcomings lay in our procedures and not in our subjects.

order of actual agreement and his estimated order of agreement
with the other 16 Ss: the more accurate an estimator, the more
nearly the same would be the order of his actual and of his perceived agreement with the other Ss, regardless of the average level
of his accuracy, in absolute terms. A shortcoming of this index
is that a high degree of accuracy may result from systematically
over- or under-estimating actual agreement, providing only that
the actual order is approximately maintained. It might also yield
an unduly low index when the estimator's range of actual agreements with others is very restricted, but this does not appear to
have occurred.

Though we shall not treat it as an index, a useful indication of
profiting by information about other Ss through increased acquaintance is the degree of increase in accuracy from early to late
acquaintance.

Table 6.7. POOLED INDIVIDUAL INDICES [a] OF ACCURACY IN
ESTIMATING OTHERS' RANK-ORDERING OF SPRANGER VALUES
(YEAR II)

	Week 2		Week 14	
Subject	Pooled index	Rank	Pooled index	Rank
34	.10	14.5	.60	1
35	.10	14.5	.25	12
36	.30	4	.16	16
37	.19	9	.21	14
38	.07	13	.46	5
39	.40	2	.32	10.5
40	.12	12	.19	15
41	.17	11	.35	9
42	.44	1	.45	6
43	.01	16	.32	10.5
44	.37	3	.24	13
45	.28	5	.48	3
46	.27	6	.43	7
47	.21	8	.38	8
48	−.03	17	.10	17
49	.18	10	.58	2
50	.24	7	.47	4

[a] See text for description of the pooled index.

Since each of the two indices described has its shortcomings, we present our findings, in Table 6.7, in terms of the mean of the two indices. The principal findings from this table are as follows.

1. At Week 2, only 1 S's index (#48) is negative, and none at Week 14.

2. There are 3 Ss (#38, 39, 44) whose pooled indices are not larger at the later time. Considering the two indices separately, however, there is no subject whose score does not improve by one index or the other.

3. Individual differences are conspicuous. One subject (#42) increases slightly in accuracy even though he ranked highest of the 17 at first. Another (#48) ranks seventeenth on both occasions. And, as if to match the 3 Ss who become less accurate with increasing acquaintance, 3 others (#34, 38, 49) increase from indices of approximately .10 to approximately .50 or even .60.

4. Finally, to anticipate a finding from Chapter 7, these differences are systematically related to at least one other variable (authoritarianism), from which fact we infer that they are not random differences.

Tendencies toward Balance

Insofar as estimates of others' rankings of the Spranger Values were influenced by forces toward balance, order of perceived agreement will be positively correlated with order of attraction. The following findings emerge from Table 6.8, in which the relevant data appear.

1. At Week 2, 2 Ss (#37, 34) and 3 at Week 14 (#36, 38, 45) do not show positive correlations.

2. The generally positive direction of the correlations is indicated by the range, at Week 2, of +.73 to −.21, and at Week 14 from +.83 to −.17. The median *rhos* are +.25 and +.20, respectively.

3. There are no differences in degree of tendency toward balance, as thus measured, between Weeks 2 and 14; at the later time *rhos* are higher for 8 Ss and lower for 9.

4. There is only the slightest indication of individual constancy in this index: the correlation between rank orders of individual positions at the two times is +.31.

By these rather crude procedures, there are very few Ss whose coefficients at both times reach the conventional levels of signifi-

Table 6.8. INDICES [a] OF TENDENCY TOWARD BALANCE IN ESTIMATING OTHERS' RANKING OF SPRANGER VALUES (YEAR II)

Subject	Week 2		Week 14		Both weeks	
	rho	Rank	rho	Rank	rho	Rank
34	−.21	17	.02	14	−.095	17
35	.25	8	.05	13	.15	10
36	.21	11	−.07	17	.07	16
37	−.06	16	.25	6	.09	15
38	.25	9	−.02	15	.115	13
39	.09	15	.22	7	.155	11.5
40	.46	3	.50	3	.48	3
41	.18	13	.19	10	.185	9
42	.26	7	.40	4	.33	6
43	.32	6	.21	8	.265	7.5
44	.18	14	.13	12	.155	11.5
45	.24	10	−.03	16	.105	14
46	.20	12	.83	1	.515	2
47	.33	5	.32	5	.325	5
48	.73	1	.20	9	.465	4
49	.54	2	.74	2	.64	1
50	.36	4	.17	11	.265	7.5

[a] For Weeks 2 and 14 the index is the individual correlation between order of estimated agreement with and of attraction to the 16 other Ss. The index in the last column represents the mean of the other two.

cance. But in view of the facts that the few negative *rhos* are very small, and that there is no individual whose coefficients are negative at both times, there is no certain individual exception to the general finding that all Ss appear to be influenced in some degree by considerations of balance. Neither, of course, can we be certain that all Ss are so influenced.

Nevertheless, individual differences appear to be conspicuous. In lieu of a better procedure, we have taken the mean of each S's *rhos* at the two times as the best available index of his tendency toward balance, according to these data, as shown in the last column of Table 6.8. According to this last index, we would conclude that at least one subject (#34) shows no tendency toward balance in estimating others' Spranger Values.

A somewhat different index of tendency toward balance may also be used. According to our theoretical formulation, the intensity of forces toward balance varies with intensity of attraction, and should therefore become most noticeable when attraction is very high. We have therefore compared each S's mean *rho* of perceived agreement with his first four attraction choices with the mean *rho* for his last four choices (Ranks 13–16). By this procedure, as shown in Table 6.9, 4 Ss show no tendency toward

Table 6.9. INDIVIDUAL TENDENCIES TOWARD BALANCE IN ESTIMATING OTHERS' RANKINGS OF SPRANGER VALUES, BY METHOD OF COMPARING ATTRACTION RANKS 1–4 AND 13–16 (YEAR II)

Sub-ject	Week 2				Week 14			
	Attrac-tion ranks 1–4	Attrac-tion ranks 13–16	Diff.	Rank	Attrac-tion ranks 1–4	Attrac-tion ranks 13–16	Diff.	Rank
34	.09	.33	−.24	17	.23	.03	.20	3
35	.44	.29	.15	12	.27	−.10	.37	5
36	.44	.14	.30	4	.36	.40	−.04	14
37	.09	.26	−.17	16	.17	.03	.14	10
38	.26	.17	.09	13	.59	.74	−.15	17
39	.57	.70	−.13	15	.62	.53	.09	11.5
40	.56	−.16	.72	1	.80	.41	.39	4
41	−.03	−.19	.16	10.5	.40	.54	−.14	16
42	.42	.14	.28	6.5	.40	.09	.31	6
43	.27	.01	.26	8	.36	.27	.09	11.5
44	.76	.77	−.01	14	.40	.38	.02	13
45	.17	−.11	.28	6.5	−.07	.00	−.07	15
46	−.53	−.69	.16	10.5	.40	−.40	.80	1
47	.54	.23	.31	5	.72	.26	.46	3
48	.93	.69	.24	9	.83	.57	.26	7
49	30	−.37	.67	2	.67	14	.53	2
50	.30	−.24	.54	3	.06	−.10	.16	9

balance at Week 2, and 4 others at Week 14; #34 is one of them at Week 2 but not at Week 14.

In general, however, the two procedures give similar results: every S lacking in balance according to the first procedure is also lacking in it by the second, and the pooled *rhos* (for Weeks 2 and 14) for the second procedure are highly correlated with those by the first procedure ($rho = .85$). And so we may conclude that 2 Ss (#34 and 37) at Week 2, and three others at Week 14 (#36, 38, 48) give no consistent evidence of being influenced by considerations of balance.

Individual Sensitivity to Strain

We shall now describe three different indices, each of which may plausibly be considered to measure, however crudely, individual differences in susceptibility to strain and balance. The three indices are based upon two sets of responses by the second population: estimates of others' attraction toward the estimator, and of others' ordering of the Spranger Values; as shown below, these three indices bear no necessary relationship to each other. Comparable data are not available from the first population.

1. *Estimates of reciprocated attraction by high-attraction others.* If we assume that the self is a highly valued object, then it follows from our theoretical assumptions that it is strain-reducing to perceive that one's highest-attraction choices reciprocate high attraction. Individuals who are relatively sensitive to balance forces will therefore estimate higher attraction from, say, their first two attraction choices than will relatively insensitive individuals. The index is in effect the sum of the estimator's attributed ranks of reciprocation.[6]

2. *Accuracy in estimating others' ordering of Spranger Values.* Insofar as individuals are sensitive to others' attitudes, they should assess them relatively accurately. Our best set of data concerning nonperson objects of attitudes was the set of orderings of Spranger

---

[6] Actually, a somewhat more complex process was required. Estimates of reciprocated attraction were made on the same 100-point scale used in rating own attraction to others. Since different Ss used different ranges of the 100-point scale, the estimates were rendered more comparable by transmuting each numerical estimate into the rank which that rating represented in the estimator's own ratings of attraction toward others.

Values; indices of accuracy in making such estimates have already been described (pp. 113–115).

3. Consistency of sensitivity concerning different objects of orientation. Other things equal, those most sensitive to strain are most likely to perceive agreement with highly attractive others, and this should be true not only with regard to the self as object of orientation (as in the first index) but also with regard to Spranger Values. Our third index therefore was the degree of correlation, for each S, between tendencies to perceive agreement with high-attraction others concerning these two objects of orientation.[7]

In terms of rank-order correlations, the three indices are not closely related to one another (see Table 6.10). We would probably have abandoned the use of these indices if we had not noted that (as reported in the following chapter) each of them correlated positively and (with the exception of the third index, significantly) with F-score at Week 14. Hence we reasoned that the three indices —in the face validity of which we put some confidence—might be contributing differential variances, each of which might have some validity in spite of their unrelatedness.

The fact that a pooling of the three indices showed a highly significant relationship to authoritarianism (see p. 130) provided some support for this hope. We computed the pooled index simply by summing the three rank positions for each subject, and re-ranking the sums. The several sets of individual rank positions appear in Table 6.10.

For various reasons, we consider the third of these indices to be more useful than either of the other two. First, it shows a consistency of tendencies in spite of altogether different objects of orientation concerning which estimates are made. And, second, it shows most consistency over time: its "test-retest reliability,"

[7] Although this index involves the same two sets of responses from which the other two indices are derived, it bears no necessary relationship to either of them. This is true, first, because the Spranger-Value data are handled in different ways: for Index 2, estimates of others' responses are correlated with estimatees' actual responses, while for Index 3 they are correlated with the estimator's own responses. Second, Index 2 represents an absolute level (of accuracy) whereas Index 3 represents a relationship (between perceived agreement about the self and about Spranger Values). In this population, correlations between accuracy and tendency to perceive agreement with highly attractive others were near zero, at both times.

Table 6.10. Individuals' Rank Positions on Indices of Sensitivity to Strain (Year II)

Subject	Week 2				Week 14			
	1	2	3	Pooled	1	2	3	Pooled
34	16	5	7.5	9.5	4.5	5.5	7	5
35	12.5	12.5	10	13	7.5	13.5	14	12
36	17	3	7.5	8	16	3	2	7
37	10.5	16	14	17	7.5	11	11	10
38	4	7	3	2	4.5	1	10	3
39	10.5	8	12	12	12.5	13.5	13	16
40	12.5	4	5.5	6	6	9	5	6
41	6	15	17	15	14	16	15	17
42	9	14	1	7	10	3	3.5	4
43	6	10	4	4	12.5	15	9	14
44	2	11	15.5	9.5	15	10	8	11
45	8	17	11	14	1.5	7	6	8.5
46	6	12.5	2	5	3	5.5	16	8.5
47	2	1	5.5	1	1.5	8	3.5	1.5
48	15	9	15.5	16	9	2	17	15
49	14	6	9	11	11	3	1	1.5
50	2	2	13	3	17	7	12	13

between Weeks 2 and 14, is .50, significant at $<.05$. That the two kinds of estimates are rather closely related at the highest levels of estimated attraction (where it is most to be expected), in spite of their different content, is shown in Table 6.11. And the consistency of responses between Weeks 2 and 14 is indicated by the fact that 13 of the 17 Ss are in the same half of the population at both times, according to this index; the p value of the distribution $\begin{smallmatrix} 6 & 2 \\ 2 & 7 \end{smallmatrix}$ is .045, by exact test.

SUMMARY: INDIVIDUAL DIFFERENCES IN ACCURACY AND BALANCE

In the second population, all subjects appear to show some effects of needs both to take account of the real world and to

Table 6.11. Numbers of Estimates at Three Levels of Reciprocated Attraction, as Related to Two Levels of Estimated Agreement about Spranger Values (Year II)

| Ranks of estimated agreement about Spranger Values | Ranks of estimated reciprocation of attraction | | | | | |
| | Week 2 | | | Week 14 | | |
	1–2	3–4	5–16	1–2	3–4	5–16
1–8	23	15	98	25.5 [a]	19.5	91
9–16	11	19	106	8.5	14.5	113
Total	34	34	204	34	34	204

$$x^2 = 4.07 \qquad x^2 = 8.64$$
$$p < .05 \text{ (1 df) } [b] \qquad p < .005 \text{ (1 df) } [b]$$

[a] Fractional frequencies result from ranks tied at 8.5 in estimated agreement about Spranger values.
[b] Estimated attraction dichotomized between Ranks 1–2 and 3–16.

establish psychological balance. With respect to both accuracy and balance there are large individual differences. With respect to accuracy there is nearly universal improvement with increasing acquaintance, but tendencies toward balance remain relatively constant with increasing acquaintance. There is no consistent relationship between accuracy and balance, and most individuals' early pattern-combinations change with further acquaintance. Individuals show increasing consistency, paralleling increasing acquaintance, in perceiving agreement with their high-attraction choices *both* with regard to the self as object of attraction and with regard to the ordering of general values.

These findings are generally consistent with those reported earlier in this chapter for the first population. Hence we conclude that, while sensitivity to strain varies with the nature of objects of orientations and with stages of acquaintance, and while individuals vary in degree and manner of showing the effects of such sensitivity, its effects were observable in virtually all of our subjects.

Personality Variables Associated with Strain and Balance

7

Insofar as individuals differ in consistent and meaningful ways in showing tendencies either toward accurate assessment of their interpersonal environments or toward psychological balance, it would not be surprising to find that these tendencies are related to other personality variables. Our attempts to discover such relationships have been limited to two variables which, on theoretical grounds, might be expected to show them.

AUTHORITARIANISM

Considerable evidence has by now been accumulated to the effect that nonauthoritarianism, as measured by *F*-scale scores (Adorno *et al.,* 1950) is commonly related to "perceptiveness of others" (Christie and Cook, 1958; their review of the relevant evidence, pp. 180–183, is the most complete that we know). Their summary, based on several directly relevant studies, includes the following statement:

> These studies strongly and consistently indicate that high and low scorers on the *F*-scale in these samples make quite different assumptions about the attitudes [i.e., *F*-scale responses] of their college peers. Low *F*-scale scorers correctly assume that they are different, and come fairly close to estimating the mean responses of others, although they cannot correctly differentiate the scores of other individuals on the basis of a brief interaction. High scorers completely misperceive the group norm and are also unable to differentiate accurately among individuals (p. 181).

Our own research setting was designed to provide enough opportunities for acquaintance so that differentiations among others might, eventually, be made. We shall therefore test the prediction that, particularly following several weeks of acquaintance, nonauthoritarians (low F-scorers) make more accurate differentiations than do high F-scorers among the attitudes of other House members. We shall then make an exploratory analysis of relationships between authoritarianism and other strain-related variables.

Accuracy, Year I

Estimates of others' preferences among House members. The correlation between nonauthoritarianism (low F-score) and individual accuracy in estimating others' ordering of House members (based upon the estimator's attraction Ranks 1 and 2 only; see Table 6.2) is only $+.01$ at Week 1, when most of the estimates could have been little better than guesses. By Week 5, however, the coefficient has dropped to $-.65$, significant at about .01. Nonparametrically, the Week-5 distribution is $\begin{smallmatrix} 2 & 7 \\ 6 & 2 \end{smallmatrix}$, and the p value, by exact test, is .045.

Thus our prediction that, following acquaintance, low F-scorers' estimates would be relatively accurate turns out to be completely wrong, in this population, with respect to other House members as objects of orientation. As we shall see (pp. 127–8), the nonauthoritarians in this population are particularly prone to perceive balance with respect to House members.

Estimates of others' attitudes toward specific issues. As previously noted, the specific items used in Year I were not very satisfactory for purposes of analyzing estimates of others' responses, with the exception of the item concerning sex activities, which was rated as being of considerable importance to most Ss (see pp. 106–7). Accuracy in estimating others' attitudes toward this issue, following several weeks of acquaintance, is related to F-score, as predicted; the data appear in Table 7.1, in which the dichotomizations are made as nearly as possible at the midpoints.

With regard to both of the other two issues (making friends, and volunteering again for the House project; pp. 107–8) which our Ss felt were of some importance to them, the estimates of low F-scorers were more accurate than those of high F-scorers, as predicted, but by nonsignificant differences.

Table 7.1. FREQUENCIES OF *S*s AT TWO LEVELS OF ACCURACY IN ESTIMATING OTHERS' ATTITUDES TOWARD SEX ACTIVITIES AND AT TWO LEVELS OF *F*-SCORE (YEAR I, WEEK 12)

N *of S*s wrongly estimated	F-score ranks [a]		
	1–8	*9–16*	*Total*
0 or 1	5	1	6
2 or more	3	8	11
TOTAL	8	9	17

$p = .046$ (exact test)

[a] Lower ranks represent relative nonauthoritarianism. *F*-scores dichotomized between Ranks 8 and 9, rather than 9 and 10, because Ranks 9 and 10 are tied.

Accuracy, Year II

Estimates of others' ordering of Spranger Values. As shown in Table 7.2, the predicted relationship between nonauthoritarianism and accuracy appears consistently on late acquaintance, but it also appears, using the absolute index of accuracy, at Week 2. That the two indices should give such different results at Week 2

Table 7.2. CORRELATIONS BETWEEN THREE INDICES OF ACCURACY IN ESTIMATING OTHERS' ORDERING OF SPRANGER VALUES AND NONAUTHORITARIANISM (YEAR II) [a]

Index	Week 2	Week 14
1 (absolute)	.64	.48
2 (relative)	.00	.47
3 (pooled)	.24	.55

[a] Rank-order correlations, with *N* of 17. See pp. 113–115 for descriptions of the three indices.

is unexpected, but in no sense contradictory. The ranking procedure involved in the relative index can easily obscure differences revealed by the averaging procedure of the absolute index. But the reasons for the unexpected superiority of the nonauthoritarians after only two weeks of acquaintance, according to the absolute index, are not self-evident.

Further analysis shows that the authoritarians tend to exaggerate actual agreement, whereas the nonauthoritarians do not. Comparing individuals' rank positions with respect to actual and estimated agreement, the high scorers overestimate actual agreement in 6 of 9 cases, and the nonauthoritarians in only 1 of 8 cases; the p value of this difference is .037, by exact test. And the effects of these differential tendencies are somewhat exacerbated by the additional fact that authoritarians tend to order the Spranger Values in atypical ways: in respect to numbers of other Ss with whom each individual is actually in close agreement, they are significantly exceeded by the nonauthoritarians ($p = .013$, by exact test).

Thus the lesser accuracy of the authoritarians at Week 2, according to the absolute index, may in part be attributed to their greater tendencies to project their own atypical attitudes to others. By Week 14, however, these bases for the superiority of the nonauthoritarians have pretty much disappeared. The authoritarians no longer respond so atypically, 6 of the 9 having changed their responses toward somewhat closer agreement with the nonauthoritarians, most of whom have hardly changed at all during the interval.[1] Meanwhile, the nonauthoritarians have come to make more estimates of very high agreement than they had at Week 2. And by Week 14 the authoritarians' inaccuracies are no longer particularly attributable to the exaggeration of actual agreement. The interesting fact, however, is that at Week 14 the nonauthoritarians are still the more accurate estimators. In particular, their estimates of high agreement are conspicuously more accurate than those of the authoritarians (by a significance level of $< .005$).

Thus the more or less constant relationship between accuracy and nonauthoritarianism, by the absolute index, represents very different states of affairs at the two periods: at Week 2 the nonauthoritarians achieve their superior accuracy by virtue of the authoritarians' tendency to project, in unwarranted manner, their own attitudes to others, whereas at Week 14 they are superior in accuracy in spite of very little unwarranted projection on the part

[1] It is of particular interest that all of the 5 lowest F-scorers were both popular (all ranking among the top 7), and stable in F-score (all having Week 2–Week 14 correlations between .83 and 1.00); only 3 of the remaining 12 Ss had coefficients as high as this, another 3 being below .50.

of the authoritarians. The nonauthoritarians have, so to speak, maintained their lead in accuracy without the handicap initially presented by the authoritarians.

Summary: Accuracy in Estimating Spranger Values, Year II

In relative terms—that is, the ability to rank-order other House members' degrees of agreement with themselves correctly, regardless of absolute level of accuracy—nonauthoritarians excel authoritarians on late but not on early acquaintance, as predicted. In absolute terms, nonauthoritarians are the more accurate both early and late; their early superiority stems in part from the authoritarians' early tendency toward unwarranted projection of their own attitudes, but their later superiority is not attributable to this factor. The association between nonauthoritarianism and accuracy of estimating others' attitudes, as previously reported by other investigators, is thus well supported by our findings, although the reasons for the nonauthoritarians' superiority appear to change with increasing acquaintance.

Tendency Toward Balance

On theoretical grounds, we see no necessary relationship between authoritarianism and tendency toward balance. It is reasonable to assume that those who are most tolerant of ambiguity should also be most tolerant of strain, but this assumption carries no clear implications for tendencies to achieve balance, as measured in Chapter 6. Those most able to tolerate strain do not, merely for that reason, prefer it; indeed, it can be argued that nonauthoritarians, in view of their demonstrated tendency to estimate others' attitudes accurately, are better able than others to recognize existing states of imbalance with others and thus to take steps to restore balance. But it can also be argued that, since common objects other than those toward which we happen to have obtained attitude responses are also operating to determine balance, the nonauthoritarians' greater accuracy results merely in their recognizing and tolerating strain regarding those attitudes that we have measured, in order to maintain balance in other and more important areas.

Hence we have no predictions concerning the relationship between authoritarianism and tendencies toward balance, and the following analyses are merely exploratory.

Estimates of others' preference among House members, Year I.
Measuring tendencies toward balance (as in Chapter 6) simply by degree of estimated agreement with the estimator's highest-ranking others in attraction—ignoring the accuracy of the estimates—we find correlations of $+.15$ at Week 1 and of .40 (almost significant at the .05 level) at Week 5. There appears to be a very slight tendency, increasing with the early weeks of acquaintance, for nonauthoritarians to perceive themselves in agreement with high-choice others regarding the relative attractiveness of other House members.

This finding suggests the possibility that nonauthoritarians, more than authoritarians, tend to increase in degree of perceived agreement with most attractive others, between Weeks 1 and 5. A comparison of individual changes indicates that this is indeed the case, as shown in Table 7.3. The low F-scorers, in spite of relatively

Table 7.3. NUMBERS OF LOW AND OF HIGH F-SCORERS WHO DO AND WHO DO NOT INCREASE IN ESTIMATED AGREEMENT WITH TWO MOST ATTRACTIVE CHOICES ABOUT OTHER HOUSE MEMBERS, BETWEEN WEEKS 1 AND 5 (YEAR I)

F-score rank	Rank at Week 5, relative to Week 1		
	Lower [a]	Not lower [a]	Total
1– 8 [b]	7	1	8
9–17	2	7	9
TOTAL	9	8	17

$p = .024$ (exact test)

[a] Lower ranks indicate estimates of greater perceived agreement, and nonauthoritarian responses.
[b] F-scores are dichotomized between Ranks 8 and 9, rather than 9 and 10, because Ranks 9 and 10 are tied.

high estimated agreement at Week 1 (mean rank of 7.8, as compared with 10.0 for high F-scorers), significantly increase their tendency to perceive agreement with most attractive others (mean ranks of 6.25 and 11.4, respectively, at Week 5).

This tendency on the part of nonauthoritarians to perceive closer agreement with highest-choice others, between Weeks 1 and 5, becomes more interesting in the light of simultaneous decreases in the accuracy with which the same estimates are made (see p. 123). It seems clear that increases in perceived agreement occur at the expense of accuracy on the part of the nonauthoritarians in this population. Why this should be more true of low than of high F-scorers is at first sight perplexing; we shall later give reasons for concluding that the low F-scorers in this population were in fact intermediate rather than high in nonauthoritarianism. If so, the more correct statement would be that in this population those intermediate in authoritarianism exceed those who are extremely authoritarian in tendency to perceive balance.

Estimates of others' ordering of Spranger Values, Year II. A suitable index of tendencies toward balance is the correlation between attraction and estimated agreement about Spranger Values. Neither at Week 2 nor at Week 14 is there any significant relationship between this index and F-score; the rank-order coefficients are —.05 and —.20 at Weeks 2 and 14, respectively $(N = 17)$.[2] From this finding we conclude simply that nonauthoritarians in this population, with respect to Spranger Values, were no less "balanced" than authoritarians in spite of being a good deal more accurate than authoritarians, as previously shown.

Another possible index is each S's mean rank, in estimated agreement, assigned to his highest-attraction choices. This index is theoretically preferable, since forces toward balance are presumed to be strongest when attraction is strong. Neither at Week 2 nor at Week 14, however, do authoritarians and nonauthoritarians differ in any consistent or significant way, by this index—as with the preceding ones.

How does it happen that estimates of others' attitudes by one subpopulation are more accurate than those of the other, but are not any more closely associated with attraction than are those of the other? It can only mean that the nonauthoritarians (the more accurate subpopulation) are more frequently *in accurate balance* than are the authoritarians. The authoritarians more frequently achieve balance via autistic distortions of others' attitudes—they tend, in other words, to overestimate agreement with most attractive others. The nonauthoritarians, on the other hand, tend to

[2] The four-fold tables, in terms of rank positions on the two variables, are $\begin{smallmatrix} 4 & 4 \\ 4 & 5 \end{smallmatrix}$ at Week 2 and $\begin{smallmatrix} 3 & 5 \\ 5 & 4 \end{smallmatrix}$ at Week 14.

achieve balance by becoming more attracted toward those with whom they are actually in agreement.

The data show that this does indeed occur at Week 14, but not at Week 2. At the earlier time the correlation between F-score and tendency to be in actual agreement with most attractive others is .12, and .33 at Week 14. A nonparametric analysis shows, however, that at Week 14 (but not at Week 2) the relationship is actually a close one. If the distribution shown in Table 7.4 is collapsed into

Table 7.4. FREQUENCIES OF Ss AT THREE LEVELS OF F-SCORE AND TWO LEVELS OF TENDENCY TOWARD ACTUAL AGREEMENT WITH MOST ATTRACTIVE OTHERS (YEAR II, WEEK 14)

Rank of non-authoritarianism	*Correlation between attraction and actual agreement on Spranger Values*	
	$\geqq +.20$	*$\leqq +.19$*
1– 5	5	0
6–12	2	5
13–17	1	4

the four-fold table $\begin{smallmatrix} 5 & 0 \\ 3 & 9 \end{smallmatrix}$, its p value is .009, by exact test. (The relationship is not a significant one if both variables are dichotomized with as nearly equal frequencies as possible, and we present this analysis simply by way of reporting what we found; as elsewhere noted, the 5 most extreme nonauthoritarians in this population are in many ways quite different from the other 12 Ss.)

Thus our finding is that, in this population with respect to Spranger Values, authoritarianism is unrelated to tendencies toward balance, although it is related to accuracy of estimates. We are thus led to inquire whether there are characteristic differences between authoritarians and nonauthoritarians in modes of coping with strain and achieving balance.

Sensitivity to Strain, Year II

Three presumed indices of sensitivity to strain have previously been described: accuracy in estimating others' ordering of Spranger Values, tendency to estimate that high-attraction choices reciprocate high attraction, and consistency in estimating highly attractive others *both* as agreeing with oneself in Spranger Values and in reciprocating high attraction. It has already been noted that all three of the interrelationships among these indices are positive at Week 14 (two of the three approaching or exceeding the .05 level of significance), but not at Week 2.

As shown in Table 7.5, each of the three indices as well as the

Table 7.5. CORRELATIONS BETWEEN NONAUTHORITARIANISM AND VARIOUS INDICES OF SENSITIVITY TO STRAIN (YEAR II) [a]

	Week 2	Week 14
Accuracy in estimating Spranger Values [b]	.24	.55
Estimation of reciprocated high attraction	−.18	.48
Consistency in estimating values, reciprocation	.08	.35 [c]
Pooled index	.21	.72

[a] See pp. 118–119 for description of these indices.

[b] Based upon the pooled index, as described on pp. 113–114.

[c] By a nonparametric test, the *p* value of this relationship is .018 (by exact test) when both distributions are dichotomized as equally as possible: 14 of 17 *S*s are in the same half of both distributions. This significant relationship contrasts with the *rho* of only .35 because one *S* (#45) ranked 1 on one variable and 17 on the other, thus reducing the coefficient very greatly.

pooled index is correlated, significantly or nearly so, with authoritarianism at Week 14. Before we offer any interpretations of these findings, we must note that in this population the indices of sensitivity are not unrelated to popularity, as shown in Table 7.6.

Table 7.6. INTERCORRELATIONS AMONG THREE VARIABLES (YEAR II)

	Week 2		Week 14	
	F-score	Pooled index of sensitivity	F-score	Pooled index of sensitivity
Popularity	.49	.36	.56	.49
F-score		.21		.72

The more popular *S*s are in a position to assume, usually correctly, that their own high attraction choices are reciprocated; further, it is more possible for them than for unpopular *S*s to associate with and thus to be able to explore the attitudes of all other Ss, and thus to judge the latter more accurately.

We conclude, however, that the much higher relationship between authoritarianism and the pooled index of strain cannot be accounted for by the relationship of both of them to popularity. For one thing, the correlation between popularity ranks at Weeks 2 and 14 is high (.80), and the Week-2 pooled index of sensitivity to strain correlates quite as well with Week-14 popularity as with Week-2 popularity. Further, as shown in Table 7.6, the only one of the three intercorrelations that changes much between Weeks 2 and 14 is the one—between F-score and sensitivity to strain—that does *not* involve popularity. Since F-scores were obtained but once (at Week 8), it is obviously changes in the index of sensitivity to strain which contribute principally to the differential intercorrelations at Weeks 2 and 14.

An analysis of the sources of change in the pooled index shows a very close relationship to F-scores. As shown in Table 7.7, 5 of

Table 7.7. RELATIONSHIP OF F-SCORES TO CHANGE IN SENSITIVITY TO STRAIN, BETWEEN WEEKS 2 AND 14 (YEAR II)

Sensitivity Changes			
Decrease > 1 rank		Increase > 1 rank	
$S\#$	F rank [a]	$S\#$	F rank [a]
45	1	46	9
34	2	39	10
42	3	44	11
49	5	43	12
36	6	40	13
37	17	41	15
		50	16

[a] Rank 1 indicates lowest authoritarianism.

the 6 Ss whose sensitivity scores show changes of >1 rank, between Weeks 2 and 14, in the direction of *increased* sensitivity, are at or below Rank 6 in nonauthoritarianism, whereas all 7 of the Ss whose sensitivity scores change >1 rank toward *decreased* sensitivity are at or above Rank 9 in nonauthoritarianism.

Among those whose sensitivity ranks changed less than one rank, two ranked very high in sensitivity at both times (#47 at

Ranks 1 and 1, and #38 at 2 and 3, at Weeks 2 and 14, respectively), their respective ranks in nonauthoritarianism being 4 and 7; and two ranked very low in sensitivity at both times (#48 at Ranks 16 and 15, and #35 at 13 and 12, at Weeks 2 and 14, respectively), their respective ranks in nonauthoritarianism being 14 and 8. In short, the 7 least authoritarian *S*s either remained highly sensitive or became more so, without exception, while all the remaining *S*s—even including #37 (who changed from Rank 17 to Rank 10 in sensitivity)—either remained relatively insensitive or became more so. The nonauthoritarians hardly changed at all, between Weeks 2 and 14, in popularity, while as many of the authoritarians increased as decreased in popularity. Hence changes in sensitivity on the part of nonauthoritarians cannot be attributed to changes in popularity.

In this population, in sum, it is possible to predict from *F*-scores those individuals who, following acquaintance, will be most sensitive (or who, at any rate will have become more so) to the phenomena of strain and balance, as here measured.

AUTHORITARIANISM AND AUTISM

Inaccurate estimates are not necessarily autistic,[3] in the sense that inaccuracies are necessarily in the direction of overestimating agreement with most attractive others—although our empirical findings support the theoretical prediction that inaccurate estimates are more frequently autistic than contra-autistic. Individuals do differ, however, in their tendencies toward autism, and we shall now test the prediction that authoritarianism and autism tend to go together. The theoretical basis of the prediction is primarily the assumption that strain, as here defined, is a special instance of ambiguity. If so, then authoritarians, who are presumed to be relatively intolerant of ambiguity (Adorno *et al.*, 1950) should also be relatively intolerant of strain, and autistic estimates represent one device for reducing strain.

---

[3] We use the term *autistic* to indicate responses influenced by balance at the cost of accuracy. *Contra-autistic* refers to responses indicating both imbalance and inaccuracy. *Realistic* responses are accurate, whether or not balanced.

Year II

We have already shown that nonauthoritarians are more accurate estimators of others' orderings of Spranger Values than are authoritarians. Nevertheless, the nonauthoritarians are far from perfect estimators, and it is possible that their errors are as frequently autistic in direction as those of the authoritarians. Table 7.8 shows, however, that this is not in fact the case at Week 14.

Table 7.8. FREQUENCIES OF DISCREPANCIES IN RANKS OF ESTIMATED AND OF ACTUAL AGREEMENT WITH FIRST THREE ATTRACTION CHOICES ABOUT SPRANGER VALUES (YEAR II) [a]

Discrepancies, actual vs. estimated ranks	Rank in nonauthoritarianism			
	Week 2		Week 14	
	1–5	6–17	1–5	6–17
> + 1 (autistic)	7	18	1	17
0 ± 1 (accurate)	4	8	8	8
< − 1 (contra-autistic)	4	10	6	11
TOTAL	15	36	15	36

$$x^2 \text{ NS} \qquad x^2 = 8.50 \text{ }^b$$
$$p < .02 \text{ (2 df)}$$

[a] Control data for each estimator's attraction ranks 4–16 do not appear in this table, since their frequencies are an artifactual residual.

[b] By way of removing the contribution of "accurate" responses to this result, the p value of the distribution $\begin{smallmatrix} 1 & 17 \\ 6 & 11 \end{smallmatrix}$ has been computed; it is .036, by exact test.

In this table each S's rank in estimated agreement with each of his three highest choices in attraction is compared with his rank in actual agreement with the same Ss. Discrepancies in which estimated ranks are higher (i.e., near to 1) than actual ranks are thus autistic. It appears from Table 7.8 that at Week 2 autism (as thus measured) is unrelated to authoritarianism, whereas at Week 14 it is associated with authoritarianism; and also that it is the nonauthoritarians, rather than the others, who have changed meanwhile, by becoming more accurate and less autistic.

This conclusion, however, is premature until we have made sure that the significant relationship at Week 14, as shown in Table 7.8, does not result from regressive effects. That is, the possibilities of both magnitude and direction of these discrepancies are influenced by extremeness of score (in this instance, extremeness of *actual* agreement rank, since this is "given" while the estimated agreement rank is taken as the dependent variable). Thus an actual agreement score which represents Rank 16 cannot be estimated at a rank greater than 16. In this case, since we are dealing at high levels of attraction, the probabilities of autism—of estimating closer agreement than actually exists—are very great.

One way of controlling for the possibility of regressive effects is to compare the upper half and the lower half, separately, of actual agreement ranks. Regressive effects involving actual agreement ranks 9–16 (low agreement) are in the same direction as autism—i.e., exaggerating agreement with attractive others; and where actual agreement ranks 1–8 are involved, regressive effects are contra-autistic. The results of applying this test of regressive effects appear in Table 7.9. While the Ns in this table are very small, it

Table 7.9. FREQUENCIES AND PERCENTAGES OF REGRESSIVE AND NONREGRESSIVE EFFECTS IN DISCREPANCIES BETWEEN ACTUAL AND ESTIMATED AGREEMENT ABOUT SPRANGER VALUES (YEAR II, WEEK 14)

Direction of actual-estimated discrepancy	5 low F-scorers: actual agreement ranks				12 higher F-scorers: actual agreement ranks			
	1–8		9–16		1–8		9–16	
	N	%	N	%	N	%	N	%
Regressive	6	55 [a]	1	25	11	55 [a]	13	81
Nonregressive	4	36 [a]	3	75	5	25 [a]	3	19

[a] Percentages do not add to 100 because of zero discrepancies, which cannot be categorized in either way.

can at least be said that the low and the higher F-scorers give no evidence of differing in regressive tendencies at actual agreement ranks 1–8, where regression is contra-autistic. At actual agreement ranks 9–16, however, where regression is autistic, the regressive tendencies of the 12 higher F-scorers are pronounced, and those of the low scorers are not; the p value of the distribution $\begin{smallmatrix} 1 & 13 \\ 3 & 3 \end{smallmatrix}$ is .058, by exact test. Hence it is clear that the higher F-scorers are more regressive than the low scorers not in general, but only when regressive responses are also autistic responses. Thus our previous conclusion that autism is associated with authoritarianism is reinforced.

One other possibly spurious basis for this conclusion remains. If the 5 lowest F-scorers are in fact in closer agreement with their highest three attraction choices, then their greater accuracy and lesser autism might be accounted for by this fact. That is to say, in case of actual agreement, balance and accuracy coincide. As Table 7.10 shows, however, this is the case only in terms of abso-

Table 7.10. FREQUENCIES OF ACTUAL AGREEMENT ABOUT SPRANGER VALUES, ACCORDING TO TWO INDICES, AS RELATED TO AUTHORITARIANISM (YEAR II, WEEK 14)

Relative Index			*Absolute Index*		
Ranks of actual agreement	*F-score ranks 1–5*	*F-score ranks 6–17*	*Rhos of actual agreement*	*F-score ranks 1–5*	*F-score ranks 6–17*
1– 4 (high)	7	10	$\geqq$ .32 (high)	11	13
5– 8	4	11			
9–16 (low)	4	15	< .32 (low)	4	23
TOTAL	15	36	TOTAL	15	36

$$\chi^2 = 1.83$$
$$p < .50 \text{ (2 df)}$$

$$\chi^2 = 4.48$$
$$p < .05 \text{ (1 df)}$$

lute level of agreement, not in terms of relative degree of agreement.

The apparent contradiction between the relative and absolute indices of actual agreement, as related to authoritarianism, is easily resolved. So many of the low F-scorers' actual agreements with their first three choices in attraction are bunched together at very high levels of agreement that they could hardly be expected to differentiate very well among them. As shown in Table 7.11, this is not at all the case for the higher F-scorers. The interesting thing, as a matter of fact, is that the low F-scorers discriminate better

Table 7.11. FREQUENCIES OF ACTUAL AGREEMENTS WITH THREE HIGHEST-ATTRACTION CHOICES ABOUT SPRANGER VALUES, AT THREE LEVELS, BY VERY LOW AND BY HIGHER F-SCORERS (YEAR II, WEEK 14)

Rhos, *actual agreement*	*F-score low (ranks 1–5)*	*F-score not low (ranks 6–17)*
$\geq$ .60	7 (1.8) [a]	3 (4.3)
.00–.59	6 (5.7)	24 (13.7)
< .00	2 (7.5)	9 (18.0)
TOTAL	15 (15)	36 (36)

$$\chi^2 = 10.13 \ (2 \ df)$$
$$p \ < .01$$

[a] Expected frequencies appear in parentheses. They are based on our own empirical count of all of the possible orderings of ranks, when $N = 6$. A coefficient of exactly .00 is not possible with an N of 6.

than the higher scorers, in spite of their concentration within a narrow range of high-agreement scores.

The total set of findings concerning authoritarianism and autism in Year II is consistent with the following interpretation. The greater sensitivity of the very low F-scorers enables them to select as most attractive those who are in fact most closely in agreement with them about Spranger Values to a considerably greater extent than is true of the higher F-scorers. The nonauthoritarians' characteristic solution to the threat of strain is nonautistic: they tend to achieve balance not by exaggerating actual agreement with those toward whom they are attracted (on other grounds), but by judging rather accurately who is in agreement with them, and letting their highest attractions be determined accordingly. The characteristic solution of the authoritarians tends to be just the reverse: instead of letting their personal preferences be determined by accurate perceptions of agreement, they tend to perceive more agreement than actually exists with those toward whom they are already attracted.

Year I

In Year I, the estimates of others' attraction orientations were much more suitable for providing indices of autism than were the estimates concerning specific issues, and the present analysis will be limited to those data. For each S's first two attraction choices, we have compared the *rhos* ($N = 15$) of estimated agreement with those of actual agreement concerning the remaining 15 Ss: the greater the tendency for estimated agreement to exceed actual agreement with highly attractive others, the greater the autism.[4] In all but 2 of the 34 comparisons, discrepancies were in the autistic direction—actual agreement was overestimated; both of the contra-autistic estimates were of the estimator's Rank-2 rather than his Rank-1 choice.

Table 7.12 shows the relationship between the two variables.

Table 7.12. NUMBERS OF SUBJECTS AT TWO LEVELS OF AUTISM IN ESTIMATING AGREEMENT WITH FIRST TWO ATTRACTION CHOICES AT TWO LEVELS OF AUTHORITARIANISM (YEAR I)

F-score ranks	Autism ranks, Week 1 [a]		Autism ranks, Week 5 [a]	
	1–9	10–17	1–9	10–17
1– 8 (nonauthor.)	3	5	1	7
9–16 (author.)	6	3	8	1
TOTAL	9	8	9	8
	p NS		p = .003 (exact test)	

[a] Low ranks indicate low levels of autism.

The relationship at Week 5 is highly significant—and in the direction opposite to that predicted. Nonauthoritarians are more autistic than authoritarians, in these estimates. And it is not a spurious finding: the low and the high F-scorers differ hardly at all in *actual* agreement with their two high-attraction choices about other men in the House (the nonauthoritarians' agreement levels are slightly lower than those of the authoritarians), but the nonauthoritarians significantly exceed the authoritarians in *estimated* agreement with them ($\chi^2 = 7.56$, $p < .01$, with 1 df).

[4] The index actually employed was the difference between actual and estimated *rhos* (two for each S), expressed as a percentage of the actual agreement *rhos;* the two percentages were summed and ranked. This was preferable to raw difference scores because an exaggeration of agreement by a given amount represents more distortion if the actual agreement is high than if it is low; in the latter case there is, so to speak, more room for distortion. Thus the index represents a percentage of "possible" exaggeration.

There are, unfortunately, several possible reasons for finding that authoritarianism is related in opposite ways to autism concerning Spranger Values in one population and to autism concerning other House members in the other. The stages of acquaintance are different; the objects of orientation are very different—and so, of course are the populations, especially in their ranges of F-scores. But none of these, alone, seems to provide any theoretical basis for expecting an opposite relationship between authoritarianism and autism. One other consideration, however, seems worth exploring. It could be that the Year-I nonauthoritarians, if they are relatively sensitive to balance—and who (if they resemble the Year-II nonauthoritarians) are more willing than the authoritarians to shift their attraction preferences in order to achieve it—are relatively autistic at Week 5 concerning House members because they are still shifting their preferences more than the authoritarians are, and are therefore less well acquainted with their highest-attraction choices of the moment. It turns out that the nonauthoritarians are indeed less stable in their choices between Weeks 2 and 5 [5] (particularly with regard to their first two choices), and by significant margins. If stability indices (correlations of rank-order preferences at the two times) are dichotomized, the distribution is $\begin{smallmatrix} 1 & 8 \\ 5 & 3 \end{smallmatrix}$, and the p value is .043, by exact test. During the 3-week interval between Weeks 12 and 15, high and low F-scorers did not differ at all in this respect, so that the difference was a temporary one.

Both Populations

Hence we may be justified in concluding that, even with such very different objects of orientation as House members and Spranger Values, our earlier assumptions regarding the greater sensitivity of the nonauthoritarians, with respect to balance, need not be revised. In both populations—though at different stages of acquaintance, and in spite of very different objects of orientation—the nonauthoritarians tend more readily to achieve balance by shifting their attraction preferences than do the authoritarians. The principal difference between the two populations' sets of data—Spranger Values at Week 14, as contrasted with House members at Week 5—is that in a relatively early stage of acquaintance the Year-I nonauthoritarians are relatively autistic, at the cost of

[5] The relevant data were not obtained in Weeks 3 and 4 of this year.

accuracy, whereas in a late stage of acquaintance the Year-II non-authoritarians are relatively accurate and nonautistic.

Thus the tentatively hypothesized relationship between authoritarianism and autism turns out not to be an absolute one. It may vary with stage of acquaintance and with objects of orientation. As to the latter, we are inclined to stress the variable of *importance;* the more valued the object, the greater the forces toward balance. In our research setting, it is quite certain that most of our subjects cared more about other House members than they did about the rather abstract Spranger Values. Hence—particularly when acquaintance was fairly recent and information about other House members' preferences still precarious—the forces toward balance were particularly strong upon the relatively sensitive non-authoritarians, with resulting inaccuracy and autism. The relevant generalization then seems to be that the relationship between authoritarianism and autism increases with acquaintance, and may be reversed at early stages of acquaintance if objects of orientation are important enough to induce very strong forces toward balance.

Need for Affiliation

Both populations were asked to write stories about TAT pictures, which were scored for content presumably indicating need for affiliation (n Aff), as indicated in Chapter 3. In this section we shall indicate the relations between these scores and the several variables previously described. On theoretical grounds it would be reasonable to predict that high n Aff is related to autism, and thus probably also to inaccuracy, simply because those most concerned about satisfactory relationships to others might be expected also to be concerned about relationships of balance with them, even at the cost of accuracy.

Authoritarianism and Need for Affiliation

In view of the relationships already shown between authoritarianism and such variables as accuracy, sensitivity to strain, and autism, we may well begin by noting whether F-scores are consistently related to n Aff scores. Table 7.13 shows that there is no significant relationship between them in either year, and that the nonsignificant relationships are in opposite directions in the two

Table 7.13. NUMBERS OF SUBJECTS AT DIFFERENT LEVELS OF
AUTHORITARIANISM AND OF NEED FOR AFFILIATION

F-score ranks	n Aff ranks, Year I		n Aff ranks, Year II		
	1–10	11–17	1–5	6–10	11–17
1–5	4	1	0	2	3
6–17	6	6	5	3	4
TOTAL	10	7	5	5	7
MEAN	7.9	10.6	13.0	7.0	7.6

populations. The most that can be said about a relationship in either population is that in Year II the 5 Ss lowest in n Aff tend to be high in authoritarianism, none of them ranking below 7 in F-score, and 3 of the 5 ranking 15, 16, and 17. A comparable breakdown is not possible for the Year-I population because of their narrow variance in n Aff score; 10 of the 17 score at zero. Thus we cannot predict from authoritarianism the need for affiliation, except perhaps for the very low F-scorers in Year II.

Autism and Need for Affiliation

In Year I, with respect to estimates of highly attractive others' ordering of House members, neither at Week 1 nor at Week 5 is there a significant relationship between need for affiliation and autism (discrepancy between estimated and actual orderings; see page 137). At Week 1, when autism tends to be more extreme, the relationship is in the predicted direction, but the p value is only .10, by exact test; the distribution is $\begin{smallmatrix} 7 & 2 \\ 3 & 5 \end{smallmatrix}$.[6]

In Year II, with respect to estimates of highly attractive others' ordering of Spranger Values, there is again no significant relationship between autism and need for affiliation. At Week 2 it is in the predicted direction and at about the .1 level of significance, but at Week 14 it is very slightly in the opposite direction. In view of the fact that, in this population, the n Aff scores showed considerable variance, we are inclined to conclude either that one or both measures were not adequate for our purposes or that the predicted

---

[6] The rank-order correlation between the indices of autism at Weeks 1 and 5 is .51 ($N = 17$), indicating a certain degree of individual consistency in spite of many changes in attraction.

relationship was so slight as to be obscured by other and stronger ones.

Need for Affiliation and Other Indices of Sensitivity to Strain

Year I. None of our indices of tendency toward balance in Year I, as described in Chapter 6, shows a significant relationship to need for affiliation. There is, however, an inverse relationship between *n* Aff and the accuracy of certain *early* estimates. First, the 7 *S*s whose *n* Aff scores are greater than zero estimate the attraction preferences of their Rank-1 choices less accurately than do the 10 *S*s whose *n* Aff scores are at zero; the *p* values of the differences are <.05 at Week 1 and approximately .1 at Week 5. Second, the 7 who are relatively high in *n* Aff estimate other *S*s' levels of reciprocated attraction (toward the estimators) less accurately than do the other 10, at Week 2; the respective scores of distortion are 79.7 and 56.2, and the *t* value of the difference is 2.34, significant at less than the .05 level (Samuels, 1956). At no later time (computations have been made for Weeks 5, 8, 9, 11, and 12) are the distortion indices related to need for affiliation. It is in the earliest weeks of acquaintance, of course, that such estimates are made with least certainty, and therefore with most opportunity for distortion. By as early as Week 5 the high *n* Aff scorers have become more accurate, while the low scorers have not; by Week 11 the high scorers have become significantly more accurate than at Week 2 (*p* < .05), while the low scorers were hardly improving at all. According to these indices, accuracy is facilitated by low need for affiliation only on very early acquaintance.

As of Week 8, however, we are able to report one interesting relationship to need for affiliation. As described in Chapter 4, we carried out an experiment in which attitudes were shown to change as attraction toward a previously unknown person, who took a strong position regarding that attitude, was first made positive and then negative. Our prediction was that attitude change in the expected direction—toward agreement with the speaker when attraction toward him was high, and toward disagreement when attraction decreased—would most probably occur on the part of those relatively high in *n* Aff. (See Burdick and Burnes, 1958.)

Results appear in Table 7.14. In the "Phase I" section of this table, 3 *S*s initially in full agreement with *E* (the speaker) are excluded from consideration, since no change in the predicted

Table 7.14. *N* OF *S*s SHOWING ATTITUDE CHANGE AT TWO LEVELS OF NEED FOR AFFILIATION

Need for affiliation	Phase I [a]		Phase II [a]	
	Change toward E	No change toward E	Change away from E	No change away from E
High	6	0	5 [b]	2
Low	2	6	1	9

$p = .009$ (exact test) $p = .017$ (exact test)

[a] Phase I refers to the period beginning with initial strangership and ending just after the speaker's initial presentation, when attraction toward him was favorable. Phase II includes the subsequent, hostile presentation by the speaker, following which attraction toward him declined.

[b] Four of these 5 *S*s were among the 6 who changed toward *E* during Phase I: they are *S*s #18, 23, 25, 30.

direction was possible for them. These *S*s could, however, change in the opposite direction, and so they are included in the "Phase II" section of the table.

These findings indicate that susceptibility to attitude change, under conditions of rather extreme provocation to change in attraction toward a person immediately associated with the issue involved, varied with need for affiliation, as predicted. Only under these conditions, however, do we find any clear relationship, in this population, between need for affiliation and sensitivity to strain.

Year II. In the Year-II population there is again an early but not a late relationship between need for affiliation and accuracy of estimates (of others' ordering of Spranger Values), but it appears only in the relative and not in the absolute index of accuracy (see pp. 113–114), and only if those very low in *n* Aff are compared with all other *S*s: the *p* value of the distribution $\begin{smallmatrix} 4 & 3 \\ 1 & 9 \end{smallmatrix}$ is .056, by exact test. The 5 *S*s lowest in *n* Aff do not seem to be handicapped as the others are in the difficult task of rank-ordering others in agreement with themselves, on early acquaintance. In this respect the findings from the two populations are quite similar, though the tasks are very different.

There are no other relationships of interest, in the Year-II population, between need for affiliation and strain-related variables, except on the part of the 5 Ss lowest in n Aff. Of these 5, 4 are in the lower half of all Ss in tendency to perceive balance in estimating others' Spranger Values at Week 2. More importantly, perhaps, 4 of the 5 are very low in the pooled index of sensitivity to strain, at Week 14 (see pp. 113–114), and they are individuals who rank 10, 15, 16, and 17 in nonauthoritarianism (Ss #37, 39, 41, 50). In this population, extreme nonaffiliativeness, extreme authoritarianism, and extreme lack of sensitivity to strain tend to be found in the same persons.

Summary

Authoritarianism is related, in both populations, to phenomena that are crucial to our formulation of interpersonal dynamics in the acquaintance process. In ways that differ with the stage of acquaintance and with the nature of objects of orientation, nonauthoritarians appear to be particularly sensitive to matters of strain and balance. With increasing opportunity for obtaining information about their fellows, they tend, more than authoritarians, to become more accurate in estimating their fellows' orientations. At early stages of acquaintance, however, their sensitivity to balance may—if the objects of orientation are of sufficiently great importance—outweigh their tendencies toward accuracy, in autistic manner.

Subjects extremely low in affiliativeness, who tended also to be extremely authoritarian, were more accurate in the earlier, but not the later, estimates of others' orientations—a temporary advantage presumably accruing from their relative insensitivity.

Nonauthoritarians—clearly in the second year and probably in the first also—came to achieve balance by discovering, with relative accuracy, who was in agreement with them and letting their attraction preferences be determined accordingly. The authoritarians, contrastingly, tended to continue to perceive more agreement than actually existed with those whom they were already attracted to.

PART FOUR

Differentiation and Structuring within Populations

In Part Two we presented findings in support of our general hypotheses concerning balance in individual and collective systems. In Part Three we showed that some degree of sensitivity to strain is common to nearly all our subjects, though it varies in degree with certain personality variables. We now turn to a consideration of the consequences of tendencies toward balance for population structuring.

Structure—whether of matter composed of molecules or of populations composed of individuals or of subgroups—refers to relationships among parts that are somehow differentiated and distinguishable. In Chapter 8 we shall describe the parts (or units, as we shall call them) that are distinguishable by virtue of properties related to interpersonal attraction, and test the general hypothesis that differentiation among the units occurs in balance-promoting ways. Then we shall go on, in Chapter 9, to consider the interrelationships among the differentiated units, in total populations. It is these relationships that constitute structure, and we shall put to the test the hypothesis that structuring also occurs in balance-promoting ways.

Within any fixed population it is to be expected that both differentiations among structural units and relationships among them will become more stable with increasing acquaintance. Insofar as we find structural changes in the direction of increasingly balanced collective systems we shall therefore inquire whether, as expected, they are also increasingly stable systems.

Early and Late Differentiation
of Individuals, Pairs,
and Triads

8

The basic datum for the identification of structural units is the degree of attraction expressed by one individual for another. During nearly every week of our data-gathering—beginning on the 3d day and ending on the 122nd day (including a two-week vacation)—272 such expressions of attraction were made, one by each of 17 Ss toward each of the other 16. For the purposes of this and the following chapter, structuring has to do with the arrangement of some or all of these 272 attraction responses. The arrangement of various sets of these 272 relationships might be so described as to show any of the following kinds of differentiated parts:

1. differentiation among *individuals,* as recipients of attraction responses from all other Ss (as sources of such responses, they are not differentiated, since each S assigned 16 ranks);

2. differentiation among *pairs* of Ss, either from the point of view of the level of their pooled scores of attraction toward each other or from the point of view of the mutuality (similarity) of their levels of attraction toward each other, regardless of absolute level;

3. differentiation among *sets* of Ss *larger than two* (triads, tetrads, pentads), in similar fashion.

Thus individuals may differ with respect to attraction received from others; and pairs or larger sets may differ either as to level or as to homogeneity (regardless of level) of members' attraction toward one another. Insofar as such differences are found, we may proceed to examine the relationships of attraction among the differentiated parts; these relationships constitute structure, for our purposes.

One assumption underlying the analyses in this chapter is that one or more kinds of differentiation actually occurs with acquaintance. Prior to any acquaintance at all, each of our populations consisted, literally, of 17 men living in 17 different cities, no one of whom had ever heard of any of the others. It could not be said that such a population contained any parts that were differentiated with respect to interpersonal attraction. The prediction that differentiation would occur where it had not been before is based upon the further assumption that individuals differ in their general capacity to elicit attraction from others, in special traits and attitudes which selectively elicit attraction in varying degrees from others, and in the traits and attitudes that they consider attractive in others. If so, then, given opportunity for interaction, differentiation of attraction relationships is bound to occur.

These considerations, however, are so general as to have no special relevance for the particular theoretical propositions with which this study is concerned. In these terms, the general hypothesis to be pursued in this chapter is not simply that differentiation will occur, but rather that it will occur in ways that promote balance, as previously defined. In terms of individual systems, this means in ways that tend to reduce the strain of perceived discrepancy. In terms of collective systems (with reference to actual, not perceived, discrepancy), it means in ways that actually reduce discrepancy.

STRUCTURING BASED UPON PERSON DIFFERENTIATION

We shall begin by considering the individual as a structural unit—that is, the individual as the locus of certain properties, including personal attributes such as he presumably brings with him to a research setting. We shall not, as in Part Three, be dealing with measurements of such attributes, but only with their measurable consequences for population structuring. Structural changes attributable to personal characteristics are, of course, affairs of interaction of persons, and not just inevitable consequences of individual traits brought to the research setting. We shall limit our consideration to personal characteristics which (as seen by other *S*s, not necessarily by the investigators) affect the *general attractiveness* of individuals. Such characteristics are both "discovered" and "created" (in the sense of being interactional effects) during the acquaintance process, and we may therefore expect that population structuring will change as a result of acquaintance.

Our theoretical formulation has nothing to say about individual differences, either in personal attributes or in susceptibility to forces of strain and balance. In this section, therefore, we shall not be primarily interested in testing predictions about differentiations among persons, paralleling acquaintance, but rather in noting the occurrence of such differentiations, since they are likely to influence differentiated *relationships* among persons—predictions which will later be tested.

Popularity Status

It is to be expected, simply on the basis of random assortments of qualities deemed desirable in populations like ours, that our subjects would soon become differentiated in respect to numbers of high-attraction responses received from others. One way of describing such differentiation is in terms of numbers of *S*s, at different stages of acquaintance, who receive fewer or more than the expected numbers of high-attraction choices—e.g., in the top half (Ranks 1–8). The obtained together with the expected numbers of *S*s receiving such responses at three levels of expected frequency are shown in Table 8.1. In Year I, as shown in this table, there is a slight tendency toward less differentiation, with increasing acquaintance; that is, there are fewer *S*s at Week 15 than at the earliest weeks who received from all other *S*s either improbably many or improbably few attraction responses in the upper half of all responses made. In Year II, on the other hand, there is an increasing tendency toward individual differentiation: by Week 15, 9 of the 17 *S*s, as compared with an expected 1.3, received either extremely few or extremely many responses in the upper half.

The same difference may be shown by comparing individual scores of popularity (the sums of all ranks received) at Week 15 for the two populations. If we take as indices of differentiation the number of individuals in each population who appear in the most extreme quarter of all 34 individual scores in both populations (the

Table 8.1. OBTAINED AND EXPECTED NUMBERS OF *S*s RECEIV-
ING VARIOUS NUMBERS OF ATTRACTION RESPONSES AT RANKS
1–8 FROM ALL OTHER *S*s

Responses received	Expected [a]	Obtained, Year I [b]			Obtained, Year II		
		Week 0	Week 1	Week 15	Week 0	Week 1	Week 15
0– 4	0.65	4	3	3	2	3	5
5–11	15.70	10	12	13	11	11	8
12–16	0.65	3	2	1	4	3	4
TOTAL	17	17	17	17	17	17	17

[a] Based upon cumulative binomial probabilities, when $Q = P = .5$; see Walker and Lev (1953), p. 459.

[b] These data are not affected by the incompleteness of response in Year I, since none were omitted at Ranks 1–8. See footnote, Table 8.3.

8 scores diverging most widely—whether very high or very low—from the average of all scores), 7 of these 8 are in the Year-II and only 1 of them in the Year-I population. This difference (in the distribution $\frac{1\ \ 7}{16\ \ 10}$) is significant at .020, by exact test. In this respect, then, the two populations differ: In Year II but not in Year I, subjects tend to become either highly popular or highly unpopular. We shall later note certain consequences of this fact for population structuring.

Frequency of Individual Involvement in High Mutual-attraction Pairs

In spite of these differences between the two populations, there is another form of individual differentiation which we may expect to find, paralleling acquaintance, in both populations: there should be an increasing number of *S*s who are involved in relatively many high mutual-attraction pairs. This prediction, unlike the previous one concerning popularity, is directly derivable from our assumptions about psychological balance. Given positive self-esteem on the part of A and high, positive attraction toward B, then A's perception of reciprocated high attraction by B is strain-reducing with respect to A as common object of orientation. Given also continued interaction with B, A's high attraction toward B is more likely to persist if he continues to perceive it as reciprocated than if he does not—and it is more likely to be so perceived if it is in fact reciprocated than if it is not. Hence it is to be expected that mutuality of high attraction will increase during a period of acquaintance within which high attraction becomes reinforced if it is reciprocated, and tends to become lower if it is not reciprocated.

The prediction that the number of Ss involved in high mutual-attraction pairs will increase with acquaintance is, in effect, a prediction of increased differentiation. Although the processes involved presuppose forces that hypothetically apply to all Ss, we may anticipate different effects of these forces upon different individuals—both because persons differ as perceivers of others and because persons differ in what they offer for others to perceive. In particular, those differences that eventually result in different popularity statuses are likely to have the further effect that very popular individuals are almost certain to have their high-attraction choices reciprocated, while this may be impossible for very unpopular ones. And so, while our prediction of the general trend is derived from our theoretical formulation, our prediction of individual differences in respect to the general trend takes into account those factors associated with varying popularity statuses, as already demonstrated.

As shown in Table 8.2, the prediction is supported; although the

Table 8.2. Numbers of Ss Involved in Various Numbers of High-Attraction Pairs [a]

| N of pairs | Year I | | | Year II | | |
	Week 0	Week 1	Week 15	Week 0	Week 1	Week 15
0–4	13	8	5	13	9	8
5–7	4	9	12	4	8	9
Total	17	17	17	17	17	17

$\chi^2 = 5.78$ (Week 0 vs. Week 15)
$p < .02$ (1 df)

$\chi^2 = 1.99$ (Week 0 vs. Week 15)
$p < .25$ (1 df)

[a] The criterion of high attraction is a pair score ≤ 48; about one-fourth of all pair scores are included, by this criterion.

relationship is not significant in Year II, it is in the predicted direction, and if frequencies for both years are combined the resulting χ^2 is 7.34, with a p value of $<.01$. In neither year are the differences between Weeks 1 and 15 significant.

In terms of individual change between Weeks 0 and 15, in each year there is a significant number of Ss who increase in the number of high-attraction pairs in which they are involved. In Year I, 11 Ss increase and 5 decrease (1 showing no change); in Year II, 10 increase, 5 decrease, and 2 show no change. Assuming equal likelihood of change in either direction, the p value of these frequencies approaches .05, in each year.[1]

Summary: Person Differentiation

Differentiation based upon individuals' personal characteristics, about which we made no predictions derived from our theoretical formulation, increased in Year II but not in Year I: in the former year a significant number of Ss, on final acquaintance, received either very few or very many high-attraction choices. In both years, however, in accordance with our theoretically based predictions, there was an increase with acquaintance in the number of individuals involved in relatively many high-attraction pairs—which is to say an increase in mutuality at high levels of attraction. Thus, in spite of the fact that, following long acquaintance, individuals presented a wider range of personal attractiveness in one population than in the other, in both years differentiation of reciprocal relationships became such that most individuals became involved, in decreasingly random manner, in a relatively large number of mutual high-attraction relationships.

STRUCTURING BASED UPON PAIR DIFFERENTIATION

As previously noted in a slightly different context, the general hypotheses of this study require the prediction that, assuming positive self-esteem,[2] with increasing acquaintance high A-to-B attraction will be reciprocated by high B-to-A attraction with in-

---

[1] There was but one instance (in Year I) of an initial score of zero; since for this individual a decrease was impossible, he was eliminated from consideration. The Ss whose scores do not change are taken as contributing .5 each to increased and to decreased frequencies.

[2] Granting the likelihood of ambivalence of self-esteem, the present assumption is merely that of a net balance of self-esteem which is positive.

creasing frequency. This prediction is based upon the assumptions (1) that the perception of nonreciprocation of one's own high attraction is strain-inducing, one likely consequence of which is reduction of attraction toward the nonreciprocator; (2) that with increasing acquaintance, judgments of reciprocation tend to become more accurate, as more information becomes available; and (3) that therefore high attraction toward individuals who do not in fact reciprocate it tends to decrease, whereas high attraction that is in fact reciprocated is reinforced, and tends to persist—and thus, in either case, a tendency toward mutuality is maintained.

Early and Late Mutuality of Attraction

In this section we shall be concerned with degree of mutuality at all levels of attraction, and not merely at high levels as in the preceding section.

Findings. In Table 8.3 appear the frequencies of within-pair discrepancies in ranks assigned to each other, at earliest and latest times for both years. The early-late differences are in the predicted direction in both populations, but are significant (at the .05 level)

Table 8.3. DISTRIBUTIONS OF DIFFERENCES IN RANKS OF ATTRACTION ASSIGNED TO EACH OTHER BY MEMBERS OF ALL PAIRS

Rank differences	Week 0			Week 15		
	Year I	Year II	Total	Year I	Year II	Total
0	12	11	23	13	12	25
1– 3	39	48	87	64	60	124
4– 9	58	70	128	49	49	98
10–15	9	7	16	10	15	25
TOTAL	118 [a]	136	254	136	136	272

[a] At Week 0 of Year I, 18 of the 272 possible responses were not made, and so the total N of discrepancy scores at this time was 118 and not 136. Six Ss reported that they could not even identify from 1 to 6 of the other men, and hence could not place them in a rank order. In most cases it was the last few ranks that were not used, since the 6 Ss ranked those whom they did know, leaving the ranks at or near 16 unassigned. Hence the last few ranks are somewhat under-represented in this week's set of responses.

only in Year I. Since at neither week are there apparent discrepancies between the two populations, they may be combined for purposes of testing differences between Weeks 0 and 15. If these combined frequencies are dichotomized into the two highest and the two lowest categories as shown in Table 8.4 (almost exactly at the midpoint), the resulting χ^2 is 6.40, significant almost at .01 with 1 df. Thus we find, as predicted, a general increase, with acquaintance, in the degree of mutuality of reciprocal attraction, without attention to levels of attraction, particularly in Year I.

Except for frequencies at levels of very large rank differences, which are far below chance expectations at all times, the obtained Week-0 distribution does not differ significantly from chance, whereas at Week 15, as shown in Table 8.4, the differences are

Table 8.4. COLLAPSED FREQUENCIES OF RECIPROCATED PAIR ATTRACTION AT TWO LEVELS OF DIFFERENCE IN RECIPROCATION

Rank differences	Week 0, both years		Week 15, both years	
	Obtained	Expected	Obtained	Expected
0– 3	110	99	149	106
4–15	144	155	123	166
TOTAL	254	254	272	272
	$\chi^2 = 1.82$		$\chi^2 = 27.92$	
	$p < .20$ (1 df)		$p < .001$ (1 df)	

very large. As thus measured, apparently the Week-0 responses were not obtained too late to reflect the essentially random reciprocation that presumably existed at the first, hypothetical moment of initial acquaintance.

The mere fact that the degree of mutuality of attraction increases with acquaintance does not tell us, however, whether this increase occurs at all levels of attraction. We have no theoretical basis for making a prediction about this, and so we have made exploratory analyses, as shown in Tables 8.5 and 8.6. In Table 8.5, four levels of mutuality are categorized according to three levels of attraction response—that is, of rank actually given by an individual S; and the obtained frequency in each cell is accompanied by the expected frequency. (The calculation of these expectancies, as of those in Table 8.4, is based upon the assumption that, if degrees of mutuality were determined only randomly, each response would

Table 8.5. Distributions of Various Levels of Mutuality, Categorized by Actual Ranks of Attraction Responses, Together with Frequencies Expected by Chance [a]

Level of mutuality in rank differences	Attraction response ranks Week 0, both years				Attraction response ranks Week 15, both years			
	1–4	5–12	13–16	Total	1–4	5–12	13–16	Total
0– 3 (high)	75	88	57	220	86	145	67	298
	(46)	(109)	(45)	(199)	(47)	(119)	(47)	(213)
4– 7	30	130	38	198	23	100	31	154
	(32)	(102)	(32)	(166)	(34)	(111)	(34)	(179)
8–11	20	32	28	80	18	27	29	74
	(32)	(39)	(32)	(103)	(34)	(42)	(34)	(110)
12–15 (low)	5	0	5	10	9	0	9	18
	(20)	(0)	(20)	(40)	(21)	(0)	(21)	(42)
Total	130	250	128	508	136	272	136	544

[a] Frequencies in this table represent responses, and not pairs; hence they are twice as great as in Tables 8.3 and 8.4. Expected frequencies are rounded to the nearest integer, and are shown in parentheses.

be reciprocated with equal frequency by every possible response, from Rank 1 to Rank 16.) The expected frequencies in Table 8.5 are not the same at all attraction levels, because at the extremes (Ranks 1–4 and 13–16) large differences can occur in one direction only.

As shown in Tables 8.5 and 8.6, the increase in high mutuality (that is, in small discrepancies, at 0–3) is almost entirely concentrated in the intermediate range of attraction. The χ^2 value of the increase from 88 of 250 high-mutual responses at Week 0 to 145 of 272 at Week 15, in the intermediate range of attraction (Ranks 5–12) is 16.43, significant at $<.001$ with 1 df; at neither of the other attraction levels are the analogous differences significant.

Tables 8.5 and 8.6 show that at both times high mutuality at the highest level of attraction (Ranks 1–4) occurs with much

Table 8.6. PROBABILITY VALUES OF DIFFERENCES BETWEEN OBTAINED AND EXPECTED FREQUENCIES OF HIGH MUTUALITY IN PAIR ATTRACTION, AT VARIOUS LEVELS OF PAIR ATTRACTION, AS SHOWN IN TABLE 8.5.[a]

Attraction ranks	Week 0, both years			Week 15, both years		
	χ^2	p	Direction [b]	χ^2	p	Direction [b]
1– 4	14.29	<.001	High	23.47	<.001	High
5–12	3.25	<.10	Low	4.67	<.05	High
13–16	2.07	<.20	High	5.87	<.02	High
1–16	1.65	<.20	High	15.18	<.001	High

[a] Ns of pairs, not of responses, were used in calculating χ^2.
[b] "High" indicates that the obtained exceeded the expected frequencies, and "low" indicates the reverse.

greater than expected frequency, but only at Week 15 does high mutuality greatly exceed expectancies at other levels also.[3]

Summary

With increasing acquaintance there occurs, quite unambiguously, increasing differentiation of mutuality in attraction. The general level of mutuality increases significantly; that is, attraction responses are increasingly reciprocated at about the same level. The initial distribution does not differ significantly from expected frequencies (except at very low levels of mutuality), but the final one does. The locus of the increase in high mutuality is primarily in the inter-

[3] These findings are in general conformity with comparable ones reported by Tagiuri, Blake, and Bruner (1953) for Week 0, but *not* for Week 15. Their data were obtained from three groups of 10 members each who met for 12 two-hour sessions for group-discussion-therapy purposes. Each person was asked, "in the middle of the series" of 12 meetings, "to indicate, without restriction on number, those in the group that they 'liked best' and those they 'liked least,' and to guess which members they thought 'liked them best' and least." Mutuality was evidently treated by the investigators as an all-or-none affair, being defined as "reciprocal choice or omission or rejection." Comparison with chance frequencies of mutuality were computed by allocating to "robots" choices and guesses "by means of a table of random numbers." They report that "A chi-square test shows that mutuality does not exceed chance, a pooled χ^2 of 5.26 with 3 df yielding a confidence level between .20 and .10." Our findings suggest that whether "mutuality does . . . exceed chance," depends both upon level of attraction and upon degree of acquaintance.

mediate range of attraction; at the end but not at the beginning, high mutuality characterizes the intermediate range of attraction—roughly, high mutuality comes to appear in three quarters instead of only one quarter of the range of attraction. Orderliness replaces randomness throughout a larger part of the range of attraction.

Degree of Within-pair Attraction

The level of reciprocal *attraction* that two individuals express for each other (as indexed by a pooling of each one's attraction level for the other) is not at all the same thing, conceptually, as the level of their *mutuality* of attraction, which we have just been discussing. The index of mutual attraction that we have employed (based upon summed squares of each pair member's attraction rank for the other) combines both variables [4] in such manner that extremely high and extremely low scores of pair attraction occur only when mutuality is high. In the intermediate ranges of the distribution, however, either mutual or nonmutual ranks assigned by two Ss to each other may result in similar or even identical pair scores (e.g., both the combinations $10^2 + 10^2$ and $14^2 + 2^2$ yield sums of 200). Since both our theoretically based predictions and our exploratory inquiries have to do primarily with high and with low levels of pair attraction, the preceding findings concerning levels of mutuality carry direct implications for extreme levels of attraction, in which we are primarily interested.

As a plausible prediction concerning increasing differentiation of high-attraction and low-attraction pairs, it might be expected that with increasing acquaintance there would be more of each. As Ss become better judges of others' attraction toward themselves, and as these judgments become stabilized, balance-induced forces should result in modifications of their own attractions such that—particularly at the extremes—mutuality increases. But we have just shown (Table 8.5) that at the highest and lowest quarters of attraction there is little early-to-late change in level of mutuality. It therefore follows—since both high and low levels of pair attraction can occur only at high levels of mutuality—that little early-to-late change is to be expected in the numbers of high-attraction and low-attraction pairs. In terms of pair-structuring of populations, this kind of increasing differentiation is unlikely.

Table 8.7 shows that this is in fact the case, and closely com-

[4] The rationale for this procedure is presented on pp. 72–74.

Table 8.7. FREQUENCIES OF PAIR SCORES OF ATTRACTION AT EXTREMES AND AT INTERMEDIATE LEVELS

Pair scores of attraction	Expected	Year I Week 0	Year I Week 1	Year I Week 15	Year II Week 0	Year II Week 1	Year II Week 15
$\leq$ 17 (high)	9.03 [a]	16	17	20	18	14	17
18–239	117.94	109	107	100	106	107	108
$\geq$ 240 (low)	9.03	11	12	16	12	15	11
TOTAL	136	136 [b]	136	136	136	136	136

[a] The expected value of 9.03 is $17/256$ of 136.

[b] For purposes of completeness, the 18 missing responses at Week 0, Year I, were entered as interpolated from Ss' remaining responses, using tied scores when necessary.

parable results appear if less extreme scores than those appearing in this table are used (see Appendix VI). At all times in each population the frequencies diverge significantly from chance expectations (χ^2 values range from 6.42 to 16.96, corresponding to p values from $<.05$ to $<.001$ with 2 df). The greater part, though by no means all, of the departure from expected frequencies is contributed by extremeness at very high rather than at very low levels of attraction. But none of the week-to-week differences is significant. Even after three days of acquaintance, high-attraction responses especially, but also low-attraction responses, tend significantly to be reciprocated at about the same levels.

As we shall show in the following section, the early high-attraction pairs tend not to persist, but the fact remains that our populations did not show increasing differentiation with respect to mutuality of pair attraction. Forces toward mutuality are apparently so strong that, whether many population members are still virtual strangers to one another or whether all are well acquainted, mutuality of high and of low attraction is the rule at all times.

STABILITY OF PAIR ATTRACTION

This finding of no increasing differentiation with respect to mutuality is of course a quantitative one, which ignores the identity of individuals involved in high-mutual pairs. It is to be expected that with increasing acquaintance more and more pairs of particular Ss with find themselves reciprocally rewarded by each other over a continuing period of time. Hence we predict that the number of *stable* high-attraction pairs will increase with acquaintance.

By way of testing this prediction, we have compared the number of pairs whose attraction scores remain stable over the earliest and the latest two-week periods—between Weeks 0–2 and 13–15. Pair scores were considered stable if they changed ≤ 20 points (on the 256-point scale) during these intervals. As shown in Table 8.8, both populations show the predicted trend. The differences are

Table 8.8. Numbers of Stable and Unstable Pairs, in Mutual Attraction, over Early and Late Two-week Periods

Change status [a]	Year I		Year II	
	Weeks 0–2	Weeks 13–15	Weeks 0–2	Weeks 13–15
Stable	29	67	45	82
Unstable	107	69	91	54
TOTAL	136	136	136	136
	$\chi^2 = 22.04$		$\chi^2 = 19.14$	
	$p < .001$ (1 df)		$p < .001$ (1 df)	

[a] See text for criterion of stability.

significant not only for each population as a whole, but also for the highest quarter, the middle half, and the lowest quarter, computed separately, in each population. In terms of proportions of stable pairs at either time, however, and especially at the later times, there are large differences between the middle half, in attraction level, and the upper and lower quarters. Between Weeks 13 and 15, only about one-third of all pairs in the middle half remain stable, as compared with more than 75 percent of all pairs in either the highest or the lowest quarter. The corresponding proportions at Weeks 0–2 are about one-sixth and one-third. Thus at all levels of attraction the same pairs of persons maintain more stable relationships of attraction at late than at early stages of acquaintance, and the proportions of stable pairs are large at high and at low levels of attraction.

These findings suggest another prediction that is more central to our theoretical formulation. Very high attraction pairs should be more stable than other pairs, insofar as their relationship of high attraction, at the beginning of the period during which stability is observed, follows adequate opportunity for pair members to explore each others' orientations. This prediction rests upon two considerations: (1) since very high attraction pairs are also characterized by high mutuality, they constitute a balanced two-person system with respect to each of the pair members themselves; and (2) during early stages of acquaintance relationships of high attraction often seemed to be based upon superficial factors, such as propinquity. According to our theoretical assumptions, stability of high attraction presupposes adequate opportunity for pair members to explore each others' orientations, and is therefore not to be expected at early stages of acquaintance.

We have tested this prediction by comparing the subsequent fate of pair relationships that are and that are not very high at Week 10. The prediction is that during the subsequent five weeks (in addition to a two-week vacation) the former will be more stable. Table 8.9, in which we have compared individual changes

Table 8.9. NUMBERS OF ATTRACTION RESPONSES ASSIGNED TO EACH OTHER BY MEMBERS OF 25 PAIRS HIGHEST IN ATTRACTION AT WEEK 10, AND BY ALL OTHER PAIRS, THAT SHOW VARYING AMOUNTS OF CHANGE BETWEEN WEEKS 10 AND 15 [a]

Change in rank	Year I attraction level			Year II attraction level		
	Very high	Others	Total	Very high	Others	Total
0	19	42	61	22	46	68
1 –2	19	93	112	21	111	132
$\geqq$ 3	12	87	99	7	65	72
TOTAL	50	222	272	50	222	272

$x^2 = 10.75$ $x^2 = 12.96$

$p < .005$ (2 df) $p < .005$ (2 df)

[a] See text for description of procedures. In Year I the period is from Weeks 11 to 15, since responses were not obtained in Week 10.

between Weeks 10 and 15 in all ranks assigned by members of high-attraction pairs and of all other pairs, between Weeks 10 and 15, shows that the prediction is well supported. "Very high" attraction is defined, in this table, as the 25 highest pairs at Week

10. It would not be justifiable to conclude that the greater stability of the high-attraction pairs is attributable exclusively to the fact of balance with respect to pair members themselves, since, as shown on pages 162–165, high-attraction pairs also tend to become involved in high-attraction triads and larger subgroups, with the result that they are balanced also with respect to one or more other House members. Since balance with respect both to pair members themselves and to extra-pair members is predictable under these conditions, it is likely that both contribute to the greater stability of high-attraction pairs.

As an incidental finding, the changes made by the 25 pairs *lowest* in attraction, during the same interval of several weeks, were in Year I very much like those made by the 25 highest pairs, but in Year II very much like those made by the pairs intermediate in attraction. It is tempting to conclude that in Year I when (as elsewhere shown; see pp. 180–188) the population was divisively structured, as it was not in Year II, the low-attraction pairs were stable as a result of autistic hostility (see Newcomb, 1947). That is, if there was little or no communication between members of low-attraction pairs in Year I (perhaps associated with their membership in the opposed subgroups) then one of the important mechanisms for increasing low attraction was not used.

In any case, there were many more pairs whose attraction relationships were stable during the final than during the early weeks of acquaintance, and, as predicted from our theoretical assumptions, it was (by significant differences) the high-attraction pairs whose stability was greatest.

STRUCTURING BASED UPON HIGH-ATTRACTION TRIADS

A triad all three of whose component pair scores, or whose summed pair scores, are very high constitutes a differentiated node, or concentration of "close" interperson relationships. Hypothetically, there should be more of these in the final than in the early weeks. The assumption here is that one of the processes by which differentiation increases is the "building up" of high-scoring pairs into high-scoring triads—very much as high individual ratings "build up" (by reciprocation) into high-scoring pairs, though presumably more slowly. Such a process would be balance-promoting, within collective systems.

At this point in our tests of the predicted increase in differentiation, we cease to be concerned with low-scoring pairs. There are good reasons for the reciprocation of low attraction, but these reasons scarcely apply to the accretive process by which pairs build up into triads and larger sets. That is, the hypothesized force toward individual strain reduction necessarily results in increasing reciprocation, over time, of both high and low individual ratings, and also in the combining of high-scoring pairs into high-scoring triads and larger sets. The reasons for the latter are that (1) strain-reducing forces tend to result in similar degrees of attraction on the part of both members of high-scoring pairs toward other persons (especially those about whom either of the pair feels strongly); and (2) those persons who become highly attractive to both members of a pair, by such processes, tend to reciprocate; thus a nucleus of one high-scoring pair tends to "grow" into a triad composed of three high-scoring pairs, or a tetrad composed of six pairs, etc. The same theoretical considerations do not, however, necessarily result in the concentration of other *low*-scoring pairs around an existing low-scoring pair—simply because, hypothetically, there are no forces toward consensus on the part of low-scoring pairs. Hence our hypotheses concerning differentiation will be tested with reference to high-scoring triads only.

In brief, the logic of the present prediction is (1) that strain-reducing forces tend to lead to the perception of "perfect triads" (as outlined on pp. 61–64); and (2) that, if and when it is discovered that such perceptions are not justified, attraction preferences tend to change in such ways that new "perfect triads," which correspond more closely to reality, are developed. Thus the dynamics of both individual and collective systems are involved.

Procedures

We shall use the simplest of several alternative procedures for identifying a high-attraction triad: any set of three Ss all three of whose pair scores (A-B, A-C, and B-C) meet a specified level of high attraction. Since the number of such sets in a total population of pairs varies with the number of pairs that meet the specified criterion, for purposes of comparison that criterion had best be stated in terms of a constant number of high-scoring pairs.[5] Thus we shall test the prediction—that there will be increasing numbers of high-attraction triads with increasing acquaintance—by counting the sets of 3 Ss all three of whose pair scores are included in the highest N of pair scores in the total population.

Findings

In Table 8.10 appear the numbers of high-attraction triads, thus computed, at Weeks 0, 1, 2, and 15 in each population; changes are

Table 8.10. NUMBERS OF HIGH-ATTRACTION TRIADS AMONG 34 PAIRS OF Ss THAT ARE HIGHEST IN MUTUAL ATTRACTION, AT TIMES NOTED [a]

| | Year I | | | Year II | | |
| | High triads | Other triads | Total [b] | High triads | Other triads | Total [b] |
Week						
0	22	49	71	14	57	71
1	10	61	71	11	60	71
2	17	54	71	13	58	71
13	13	58	71	19	52	71
14	14	57	71	19	52	71
15	15	56	71	20	51	71

[a] See text for criterion of high-attraction triads.
[b] The maximum number of different triads that can be constructed from 34 pairs is 71.

rather considerable in the early weeks, and negligible in the final ones.

If (according to the rationale presented below), Week 1 is compared with Week 15, and if the two populations are combined,

[5] At certain weeks in either population tied pair-scores made it necessary to include one or two more than the specified number of them; in such cases only as many of the tied pair scores as required to complete the specified number were included in the computation of triads, each of the tied scores being considered alternatively (rounded to the nearest integer), and the average number of triads resulting from all possible alternatives among the tied scores was taken as the triad count at the specified criterion level.

the increase in numbers of high-attraction triads is significant at almost exactly the .05 level ($\chi^2 = 3.76$, with 1 df).[6]

In both populations, but especially in Year I, there is a decrease between Weeks 0 and 1 in the number of high-attraction triads. In Year I there are actually more of them on the third day of acquaintance than at the end of the fourth month—apparently because on the third day most Ss' acquaintance was very limited; high attraction was in nearly every instance reciprocated by roommates, who often, also, struck up early acquaintance with the same individuals in other rooms. By the tenth day of acquaintance, in both populations, the lines were beginning to reform, with attendant decreases in the numbers of high-attraction triads in Week 1. In a certain sense, therefore, the Week-1 data are more suitable than those of Week 0 for testing the prediction of increasing numbers of high-attraction triads with increasing acquaintance—that is, if one is interested in testing the prediction that at both of the times to be compared attraction choices are made with some knowledge of *all* Ss who are being ranked in attractiveness.

Since we initially described the problem of this study in terms of *stable* interpersonal relationships, these same data may also be analyzed in terms of *persisting* high-attraction triads. For purposes of testing the present prediction, we may consider that any triad which meets the criterion of high attraction both at the beginning and at the end of a two-week interval is a persisting one. In Table 8.11 (which is taken from the data in Table 8.10) we have therefore shown the numbers of high-attraction triads that persist from Week 0 to Week 2 and from Week 13 to Week 15. As shown in Table 8.11, the number of persisting high-attraction triads increases sharply from earliest to latest fortnights; in terms of proportions, the increase is from about 12 percent to 54 percent in Year I, and from 23 percent to 73 percent in Year II.

[6] These findings are not a unique result of the particular criterion level chosen, nor of the particular mode of computing levels of triad attraction. We have computed frequencies analogous to those in Table 8.10, except that (1) a minimum *mean* (on the 256-point scale) of the three pair-scores included in each triad, rather than a minimum for *each* of the three pair-scores, was taken as the criterion; and (2) a somewhat higher level of attraction was used as the criterion (25 rather than 34 highest pairs). Results parallel those in Table 8.10: frequencies of high-attraction triads, at the same weeks, are 7, 4, 5, 9, 10, 11 in Year I; and in Year II they are 5, 4, 4, 9, 10, 9. The differences between Weeks 1 and 15 are significant at $<.025$; $\chi^2 = 5.21$, with 1 df.

Early and Late Differentiation ———————————

Table 8.11. NUMBERS OF HIGH-ATTRACTION TRIADS THAT PER-
SIST OVER A TWO-WEEK PERIOD, ON EARLIEST AND ON LATEST
ACQUAINTANCE

	Year I			Year II		
Weeks	Persisting triads	Other triads	Total [a]	Persisting triads	Other triads	Total [a]
0– 2	2	15	17	3	10	13
13–15	7	8	13	14	5	19
		$p = .036$ (exact test)			$p = .017$ (exact test)	

[a] The N of total triads is considered to be the maximum that could persist—i.e., the smaller of the numbers of high-attraction in the two weeks
under consideration.

Population Differences

The findings already presented suggest certain differences between the two populations. As shown in Table 8.12, there is a
significant tendency for more high-attraction triads to appear in
Year II than in Year I (Week-0 frequencies are ignored in this
table, for reasons already discussed).

Table 8.12. NUMBERS OF WEEKS, BETWEEN WEEKS 1 AND 15,
IN WHICH HIGH-ATTRACTION TRIADS APPEAR IN THE TWO POPU-
LATIONS, AT TWO LEVELS OF FREQUENCY

N of triads	Year I	Year II	Total
10–14	9	4	13
15–20	3	10	13
TOTAL	12	14	26

$\chi^2 = 3.87$ $p < .05$ (1 df)

These differences in triad structuring between the two populations are clearly related to their differences in popularity statuses,
as previously noted. At Week 15, there was greater consensus in
Year II about the unpopularity of 4 Ss than about any S in Year
I; hence, in effect, there were fewer Ss in Year II who were
"eligible" for membership in high-attraction triads, and high attraction ranks were concentrated among fewer individuals. Further,

at Week 15 there was greater consensus about the popularity of 3 Ss in Year II than about any S in Year I: this meant, again, that high-attraction ranks were concentrated among fewer individuals in Year II than in Year I. Given these circumstances, the greater frequencies of high-attraction triads in Year II were an almost inevitable outcome. In Chapter 9 we shall discuss, in terms of our theoretical framework, some of the reasons for these differences between the two populations.

Summary: Structuring Based upon High-attraction Triads

As predicted from theoretical considerations, there are increasing numbers of high-attraction triads with increasing acquaintance between Weeks 1 and 15, but (contrary to expectation) not between Weeks 0 and 15. Informal evidence suggests that the unexpectedly large number of such triads on the third day of acquaintance resulted from limited acquaintance; small coteries of individuals, within which but not between which individuals had had some informal contact, appear to account for the phenomenon. This interpretation is reinforced by the fact that the numbers of high-attraction triads that persisted (that included the same 3 Ss) over a two-week period increased sharply between the earliest and the latest two-week periods. These tendencies are more extreme in Year II than in Year I, as a result of greater extremeness of individuals' popularity and unpopularity in Year II.

SUMMARY: EARLY AND LATE DIFFERENTIATION

The general hypothesis of this chapter is based upon the assumption that, as initial randomness of attraction relationships among individuals gives way to orderliness, there will be increasing differentiation among individuals, among pairs, and among larger sets of individuals. The general hypothesis itself is that, insofar as such differentiation is not attributable to personal qualities (with regard to which individuals differed before entering the research situation, and about which our theoretical formulation has nothing to say), it will occur in balance-promoting ways.

We found, though we made no prediction, that *individual* differentiation with respect to popularity status increased only in Year II, when a significant number of Ss, on final acquaintance, were either very popular or very unpopular. In both years, however, as predicted, there was an increase in the number of individuals involved in relatively many high-attraction pairs.

There was also increasing differentiation, with increasing acquaintance, among *pairs,* in the sense of increasing numbers of pairs whose members' attraction toward each other is at about the same level. Most of this increase does not occur at very high or very low but at intermediate levels of attraction; particularly at high levels of attraction, the hypothesized forces toward mutuality are constant at all times.

Our prediction that with acquaintance there would be increasing numbers of high-attraction *triads* was supported by comparisons between Weeks 1 and 15, but not between Weeks 0 and 15. As early as the third day of acquaintance, limited acquaintance within small subgroups resulted in large numbers of high-attraction triads, especially in Year I. In neither year, however, did these early triads persist, whereas triads formed toward the end of the acquaintance period were quite stable.

Early and Late Structuring
of Total Populations

9

We have shown that, in accordance with predictions derived from our hypothesis concerning strain and balance, increasing acquaintance is paralleled by an increasing tendency toward mutuality of high attraction, with the result that there is increasing differentiation of high-attraction pairs and triads. In this chapter we shall inquire into the changing relationships of these differentiated units—relationships that constitute the structure of the total population.

The central hypothesis of this chapter is that, in two-person systems, forces toward balance with respect to third, fourth, and nth persons result in an accretive process such that, with increasing acquaintance, there come to be larger sets of persons, all characterized by high attraction toward one another. This description of the process is not meant to imply that every high-attraction unit of three or more persons necessarily has its origin in only one of its constituent two-person systems; rather, similar processes are occurring, hypothetically, on the part of all high-attraction pairs simultaneously. And so we predict increasing numbers of larger high-attraction units, with acquaintance.

The process of "building" larger units out of smaller ones obviously involves selection; if the process goes on at all it must be a limited one, for otherwise all high-attraction pairs would merge into a single, large unit all of whose intermember attractions were high—a most improbable development, under the conditions of our research setting. Further, the process may also involve competition or conflict, with the result that two or more large units, each characterized by internal relationships of high attraction, develop interunit relationships of indifference or even hostility. Under ideal conditions (either a large number of populations selected in comparable manner, or two or more populations selected as different by experimental criteria), one might test the following prediction, derived from our hypotheses: high-attraction units characterized by interunit relationships of hostility are more likely to develop when preacquaintance attitudes toward common objects of importance are polarized within a population (i.e., when there are many pairs in strong disagreement, and many in close agreement) than when they are not. But we cannot test such a prediction with only two populations selected in the same manner, and so our inquiries concerning the development of opposed high-attraction units will be only exploratory ones.

It is of course to be expected that initial randomness of interpersonal attraction will give way to increasing orderliness and complexity of structure. The purpose of this chapter is not so much to show that this does in fact happen as to show that it happens in ways that are predictable from our theoretical formulation. And, since there are many alternative ways in which structuring might develop in ways consistent with that formulation, we shall also be interested in noting some of the alternative forms of structuring.

The Unit Structure of Total Populations

General Nature of Differentiated Units

Every member of either population had some sort of personal attraction status (such as popularity), of course. Each member had some sort of attraction relationship to each other member, so that each of the 136 pairs can be described by a pair score. Each of the 680 possible triads, and of the 2380 possible tetrads, and so on, can be assigned an index of within-unit attraction. But many individual statuses were not very different from many others, nor most of the possible pairs from most other pairs, nor most triads from most other triads, etc. For the purposes of this study, it is the differentiations at the extremes of attraction that are of interest.

We therefore define two categories of structural units: (1) any set of individuals the totality of whose attraction relationships to one another exceeds a rather high criterion; and (2) any single individual none of whose attraction relationships to any other individual reaches the same criterion. There are two consequences, both relevant to the predictions that we are interested in testing, of having chosen these definitions. (1) Relatively popular *S*s are not regarded as units, because such individuals are necessarily included in larger units (pairs, triads, etc.), as is not the case with very unpopular *S*s. (2) Low-scoring pairs, triads, and tetrads are not regarded as units, primarily because we have no predictions of importance to test about neutral, heterogeneous, or low-attraction sets of individuals.

Thus we shall be dealing with units consisting either of a single person (if his attraction relationships with no others reach the criterion, in which case he will be termed an *isolate*) or of multiperson units characterized by high "internal" attraction. This procedure has the advantage that the attraction relationships of every member of a population are taken account of in describing the total-population structure.

Operational Definition of High-attraction Units

For purposes of combining the ranks of attraction that are assigned by the members of any multiperson unit to each other we have summed the pair scores (on the 256-point scale; see pp. 72–74) of all pairs included in that unit; and, to make indices of within-unit attraction comparable with those of pairs, we then divided this sum by the number of pairs included in the multiperson unit (3 pairs in the case of a triad, 6 pairs in a tetrad, etc.). Our index is thus equivalent to the mean pair-score value of all within-unit pairs.

As a criterion of *high* within-unit attraction we have (since such a criterion may, for purposes of comparison only, be selected by any reasonable standard of convenience) chosen the rather severe cutting-point of *95 percent of the maximum possible* degree of within-unit attraction for the size of the unit involved. It is necessary to state the criterion relative to the maximum possible, rather than in terms of a fixed score, because the maximum possible degree of internal attraction declines with increasing numbers of persons in the unit. This is a consequence of the fact that attraction responses are made in *ranks*. Since an individual can assign each rank (from 1 to 16) only once, it follows that a pair is the only multiperson unit all of whose members can assign to each other only the maximally high rank of 1. In a triad, only half of the ranks assigned by members to each other can be at Rank 1, the maximally high combination being 1-1-1-2-2-2; in a tetrad only one-third, the maximally high combination being 1-1-1-1-2-2-2-2-3-3-3-3; in a pentad only one-fourth, etc. Thus the maximum possible index of within-unit attraction necessarily must decline with increasing size of the unit.

As to the reasons for settling upon 95 percent rather than some higher or lower value, it need only be said that experience has shown that any value much higher than this results in too many isolated individuals, and any value much lower in too few non-overlapping units, for purposes of clear comparison between different times or between the two populations.

The exact procedure of identifying high-attraction units is described in Appendix VII, with special attention to the steps of combining smaller units into larger ones.

Frequencies of Units of Various Sizes

In Figures 9.1 to 9.6 there appear graphic representations of the structuring of attraction relationships in both populations, in terms of units of all sizes that meet the 95-percent criterion at Weeks 0, 1, and 15. These three weeks are selected because the earliest and latest periods are most crucial for noting changes with acquaintance, and because (particularly in Year I) there are noticeable changes between Weeks 0 and 1, whereas subsequent week-to-week changes are not very marked.

The same data are summarized in quantitative form in Table 9.1. In this table all pairs, triads, and tetrads are included, even

Table 9.1. FREQUENCIES OF UNITS OF VARIOUS SIZES

N of persons in unit	Year I Week 0	Week 1	Week 15	Year II Week 0	Week 1	Week 15	Both years Week 0	Week 1	Week 15
1	3	2	2	2	3	4	5	5	6
2	19	19	24	17	18	25	36	37	49
3	11	4	13	4	6	15	15	10	28
4	5	0	3	0	1	5	5	1	8
5	1	0	0	0	0	1	1	0	1

Table 9.2. Numbers of *S*s Appearing in Units of Various Sizes, Each *S* Appearing in the Largest Unit of Which He Is a Member

N of persons in unit	Year I			Year II			Both years		
	Week 0	Week 1	Week 15	Week 0	Week 1	Week 15	Week 0	Week 1	Week 15
1	3	2	2	2	3	4	5	5	6
2	7	7	3	5	7	0	12	14	3
3	2	8	3	10	3	8	12	11	11
4	0	0	9	0	4	0	0	4	9
5	5	0	0	0	0	5	5	0	5
TOTAL	17	17	17	17	17	17	34	34	34

though the same units may also appear in larger sets.[1] In Table 9.2 the same data are so presented that each individual appears only once—in the largest unit of which he is a member, by the criterion employed.

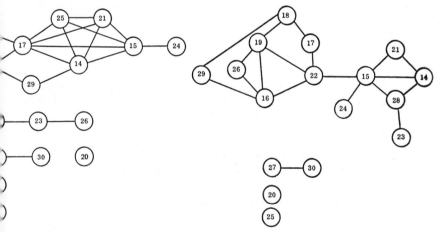

Fig. 9.1. Week 0, Year I   **Fig. 9.2.** Week 1, Year I

Sociograms showing all pairs and larger sets of individuals whose attraction relationships reach the 95-percent criterion. Unconnected individuals have no such relationships.

---

[1] In comparing the frequencies in Tables 9.1 and 9.2 with the sociograms in Figures 9.1–9.6, it should be remembered that the size of any unit is the

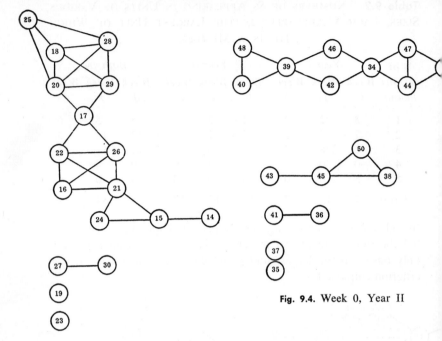

Fig. 9.4. Week 0, Year II

Fig. 9.3. Week 15, Year I

Sociograms showing all pairs and larger sets of individuals whose attraction relationships reach the 95-percent criterion. Unconnected individuals have no such relationships.

Table 9.1 shows a tendency toward more units of all sizes at the end than at the end of the acquaintance period, but this results from the fact that the same individuals are multiply counted (for example, four individuals in a tetrad constitute not only a tetrad but also four triads and six pairs); the increases at Week 15, as shown in Table 9.2, actually stem almost entirely from the greater number of larger units.

---

largest number of Ss the average of *all* of whose pair-scores reaches the 95 percent criterion; thus, in Figure 9.4, for example, Ss #34, 44, 47, and 49 are considered to constitute two triads, not one tetrad, because the mean of all six of the possible pair scores among these four Ss does not reach the criterion, whereas two of the possible four triads do reach the criterion.

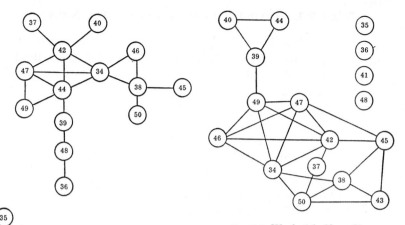

Fig. 9.6. Week 15, Year II

Fig. 9.5. Week 1, Year II

Sociograms showing all pairs and larger sets of individuals whose attraction relationships reach the 95-percent criterion. Unconnected individuals have no such relationships.

The column totals in Table 9.1 are meaningless, since the same individuals may appear varying numbers of times in the same column. But from Table 9.2 we may test the prediction that there will be larger numbers of Ss in larger units on late than on early acquaintance. If the frequencies for both years are combined, the prediction is significantly supported by comparisons of either Week 0 or Week 1 with Week 15: the χ^2 values are, respectively, 6.76 and 9.02, significant at $<.05$ and $<.02$, respectively, with 2 df.

In terms of numbers of units (rather than of Ss), Table 9.3 shows that more high-attraction units larger than two exist at the later time. In each of the two populations (if the very transient pentad of Week 0, Year I, be ignored), there are more larger units at Week 15 than in either of the earliest weeks. Particularly as compared with Week 1, there are at Week 15 fewer units as small as pairs and more of larger size.

Table 9.3. FREQUENCIES OF UNITS OF ALL SIZES [a]

Size of units	Year I Week 0	Year I Week 1	Year I Week 15	Year II Week 0	Year II Week 1	Year II Week 15	Both years Week 0	Both years Week 1	Both years Week 15
1	3	2	2	2	3	4	5	5	6
2	4	5	2	2	7	3	6	12	5
3	1	6	3	6	2	5	7	8	8
4	0	0	3	0	1	0	0	1	3
5	1	0	0	0	0	1	1	0	1

[a] No set of any size appears more than once in this table, though the same S may appear more than once. Every attraction relationship appears in the largest unit where it can appear.

Overlapping Triads

In a highly structured population one would expect not only a considerable number of high-attraction units larger than two; it is also to be expected that a considerable number of high-attraction pairs in such units would be involved in more than one unit larger than two. This could come about in either of two ways: (1) by inclusion of the pair in a high-attraction tetrad or pentad (each pair within a tetrad is included within two triads, and each pair within a pentad in three triads); or (2) by inclusion of the pair in two or more triads composed of that pair and different third individuals—for example, triads A-B-C and A-B-D, when the C-D pair score does not meet the specified criterion.

In Table 9.4 appear the data by which the prediction may be tested that with increasing acquaintance there will be increasing

Table 9.4. NUMBERS OF HIGH-ATTRACTION PAIRS INCLUDED IN ≤ 1 AND IN ≥ 2 HIGH-ATTRACTION TRIADS

N of pairs in	Year I Wk 0	Year I Wk 15	Year I Wk 1	Year I Wk 15	Year II Wk 0	Year II Wk 15	Year II Wk 1	Year II Wk 15	Both years Wk 0	Both years Wk 15	Both years Wk 1	Both years Wk 15
≤ 1 triad	10	15	4	15	2	12	6	12	12	25	10	27
> 1 triad	9	9	16	9	16	13	12	13	25	22	28	22
	NS		$x^2 = 6.37$ $p < .02$		$x^2 = 4.91$ $p < .05$		NS		$x^2 = 4.16$ $p < .05$		$x^2 = 6.12$ $p < .02$	

numbers of high-attraction pairs that are included in more than one larger unit. (Frequencies of inclusion in triads rather than in larger units are taken as the criterion simply because larger units are too infrequent.) Although the two populations differ somewhat in their earliest weeks, the general trend is toward the development of more high-attraction units of larger size, as predicted, and toward greater complexity of structuring, as evidenced by inclusion of the same high-attraction pairs in larger numbers of units.

RELATIONSHIPS AMONG THE STRUCTURAL UNITS

We now approach the central problem of population structuring: what is the nature of the changes in relationships among differentiated units, with increasing acquaintance? As we have already noted, we shall not attempt to predict which of the many alternative forms that are consistent with our theoretical formulation will be followed, in either or both of our populations. Our purposes are primarily descriptive and exploratory. We think it worth while simply to document the point that structuring takes different forms at different stages of acquaintance.

As more and larger high-attraction units emerge, and as they increasingly overlap via the high-attraction pairs that they have in common, it is possible for the attraction relationships *among* the units to change in either of two general ways. Some units might become increasingly opposed to each other—they might be characterized by reciprocal negative attraction. Or it might happen that, for any given unit, attraction relationships with other units would be little differentiated, in the sense that between-unit attraction, while not so high (by definition) as within-unit attraction, might be about the same with all other units.[2]

Procedures

Our use of individual ranks as an index of attraction raises the question of artifactual effects in our analyses. Since the ranks of

[2] Isolates, elsewhere treated as units, are excluded from the following analyses, since their relationships with other units are, by definition, predetermined.

high attraction are necessarily included within high-attraction units, does it not follow that for the individuals in such a unit only low-attraction ranks are left for between-unit relationships? And, by the same reasoning, if there is an increase of within-unit attraction is not a decrease in between-unit attraction artifactually required? We shall argue that only under a special set of circumstances are such artifactual effects to be expected, and that if they presuppose a special set of circumstances they are not inevitable. The set of circumstances is as follows: (1) a considerable degree of consensuality in the attraction of unit members toward all members of other units; and (2) the exclusive assignment by members of a high-attraction unit of highest ranks of attraction to each other, so that they cannot assign such ranks to non-unit members. Our methods of identifying high-attraction units require neither of these conditions. It could happen—and, as we shall show, it does happen —that members of the same unit express very different levels of attraction to the same members of other units, and that some of these are at very high levels. It is true by our operational definition, of course, that within-unit attraction is higher than between-unit attraction; but the units are only relatively, not absolutely high in internal attraction, which may be but little higher than between-unit attraction. There are enough degrees of freedom in the distribution of each unit member's distribution of 16 ranks so that a unit's internal attraction and its external attraction to one or more other units may increase at the same time. The increase in the one does not necessarily result in a decrease in the other.

The basic datum for analysis will be the mean of all attraction pair-scores included within each unit.[3] For some purposes we shall also be interested in the distributions of between-unit values (the latter being averages of between-unit pair-scores), and for others in comparisons of within- and between-unit values. For any given analysis, no individual will be considered as belonging to more than one unit, and in no case does the same pair appear more than once in the same analysis. The problem of computing between-unit values when those units include one or more of the same persons, is discussed in Appendix VIII.

[3] Means are computed from rank scores on the 256-point scale of pair scores.

Findings

Interunit levels of attraction. Table 9.5 shows the distributions of levels of mean interunit attraction at early and late times, for both populations; for each comparison the marginal frequencies are trichotomized as nearly equally as possible.

Table 9.5. FREQUENCIES OF MEAN INTERUNIT ATTRACTION VALUES, SHOWING COMPARISONS AT DIFFERENT TIMES OR FOR THE TWO POPULATIONS

| Mean attrac- | Year I | | Mean | Year I | |
tion level	Week 0	Week 15	level	Week 1	Week 15
$\leqq$ 119 (high)	6	5	$\leqq$ 119	15	5
120–139	6	8	120–149	13	12
$\geqq$ 140 (low)	10	8	$\geqq$ 150	13	4
TOTAL	22	21		41	21

$$x^2 = 0.61 \qquad\qquad x^2 = 3.67$$
$$p < .75 \ (2 \ df) \qquad\qquad p < .25 \ (2 \ df)$$

| Mean attrac- | Year II | | Mean | Year II | |
tion level	Week 0	Week 15	level	Week 1	Week 15
$\leqq$ 89 (high)	2	12	$\leqq$ 89	4	12
90–129	6	9	90–119	14	6
$\geqq$ 130 (low)	13	2	$\geqq$ 120	15	5
TOTAL	21	23		33	23

$$x^2 = 15.74 \qquad\qquad x^2 = 10.69$$
$$p < .001 \ (2 \ df) \qquad\qquad p < .25 \ (2 \ df)$$

| Mean attrac- | Week 0 | | Mean | Week 1 | | Mean | Week 15 | |
tion level	Yr I	Yr II	level	Yr I	Yr II	level	Yr I	Yr II
$\leqq$ 119 (high)	6	7	$\leqq$ 109	10	10	$\leqq$ 99	1	14
120–149	9	6	110–139	10	13	100–129	9	7
$\geqq$ 150 (low)	7	8	$\geqq$ 140	21	10	$\geqq$ 130	11	2
TOTAL	22	21		41	33		21	23

$$x^2 = 1.59 \qquad\quad x^2 = 3.41 \qquad\quad x^2 = 17.70$$
$$p < .50 \ (2 \ df) \qquad p < .25 \ (2 \ df) \qquad p < .001 \ (2 \ df)$$

Early and Late Structuring ———————————— **177**

In Year I there are no significant differences in level of interunit attraction between Weeks 0, 1, and 15, whereas in Year II the level of interunit attraction is significantly higher at Week 15 than at Weeks 0 or 1; there is no significant change between Weeks 0 and 1 of Year II. And only at Week 15 is there a significant difference between the two populations, the level being much higher in Year II. The distribution at Week 15 of Year II differs very significantly from all others, in either year, and no others differ significantly from one another.

At no time in Year I did a majority of the obtained interunit values fall into the upper half of the expected distribution (≤128), whereas in Year II a majority of them were in the upper half at all times except Week 0, and at Week 15 only 2 of 23 such values were in the lower half. Thus it may be concluded that in Year II but not in Year I there was a consistent tendency, following acquaintance, toward high levels of attraction among the distinguishable, nonoverlapping, very high-attraction units of more than two persons each.

Between-pair opposition. The over-all structuring of two populations will be quite different if within one of them there are many pairs of high-attraction pairs that are opposed to each other (in the sense that all four between-pair attractions are low), whereas in the other population there are few or no such pairs. The former might be referred to as divisively, and the latter as cohesively, structured.

Any criterion of what constitutes such a pair of "opposed" pairs of Ss must necessarily be an arbitrary one. We shall begin with this criterion: (1) only those pairs of Ss will be considered whose pair-scores ranks of mutual attraction are ≤20—approximately the highest 15 percent of all pairs, as obtained (varying a little from week to week), and 7.8 percent of the expected frequency: and (2) among such pairs of Ss, any pair of pairs will be considered opposed if all four of the between-pair pair-scores are ≥128—i.e., in the lower half of all pair scores (the obtained and expected frequencies at this level are almost identical).

The frequencies of opposed pairs obtained at various times are shown in Table 9.6. The two populations do not differ significantly at either Week 0 or Week 1, nor is there any significant change in either population between these two times. But the two populations do differ significantly at Week 15 ($\chi^2 = 12.61$; $p < .005$ with

Table 9.6. FREQUENCIES OF OPPOSED AND OF OTHER PAIRS
OF HIGH-ATTRACTION PAIRS, AT TIMES NOTED [a]

Pair re-lationship	Year I			Year II		
	Week 0	Week 1	Week 15	Week 0	Week 1	Week 15
Opposed	11(8)	9(8)	15(10)	8(9)	15(8)	0(8)
Overlapping	44	38	46	39	36	41
Others	116(119)	124(125)	149(154)	143(142)	120(127)	130(122)
TOTAL	171	171	210	190	171	171

[a] See text for criteria of opposed and of high-attraction pairs. Overlapping pairs refer to those which have one member in common. Expected frequencies (with decimals omitted) appear in parentheses; they are computed on the basis of obtained totals excluding overlapping pairs. Total Ns represent all possible combinations of the Ns of pairs at $\leqq 20$ (19, 19, 21, 20, 19, and 19, reading from left to right in the table).

2 df), and in Year II the difference between Weeks 1 and 15 is also significant ($\chi^2 = 15.72$; $p < .001$ with 2 df). Only at Week 15 of Year II does the distribution differ significantly ($p < .01$) from that expected by chance.[4] The findings are not dependent upon the particular criterion level chosen.[5]

What is most instructive about these analyses is the difference between the two populations: they change, from first to last, in opposite directions. Between-pair opposition *in*creases in Year I, though not significantly; in Year II there is a significant *de*crease (to zero) in the number of opposed pairs.

The higher frequency of opposed pairs in Year I than in Year II, at Week 15, is consistent with the appearance of the corresponding sociograms, as shown in Figures 9.3 and 9.6. According to

[4] Expected frequencies are calculated on the assumption that 0.5^4 or 6.25% of all sets of four between-pair pair scores (ignoring the pairs of pairs that have an overlapping member) would be in the lower half of the distribution. The expected frequencies of opposed pairs in Table 9.6 range between 7.94 and 10.20. There is no way of computing expectancies for overlapping pairs.
[5] Since, by this criterion, frequencies of opposed pairs of pairs are small, a more lenient criterion of opposition was also employed—namely, that all four between-pair scores should be $\geqq 64$, or in approximately the lowest three-quarters of the obtained distribution. The frequencies of opposed pairs of pairs, by this criterion, are closely comparable to the preceding ones, though the significance levels are more extreme. The χ^2 value of the two Week-15 comparisons is 27.72 and $p < .001$. In Year II, both Weeks 0 and 1 differ from Week 15 at comparable levels, while in Year I Weeks 1 and 15 differ at $< .05$ ($\chi^2 = 5.98$, with 1 df).

the Year-I sociogram there are two clusters of Ss, with no high-attraction bonds between them except via one individual (#17); and all 15 of the opposed pairs at this time are either between these two clusters (considering #17, for the moment, as belonging to neither cluster), or are oppositions between pair #27–30 (two near-isolates who have no other high-attraction bonds) and pairs in one or the other of the two clusters. Thus at Week 15 of Year I there are, in effect, three high-attraction sets (of 2, 5, and 7 Ss) [6] each of which includes one or more pairs opposed (by our criterion) to one or more pairs in each of the other sets.

At no early time in either year does this degree of structured pair-to-pair opposition occur. At earlier times, in both populations, a very large proportion of all between-pair oppositions is accounted for by wide-spread opposition to only two or three pairs, and this concentration of opposition is accompanied by high-attraction connections which cut across what would otherwise be separate and opposed pairs (as at Week 15 of Year I). In these respects the two populations were similar in the early weeks, but this similarity gradually disappeared as divisiveness became more prominent in Year I and virtually disappeared in Year II.

Summary. With respect to numbers of "opposed" high-attraction pairs (in which all four *inter*pair relationships are at *low* attraction levels), the two populations move in opposite directions from early to late acquaintance. By the criterion employed, there were at Week 15 of Year II no opposed pairs at all—a significant decrease from the early weeks, and significantly less than expected. At Week 15 of Year I, on the other hand, the frequencies of opposed pairs are nonsignificantly higher than at Week 1. Initially nonsignificant differences between the populations become significant. The pair-to-pair opposition at the end of Year I, but not at earlier times in either population, was structured, in the sense that all of the opposed pairs were in one of three sets of Ss, each of which showed a good deal of opposition to both of the others.

THE CENTRALITY OF POPULATION STRUCTURING

We have several times noted differences between our two populations, particularly on final acquaintance. They differ, for

[6] These 14 Ss exclude two isolates (#19, 23) and one between-cluster S (#17).

example (as shown in Chapter 8) with respect to the concentration among relatively few Ss of high-attraction choices received or of involvement in relatively many high-attraction pairs. And a glance at the sociograms in Figs. 9.3 and 9.6 suggests that the final structuring of high-attraction relationships was quite different in the two populations; the Year-II structure seems to be more centrally organized than that of Year I. By *centrality* we refer to compactness, as opposed to extendedness, of the network of high-attraction bonds. It is a population variable that is best described in terms of multiplicity of interconnections of person-to-person attraction. The significance of the variable lies in the fact that centrally structured populations tend to be stable, since the multiplicity of interconnections makes it unlikely that a decrease in the attraction level of only a few person-to-person connections would fundamentally alter the structure. In a noncentral structure, on the other hand, a very few such changes might totally alter the structure.[7] In this sense, such a structure is a tenuous one.

Since our theory has necessitated the conceptualizing of structure in terms of high attraction, it seems likely that there will be different structural consequences of narrow vs. wide distribution among the recipients of high-attraction ranks. But we see no reason why concentration of high-attraction choices among a few Ss should, of itself, necessarily result in either kind of structuring. Given two populations alike in concentration of attractiveness among a few Ss, different patterns of structuring could emerge in the two populations as a result of differences in the attraction relationships among the few Ss in whom attractiveness is concentrated. If the popular Ss assign high ranks to each other, then a central structure becomes virtually inevitable, since each of the popular Ss is sure to be involved in many high-attraction pairs, and since (as we have shown in Chapter 6) high-attraction pairs tend (by way of agreement regarding attractive third persons) to "grow" into high-attraction triads and large units. Each of the popular Ss, so to speak, carries along with him several high-attraction pairs and/or larger units into the structure of which popular Ss are at the center. If, on the other hand, none of the popular Ss assign high ranks to each other, then (by the same processes) each of them tends to become the center of a substructure, and there would not be a

[7] This definition of centrality applies also to substructures within a total population, but we are here interested only in total populations.

high probability of high-attraction relationships among these sub-structures. Thus we suspect that centrality is influenced by concentration of popularity among a few Ss only insofar as there is high attraction among the popular Ss.

These two variables seem to us to be necessary, artifactual determinants of centrality. But they may not be the only determinants, and hence we shall note the extent to which each of them, and both together, succeeds in differentiating the two populations which appear to be differently structured on final acquaintance.

Comparative Centrality of the Two Populations

We need, first, to test our impression that the population is more centrally structured in Year II than in Year I. Since we have defined centrality as the opposite of tenuousness in structuring, the degree to which an interconnected network of individuals is dependent upon a single one of them for maintaining its interconnectedness is an indicator of tenuousness. That is, if (as in Fig. 9.6) 13 Ss are all interconnected, directly or indirectly, by high-attraction bonds, then we may ask to what degree this interconnectedness is broken down by the removal of any single S. For example, if S #49 is removed, in Fig. 9.6, 5 of the 25 interconnecting bonds are removed, and there are now two sets of interconnected Ss (one of 3 and one of 9) with no interconnections between them—that is, two separate substructures. The more vulnerable a population's interconnectedness to such effects of removing one or a very few Ss, the less central its structuring.

In Table 9.7 we show the results of removing, successively, the single individual upon whom the structure is maximally dependent for maintaining interconnectedness. As shown in Table 9.7, the removal in Year I of 3 "key" individuals among the 13 who are interconnected, directly or indirectly, reduces the number of connected pairs from 78 in a single set to 16 in 3 unconnected sets. In Year II, however, removal of 3 Ss reduces the number of connected pairs only to 31, which are in only 2 unconnected sets. And the maximum number remaining in a single connected set is 10 in Year I, as compared with 28 in Year II.

By this operational definition, then, there is more centrality in Year II than in Year I, on final acquaintance.[8] Pairs of Ss whose

---

[8] Whether or not the difference is a significant one is another question. If it be legitimate to compare Ns of connected and unconnected pairs

Table 9.7. INTERCONNECTEDNESS AMONG *S*s AS DEPENDENT UPON A VERY FEW HIGHLY CONNECTED INDIVIDUALS (WEEK 15)

N of *S*s considered [a]	N of pairs connected with one another [b]	
	Year I	Year II
13	78	78
12	21, 10	36, 3
11	10, 3, 3	28, 3

[a] Excluding isolates and pairs otherwise unconnected.

[b] Two or more entries indicates that there are two or more sets of *S*s having no between-set connections. Frequencies refer to all within-set pairs, whether or not directly connected via pair-scores that meet the 95 percent criterion.

direct connections with each other are not at the highest level are more likely, in Year II, to be connected, indirectly, via more than one mediating individual. It is this network of multiple connectedness that makes for high centrality.

Attraction Power

In devising an index of concentration of attractiveness within a population, it is necessary to bear in mind that the indices by which we have determined structuring are based upon high levels of attraction. Since the results of rank-ordering of total popularity scores (based upon all 16 ranks received by each *S*) are not necessarily the same as rank-ordering based upon the receipt of high ranks only, it seems wiser to use an index derived from the latter, which we shall refer to as attraction power—in the sense of capacity to elicit high-attraction choices from others.

Scoring procedures were determined by the following facts. (1) Inspection shows that in no case did an A-to-B rank of >7 ever result in the inclusion of that A-B pair in any structural unit that met the 95 percent criterion. Only attraction ranks from 1 to 7 were therefore considered, in computing individual scores of attraction power. (2) The very highest attraction ranks should be heavily weighted. We therefore (as in computing pair-scores of attraction; see pp. 72–73) squared each rank between 1 and 7 that was received by any *S* and, for convenience, subtracted the squared value

among 11 *S*s in the two populations, the resulting χ^2 is 3.88, significant at $<.05$.

from a constant (50); and, finally, all the resulting values were summed for each S. Thus, for ranks successively less close to 1 (the highest possible), progressively greater values were subtracted from the index of attraction power. An example, based on ranks received by one individual, follows:

Rank received	Rank value	Fre- quency	Value × frequency
1	49	1	49
2	46	4	184
3	41	3	123
4	34	0	0
5	25	1	25
6	14	2	28
7	1	0	0

SUM (individual attraction power): 409

As shown in Table 9.8, the degrees of concentration of attraction power at different times, or in the two populations, may be compared from the first few entries in the columns showing cumulative totals. (Only the higher ranks contribute to population structuring, according to the 95-percent criterion.) Such comparisons show

Table 9.8. RANK ORDERS OF INDIVIDUAL ATTRACTION POWER, AT TIMES NOTED

	Year 1, Week 0			Year 1, Week 1			Year 1, Week 15		
		AP			AP			AP	
Rank	S #	value	Cum. Σ	S #	value	Cum. Σ	S #	value	Cum. Σ
1	17	528	528	17	414	414	21	370	370
2	14	439	967	14	410	824	28	360	730
3	15	422	1389	29	377	1201	20	323	1053
4	18	274	1663	15	364	1565	22	271	1324
5	21	264	1927	19	339	1904	18	270	1594
6	28	241	2168	21	302	2206	15	261	1855
7	29	227	2395	16	243	2449	29	257	2112
8	25	182	2577	28	199	2648	16	256	2368

	Year I, Week 0			Year I, Week 1			Year I, Week 15		
Rank	S #	AP value	Cum. Σ	S #	AP value	Cum. Σ	S #	AP value	Cum. Σ
9	16	179	2756	26	171	2819	26	242	2610
10	26	169	2925	22	147	2966	25	219	2829
11	19	153	3078	18	134	3100	17	179	3008
12	27	135	3213	24	125	3225	14	158	3166
13	24	123	3336	27	108	3333	24	135	3301
14	22	69	3405	30	63	3396	23	120	3421
15	20	66	3471	25	63	3459	30	97	3518
16	30	50	3521	20	62	3521	27	51	3569
17	23	49	3570	23	49	3570	19	1	3570

	Year II, Week 0			Year II, Week 1			Year II, Week 15		
	S #	AP value	Cum. Σ	S #	AP value	Cum. Σ	S #	AP value	Cum. Σ
1	34	517	517	34	480	480	34	559	559
2	40	409	926	42	400	880	47	417	976
3	39	381	1307	47	384	1264	42	401	1377
4	42	268	1575	38	268	1532	39	314	1691
5	47	250	1825	39	266	1798	49	280	1971
6	44	234	2059	44	254	2052	45	270	2241
7	36	208	2267	46	235	2287	50	265	2506
8	41	204	2471	50	190	2477	38	236	2742
9	45	200	2671	48	177	2654	43	202	2844
10	46	156	2871	45	174	2828	44	197	3141
11	38	147	2974	40	166	2994	40	127	3268
12	35	120	3094	49	136	3130	46	112	3380
13	48	114	3208	41	115	3245	37	90	3470
14	50	113	3321	37	115	3360	35	46	3516
15	49	104	3425	36	96	3456	36	40	3556
16	43	94	3519	35	74	3530	48	14	3570
17	37	51	3570	43	40	3570	41	0	3570

that (1) as expected, there is most concentration of attraction power at Year I, Week 0 and at Year II, Week 15 (though the concentration at Year II, Week 0 approaches these values more closely than anticipated). The greater concentration at the three highest ranks, at Week 0, probably reflects some instances of very early, "accidental" prominence accorded to a few individuals; by Week 1 attraction was presumably beginning to be based upon more substantial grounds.

Attraction among Ss High in Attraction Power

The second "artifactual" determinant of centrality of structuring is the amount of reciprocated high attraction among those Ss highest in attraction power. As an index of this, it is not appropriate to average all the pair scores involved among the Ss highest in attraction power, since only very high scores contribute to structuring, by our procedures. We have therefore chosen, as an index, the maximum number of pairs, among the 6 Ss highest in attraction power, that appear in overlapping triads which reach the 95-percent criterion at any given time. This description of our index may be clarified and justified as follows. (1) *Triads,* all of whose component pair scores reach criterion, rather than mere chains of high-attraction pairs, are considered because it is the "closing" of chains of three or more persons that makes for centrality. (2) Only *pairs* in overlapping triads—that is, with at least two members in common—are counted, because unconnected or singly connected triads can make for dispersion rather than centrality. (3) Hence, in case of two or more sets of nonoverlapping triads, only that set including the *largest* number of pairs is counted. (4) The justification for counting the number of above-criterion pair connections among the *six highest* (rather than some other arbitrary number) in attraction power is simply that of convenience for the purpose: at all times, in both populations, a little more than half of the attraction power of the total population is concentrated in the 6 Ss who rank highest, and any number less than six would have resulted in very small counts and very little variance.

These indices—maximum numbers of pairs that appear in connected triads reach the 95-percent criterion—are as follows:

	Year I	Year II
Week 0	6	3
Week 1	3	6
Week 15	3	8

The trends of these indices over time, for both populations, correspond to the appearance of the sociograms, and to the differences in centrality as shown in Table 9.7. The indices reflect the apparent differences between the two populations at all times.

Joint Effects of the Two Determinants of Centrality

Since centrality is determined by at least two factors—degree of concentration of attraction power among a few Ss, and high-attraction relationships among those high in attraction power—the two indices that we have described may be combined. Any procedure for doing so is necessarily an arbitrary one, but the following seems as reasonable as any: the *percentage of all attraction* power that is concentrated in the 6 Ss ranking highest, multiplied by the *percentage of possible high-attraction pairs* (15, in all cases) that is obtained among overlapping triads. The results appear in Table 9.9.

Table 9.9. COMBINED INDEX OF CENTRALITY

	Concentration of AP (%)	High attraction among Ss high in AP (%)	Product
Year I			
Week 0	60.7	40.0	.243
Week 1	60.8	20.0	.121
Week 15	51.9	20.0	.104
Year II			
Week 0	57.7	20.0	.115
Week 1	57.5	40.0	.230
Week 15	62.8	53.3	.334

These combined index values seem to correspond fairly closely to the degrees of centrality, judging from the appearance of the sociograms, of the two populations at various times, and also to the population differences shown in Table 9.7. We are not suggesting, of course, that this apparent correspondence validates the index. Our point is more nearly the opposite one—that the two components of the index, which necessarily must be determinants of the degree of structural centrality (though not necessarily the only ones), confer some validity upon inferences likely to be drawn from the appearance of the sociograms.

Quite similar findings emerge if a fixed cutting point for high-attraction pairs, rather than the 95-percent criterion, is employed. Relevant data appear in Table 9.10, in which the criterion of pair

Table 9.10. NUMBERS OF Ss INVOLVED IN HIGH-ATTRACTION PAIRS, AND NUMBERS OF HIGH-ATTRACTION PAIRS AMONG THOSE Ss [a]

	Year I		Year II	
	Week 0	Week 15	Week 0	Week 15
N of Ss involved in 5 high-attraction pairs	3	4	2	5
N of high-attraction pairs among these Ss	3	1	1	7
Product of above Ns	9	4	2	35

[a] See text for description of high-attraction criterion.

scores ≤ 48 (constituting about the highest quarter of all pair scores) is employed. There is no special justification, of course, for taking the product of (N of Ss involved) and (N of pairs among these Ss) as an index; perhaps, for example, some root of the second N should be employed. Some multiplicative relationship is required, and the relative positions of the indices would not be affected in any case.

These relative positions of the two populations, each early and late, correspond both to the appearance of the sociograms and to the results from the use of the 95-percent criterion of unit-membership.

Balance-promoting Tendencies as Determinants of Centrality

We shall now consider some implications of these findings for our theoretical formulation. If, as appears to be the case, the greater centrality in Year II than in Year I, on final acquaintance, stems in considerable part from the relationships of high attraction among Ss high in attraction power, then we must ask why these individuals are attracted to one another. And, in particular, we must inquire whether (as required by our theory) these generally attractive individuals who in Year II were highly attracted to one another were characterized to an unusual degree by agreement concerning matters of importance to them. We shall therefore test the prediction that at Week 15 there was higher agreement in Year II than in Year I among the Ss highest in attraction power. Insofar as this prediction is supported, we shall have a theoretical basis, drawn from our own formulation, for explaining the greater centrality in the second population.

The bases for comparing the two populations are limited, since (as explained on pp. 38–41) several kinds of responses were obtained in Year II but not in Year I. Our most nearly comparable indices of agreement are those based upon miscellaneous inventories of attitude items. Though, as explained, on pages 38–41, the content was quite different in the two years, we have shown that they give quite comparable results in testing other predictions. In the present case, however, they give quite different results—as called for by the present prediction. As shown in Table 9.11,

Table 9.11. Numbers of Pairs, among 6 Ss Highest in Attraction Power at Two Levels of Agreement Concerning Attitude Inventories, as Compared with all Other Pairs (Week 13)

Agreement level [a]	Year I		Year II	
	Among 6 Ss	All other pairs	Among 6 Ss	All other pairs
High	5	58	10	43
Low	10	63	5	78
Total	15	121	15	121
	x^2 NS		$x^2 = 4.66$ $p < .05$ (1 df)	

[a] Because the general level of agreement was much higher with the Year-I than with the Year-II inventory, the cutting point is higher in Year I; the two categories of agreement have been made as nearly equal as possible.

the 15 pairs made up of the 6 Ss highest in attraction power are in significantly closer agreement about these miscellaneous issues than are the remaining pairs of Ss, in Year II but not in Year I. As a matter of fact, there is somewhat *less* agreement (nonsignificantly) among the 15 pairs of Ss highest in attraction power than among all other pairs in Year I.

The prediction as to differences between the two populations in agreement among the 6 Ss highest in attraction power is also supported by F-scale responses. In Year II the F-score ranks of the 6 Ss in nonauthoritarianism are 1, 2, 3, 4, 5, and 10; the range of scores for the lowest-ranking five of these is 62–77, and for the sixth the score is 109. Agreement among them could hardly be closer. But in Year I the F-score ranks of the corresponding 6 Ss are 2, 8, 9.5, 9.5, 15.5, and 17—virtually the entire range, from 85–175.

These are the only comparable responses of attitudinal nature that were made by both populations, but it is also worth noting that in Year II, when responses concerning values were obtained, the 6 Ss were again in relatively close agreement. With respect to Spranger Values, the 6 Ss are considered by the entire population to be in close agreement (see Chap. 15), and are so considered by themselves (their own estimates of agreement with each other are significantly higher than all other estimates in the population; $p < .001$). In actual agreement, about Spranger Values, 5 of the 6 are in significantly higher agreement with each other than are all other pairs ($p < .005$). And with respect to the Ten Values, the 6 Ss are also significantly more closely in agreement than are all the remaining pairs ($p < .01$).

Summary

We have no way of being sure, of course, that in Year I, had the same value responses been obtained, agreement among the 6 Ss highest in attraction power would have been less than in Year II, though the inferential evidence suggests that this is likely. At any rate we know that in Year II, when the final population structuring was a relatively central one, the most generally attractive individuals were highly attracted to each other, as was not the case in Year I. We also know that these same individuals were quite consistently (with the partial exception of one of them) in close agreement with each other on every attitudinal measure that we used. And we know, insofar as we can judge by the attitudinal responses obtained in Year I, that the highly attractive individuals did not agree with each other more closely than did other pairs of Ss. Thus it is a reasonable conclusion that the centrality of structuring in Year II was in some degree determined by agreement among highly attractive individuals, the apparent absence of which in

Year I may account for the relative absence of centrality in that year's population structure.

SUMMARY: STRUCTURING OF
TOTAL POPULATIONS

With increasing acquaintance the general trend in both populations is toward the development of more high-attraction units of larger size. Thus, in balance-promoting ways, high-attraction pairs tend to "build up" into high-attraction triads, tetrads, and even larger units. The relations between these units of increasing size are not necessarily those of high attraction. In Year I there were increasing numbers of high-attraction pairs in opposition to each other—that is, whose interpair attraction was low; in Year II there were significantly decreasing numbers of them. Either trend is consistent with our theoretical formulation: increasing opposition of high-attraction units is, hypothetically, most likely when a population's pre-acquaintance attitudes are strongly held and widely dispersed, but our data did not permit us to put this hypothesis to test.

Consistently with the latter findings, the attraction structure became more centrally organized in Year II than in Year I. The difference lay not so much in differing degrees of concentration of personal attractiveness among a few individuals, but rather in the fact that in Year II but not in Year I the most generally attractive individuals became highly attracted to one another. Since, as we have shown in Chapter 5, agreement has good predictive power for high attraction, we should therefore expect that in Year II but not in Year I the highly attractive individuals would show close agreement with one another; this is indeed the case—close agreement is quite clearly present in Year II and presumptively absent in Year I. We thus conclude that the differences in the structuring of the two populations are partly to be accounted for as balance-promoting changes that occur in collective systems with acquaintance.

PART FIVE

Process and Change with Continuing Acquaintance

We have seen that individual systems tend to be in balance at all stages of acquaintance, and collective systems increasingly so with continued acquaintance. And we have observed, as outcomes of tendencies toward balance over a period of time, the emergence of increasing numbers of high-attraction pairs, triads, and larger subgroups—especially, stable ones. But we have not looked very closely at the processes involved in these changes, and we have not dealt at all systematically with influences other than tendencies toward balance that contribute to the observed changes.

And so, in Chapter 10, we shall look at week-to-week changes in attraction relationships throughout the entire sixteen weeks that we observed each of our populations, noting the shape of the time-curve which portrays the stabilization of those relationships. In Chapter 11 we shall inquire, in more detail than we did in Chapter 5, into the short-run and long-run effects of proximity (in the form of living in the same room or on the same floor) on interpersonal attraction. Then, in Chapter 12, we turn to a hitherto neglected problem: the contribution of individuals' personal characteristics to their relationships of attraction. Tendencies toward balance operate in individuals who perceive their peers not as identical but as presenting very different packages of personal characteristics, and so we must anticipate interaction-effects between forces toward balance and individuals' assessment of each others' characteristics. And finally, in Chapter 13, we shall look at another set of interaction effects—involving an early, consensual "typing" of the House members in the second population, their individual tendencies to authoritarianism, their individual popularity statuses, and the developing structure of the total population. In this chapter, which is in a sense a developmental case study of a population (and thus not a basis for generalizing to other populations), we see in somewhat greater detail how forces toward balance operate within a context of other relevant variables.

Thus Part Five is devoted not so much to hypothesis testing as to analyses, primarily exploratory, of the multivariable contexts within which the acquaintance process develops in general conformity with our hypotheses.

Week-to-Week Changes in Attraction Relationships* ──────── 10

Elsewhere we report findings for selected weeks only—a procedure justified by the empirical fact that our *S*s showed little or no attitude change from first to last, and relatively few changes in attraction after the earliest weeks. This latter fact will be documented in the present chapter, which will also serve to show the nature of such changes as did occur.

STABILITY OF ATTRACTION CHOICES

In the initial stages of acquaintance, information about another person's attitudes is meager, which means that perception of others' attitudes is more likely to be influenced by autistic factors than when more information is available. It is to be expected, therefore, that in earlier as opposed to later stages of acquaintance the "real" attitudes of others are less accurately assessed and thus less stable. As time passes and more information becomes available, both from intentional and unintentional communication, increasingly accurate assessments tend to stabilize, as the likelihood of acquiring any new information decreases. We therefore expect that on early acquaintance attraction choices, which are hypothetically a function of perceived similarity of attitudes (agreement), will tend to be less stable than at later stages of acquaintance. This is such an obvious prediction that the finding of empirical support for it may be taken as one kind of validation of our basic data,

* This chapter is based upon the work of Peter G. Nordlie (1958), from which much of the text, most of the tables, and all of the figures in the chapter have been taken.

rather than as a new discovery, or one that stems only from the present formulation.

As a measure of any S's stability of attraction choices, a rank-order correlation coefficient was computed between his ranking of the other 16 Ss at one time with his ranking of the same Ss a week later. Such a *rho* was computed for each pair of adjacent weeks. The mean *rhos* of the 17 Ss in each population, for each weekly interval, appear in Table 10.1.

Table 10.1. MEANS OF 17 INDIVIDUAL CORRELATIONS (*rhos*), FOR PAIRS OF ADJACENT WEEKS, IN RANK-ORDERING ATTRACTION TOWARD OTHER 16 Ss

Weekly intervals	Year I	Year II
0– 1	.51	.65
1– 2	.82	.81
2– 3	—[a]	.85
3– 4	—[a]	.84
4– 5	—[a]	.88
5– 6	.81	.91
6– 7	.85	.92
7– 8	.90	.90
8– 9	.87	—[a]
9–10	—[a]	—[a]
10–11	—[a]	.89
11–12	.81	.89
12–13	.88	.92
13–14	.91	.90
14–15	.91	.90

[a] Responses were not obtained at one or both weeks of this interval.

The coefficients for the two populations are similar. To test the possibility that the means of all the *rhos* of the two populations might be significantly different, a sign test of the population difference for the nine weeks in which *rhos* were available in both years was made (Edwards, 1954, p. 288). An obtained p value of .37 supports the null hypothesis of no difference between the populations.

The significance of the difference between each pair of *rhos* at the same weekly interval was also evaluated. The largest difference (in terms of z' values, interval 5–6) yields a p value of only .29; no pair of *rhos,* therefore, from the same week can be considered significantly different. Hence the *rhos* from the two populations were combined, and are presented in Figure 10.1 for visual inspection.[1]

The curve in Figure 10.1 shows a sharp increase in stability in the first three weeks, and only a slight increase thereafter. The significance of this increasing trend was tested by correlating magnitudes of the mean *rhos* with order of the weeks. The fourteen mean *rhos* were rank-ordered, the highest being assigned a rank of 1; the successive weekly intervals were similarly ranked, the latest being assigned a rank of 1. If the prediction were to be perfectly substantiated, a *rho* of +1.00 between the two sets of ranks should result. The actual finding was a *rho* of +.86, significant beyond the .01 level of confidence. (The same test applied to the first and second populations, separately, yields *rhos* of +.74 and +.67, respectively; both are significant beyond the .01 level of confidence.) This significant increase of stability over time appears in spite of the fact that there was very little change in the mean *rhos* beyond the third week.

The considerable degree of stability that is indicated by the mean correlations of about .9 in each population (Table 10.1) in the last few weeks is also shown by the group reports of subgroup membership (as described on pp. 34–36). Table 10.2 shows the frequencies with which the same pairs of Ss are mentioned as in the same subgroups at Weeks 12 and 14. The χ^2 values of the collapsed distributions are 60.45 and 85.01, for Years I and II, respectively, significant at $<.001$ with 4 df.

Stability and Popularity

Balanced systems, we have assumed, are likely to be stable ones. We have also assumed that, among other objects with regard to which a two-person system may or may not be balanced,

---

[1] When *rhos* from both groups were available, the mean for a weekly interval was computed on the basis of 34 individual *rhos.* Where *rhos* for only one population were available (because data were not obtained in some weeks), the mean *rho* of the other population was determined by interpolating from a straight line drawn between the mean of the immediately preceding and succeeding weeks, for that population. The combined mean *rho* for certain intervals is therefore based on actual *rhos* for one population and an interpolated mean *rho* for the other. The week-to-week *rhos* for each S appear in Appendix X.

Changes in Attraction Relationships —————— **197**

Table 10.2. Numbers of Pairs of Ss that Are Reported as Belonging to the Same Subgroups, with Frequencies Indicated, at Weeks 12 and 14

Reported frequency, Week 12	Reported frequency, Week 14							
	Year I				Year II			
	0–1	2–4	≧ 5	Total	0–1	2–4	≧ 5	Total
0–1	66	9	2	77	53	15	1	69
2–4	19	6	5	30	16	14	5	35
≧ 5	3	9	17	29	1	6	25	32
Total	88	24	24	136	70	35	31	136

are those persons themselves. Thus—assuming positive self-regard on the part of each of them—a two-person system that is balanced not only with regard to some external object but also with regard to each of those persons is, so to speak, doubly anchored, and therefore, presumably, particularly stable. Such a system is one of reciprocal high attraction.

In a population some of whose members are more generally attractive, or popular, than others, the popular ones have a greater likelihood of attaining this form of balance with a large proportion of other members than have unpopular ones. This is a consequence of the fact that the more popular Ss have more opportunity to match their own high positive choices with high positive choices received from those so chosen, whereas the unpopular Ss have difficulty in matching their high positive choices with reciprocated ones. Thus the popular Ss are less subject to forces toward system change than are those less able to attain this form of balance. And, since changing one's attraction toward a person is one possible way of reducing strain, we predict higher stability of attraction toward others for popular than for unpopular Ss.

One way of testing this prediction is based upon the assumption that the order of popularity of individual Ss remains relatively constant. The order of popularity was determined by summing all ranks received by each S during all weeks and ranking the resulting sums, assigning rank 1 to the most popular S. The week-to-week *rhos* of attraction ranks assigned by each S were then averaged, and similarly ranked from highest to lowest. The prediction would

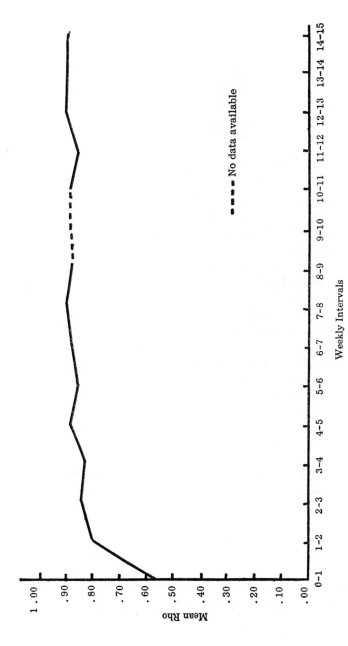

Fig. 10.1. Mean week-to-week *rhos* of attraction rankings (Year I and Year II combined).

be supported by a significant positive correlation between these two rank orders. The obtained coefficients were as follows:

Year I: $rho = +.22$ $(p < .50)$
Year II: $rho = +.69$ $(p < .01)$.

The prediction is thus supported in Year II but not in Year I.

The assumption of relative stability of individual popularity was then tested, by correlating the order of popularity at Week 2 (after choices had begun to stabilize) with the final order of popularity at Week 15. Results were as follows:

Year I: $rho = +.37$ $(p < .20)$
Year II: $rho = +.78$ $(p < .01)$.

From these two sets of findings it may be inferred that, given relatively high stability of individual popularity over a period of weeks, the stability of attraction toward others is higher for popular than for unpopular Ss.

The prediction may also be tested by examining this same relationship at different points in time. For each weekly interval, mean *rhos* of attraction choices were computed for a group of popular and for a group of unpopular Ss, the former consisting of the 6 highest and the latter of the 6 lowest in popularity, in each population.[2]

The mean *rhos* of these sets of popular and unpopular Ss are plotted against time in Figure 10.2, which shows that during the first three weeks of acquaintance there was no difference in the stability of rankings made by the popular and the unpopular Ss, but thereafter the mean *rho* for popular Ss was higher than for unpopular Ss. The significance of the obtained differences was assessed by a sign test. If there were no consistent differences between the mean *rhos* of popular and unpopular Ss, we would expect the mean *rhos* to be higher for either group about half of the time. In fact, at eleven of the fourteen weeks the mean *rho* for popular Ss was higher than for unpopular Ss—a proportion that is significant beyond the .05 level of confidence. And the fact that all of the three exceptions occur at the three earliest weeks, when sta-

---

[2] As already noted, for some weeks data were available for only one of the two populations. In such instances, the missing data were supplied by interpolating between the mean *rhos* for the weeks preceding and following the missing week.

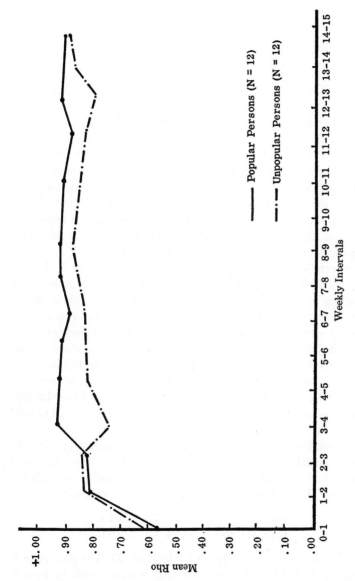

Fig. 10.2. A comparison of the mean *rhos* of attraction stability from week to week of popular and unpopular persons (Year I and Year II combined).

bility of choices given is known to be lowest, lends further support to the *post hoc* hypothesis that, given a certain minimum level of stability of expressed attraction toward others, such stability varies with popularity.

POPULARITY AND AGREEMENT

An adequate test of our hypotheses concerning balance and strain presupposes an object of orientation that has high importance and common relevance for all Ss. Under the conditions of this study, there was no category of objects of orientation that so well met these criteria as House members themselves—members other than those included in any given two-person system. In testing predictions concerning the relationship between attraction and similarity of orientation toward common objects, we may use as an index of the latter the coefficient of correlation on the part of any 2 Ss' rank-orderings of the remaining 15 Ss. Our general hypothesis is that the higher the attraction between 2 Ss the higher this index of similarity, or agreement in rank-ordering other Ss.

One prediction to be derived from this hypothesis is that individuals with whom others tend to be in agreement (about the remaining 15 Ss) should also be individuals toward whom others are most attracted; persons who are in general agreed with are also generally attractive persons. This prediction follows from our general postulates to the effect that the greater the attraction that characterizes a two-person system the greater the likelihood of agreement on the part of those persons about important and relevant objects; and from the assumption that, for each S individually, all other Ss' tendencies to agree with him and to be attracted toward him may be summed.

This prediction has been tested, first, by correlating each S's mean popularity rank over all weeks with the rank of his mean coefficient of agreement with all other Ss (in each case with the remaining 15 Ss) over all weeks. Results are as follows:

Year I: $rho = +.66$ ($p < .01$).
Year II: $rho = +.44$ ($p < .10$).

These two coefficients differ at a p level of .38. The prediction is clearly supported by this particular test, however, only in Year I.

The prediction may also be tested (in somewhat different form) by considering these same data at each week, instead of summing over weeks. There are good reasons for assuming that the predicted relationship should be stronger following long than following only brief acquaintance. As we noted in Chapter 2, it is assumed that actual balance in multiperson systems can be achieved only via communication, some minimal degree of which, at least, is presupposed on the part of *all* pairs of Ss by the present manner of testing our prediction. Hence we shall test the dual prediction that the relationship between popularity and being agreed with concerning other House members (1) increases with successive weeks, and (2) differs significantly from zero in the later weeks.

The results of computing rank-order correlations between popularity and being agreed with for each week, separately, appear in Table 10.3, and in Figure 10.3 (in which coefficients for the two populations are averaged). Sequential discontinuities appear in

Table 10.3. MEAN *rhos* BETWEEN INDIVIDUAL POPULARITY AND AGREEMENT WITH EACH OTHER S ABOUT ATTRACTIVENESS OF REMAINING SUBJECTS [a]

Week	Year I	Year II
0	.35	.25
1	.31	.34
2	.57	.47
3	— [b]	.29
4	— [b]	.19
5	.36	.48
6	.43	.48
7	.56	.44
8	.57	.47
9	.55	— [b]
10	— [b]	.44
11	.50	.47
12	.62	.47
13	.55	.38
14	.17	.65
15	.49	.82

[a] $N = 17$ for each mean *rho*.
[b] Responses were not obtained.

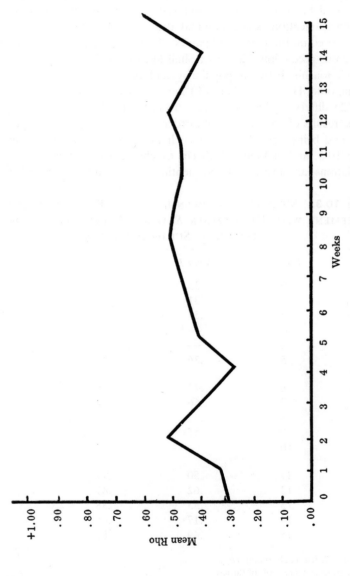

Fig. 10.3. *Rhos* between popularity and mean pair agreement *rho* each week (Year I and Year II combined).

each population,[3] but the null hypothesis of no difference in *rhos* between the two populations is supported by a *p* value of .28 (sign test). In addition, the significance of the differences between *rhos* at each week was determined: the *largest* difference (in terms of z' values, at Week 15) yields a *p* value of .10, supporting the conclusion that in general the two populations do not differ significantly at the same point in time. These findings justify our pooling results from the two populations, as in Figure 10.3.

The prediction of an increasingly close relationship between popularity and being agreed with is supported by a correlation of $+.54$ ($p < .05$) between number of elapsed weeks and magnitude of *rhos* (averaged for the two populations).

The prediction of correlations differing significantly from zero in the later weeks is supported by the finding that at all times between Weeks 7 and 15, except at Week 14, the combined *rhos* for the two populations approximate or drop below the *p* value of .05. Prior to Week 7, there is no time except Week 2 when the corresponding *p* values are as low as this. The probability that 8 of the 9 mean correlations in later weeks will exceed 6 of the 7 in earlier weeks is of course very small.[4]

PAIR ATTRACTION AND PAIR AGREEMENT

A pair of predictions that test, more directly than the preceding one, the hypothesis of covariation between attraction and agreement is that for the total population of 136 pairs (regardless of individual popularity) the relationship between the two variables will (1) increase with successive weeks, and (2) differ significantly from zero in the later weeks. Pair scores of attraction ($N = 136$) were correlated with the pair scores just described as indices of agreement in rank-ordering the attractiveness of the remaining 15 Ss. The resulting product-moment coefficients were computed for each week for both populations, as presented in Table 5.1.

Again, the possibility of a difference between the two populations was tested by a sign test, with a resulting *p* value of .12. The

[3] See Nordlie (1958, pp. 59–61) for a discussion of the more conspicuous irregularities.

[4] By exact test (following the conservative procedure of comparing the first half with the latter half of the 16 weeks), the *p* value of the distribution $\begin{smallmatrix} 6 & 1 \\ 2 & 7 \end{smallmatrix}$ is .0105.

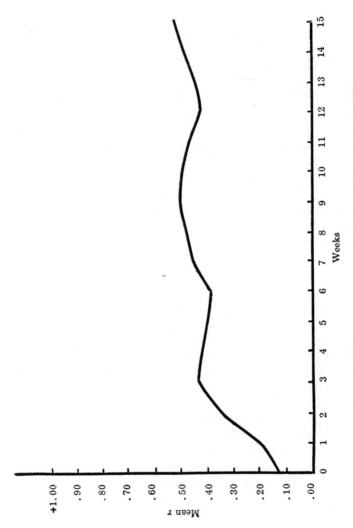

Fig. 10.4. Correlations between pair attraction and pair agreement at different weeks (Year I and Year II combined).

difference between each of the pair of coefficients at the same week was similarly tested; the largest of these differences has an associated *p* value of .50. On the basis of these two kinds of tests it appears that the two populations were sufficiently similar to justify combining coefficients as of the same weeks, as shown in Figure 10.4.

The significance of the increasing trend of the correlations with time was tested by correlating the rank order of the weekly correlations with the number of weeks of acquaintance, for both years combined. The resulting *rho* of .79, as reported on page 75, is significant beyond the .01 level of confidence. The prediction of significant relationships between attraction and agreement in the later weeks was also supported: for both populations combined, all the coefficients at Week 2 and thereafter are significant at less than the .01 level, and beginning with Week 3 at the .001 level (df 134).

Summary

In spite of certain differences between the two populations, week-to-week changes in attraction proceed in orderly fashion. By various tests, we have found support for the hypothesis that interpersonal relationships of attraction stabilize—at relatively early stages of acquaintance—as individuals cease to acquire new information about each other, and that with such stabilization the relationship between attraction and agreement about other House members increases, and becomes a significant one. Such findings are consistent with those that are required by our assumptions about two-person systems of orientation.

The Attraction of Floormates and Roommates toward One Another

11

We assume that proximity promotes readiness of communication, as a result of which individuals have an opportunity to discover each others' common attitudes. Such discovery may—or may not—lead to reciprocated high attraction, in the long run, depending upon what common attitudes of importance there are to be discovered. We shall therefore test the null hypothesis that (in our research setting, where populations were small and where there was adequate time for exploration of each others' attitudes), following ample opportunity for acquaintance, high attraction is not related to proximity, as defined by residence on the same floor of the House.

FLOORMATES

In Table 11.1 we present the frequencies of pairs at three levels of attraction, at five different times, separately totaled for within-floor and between-floor pairs, in Year I. The differences between this table and the corresponding one for Year II are so slight that we shall not present the latter. The following findings emerge from the two sets of data, combined.

1. Summing all within-floor pairs at each of the five weeks, at no time do the distributions differ significantly from those expected by chance. At Week 0, however, within-floor attraction exceeds between-floor attraction at a significance level $<.10$.

2. Similarly, at no time do the distributions of between-floor attraction significantly differ from expectations, though the dif-

Table 11.1. NUMBERS OF PAIRS AT THREE LEVELS OF ATTRAC-
TION, CATEGORIZED AS WITHIN EACH OF TWO FLOORS OR BETWEEN
FLOORS (YEAR I)

Attrac- tion level	Week 0	Week 1	Week 2	Week 5	Week 15
Floor II					
High [a]	15 (7.9) [a]	12 (8.5)	9 (7.7)	9(10.1)	9 (9.8)
Intermediate [a]	10(11.2)	12(10.0)	13(10.3)	6 (7.1)	5 (7.1)
Low [a]	11(16.9)	12(17.5)	14(18.0)	21(18.8)	22(19.1)
TOTAL	36	36	36	36	36
Floor III					
High	4 (6.2)	3 (6.6)	4 (6.0)	7 (7.8)	10 (7.6)
Intermediate	8 (8.6)	8 (7.8)	9 (8.0)	8 (5.6)	7 (5.6)
Low	16(13.2)	17(13.6)	15(14.0)	13(14.6)	11(14.8)
TOTAL	28	28	28	28	28
Across floors					
High	11(15.9)	17(16.9)	16(15.3)	22(20.1)	18(19.6)
Intermediate	24(22.2)	18(20.2)	17(20.7)	13(14.3)	15(14.3)
Low	37(33.9)	37(34.9)	39(36.0)	37(37.6)	39(38.1)
TOTAL	72	72	72	72	72

[a] "High" indicates approximately highest one-fifth of expected frequencies; and "low" indicates lower half of expected frequencies. The entries
in parentheses indicate expected frequencies, given the obtained frequencies
among the total population of pairs at each level of attraction.

ference is greatest at Week 0, when the expected level exceeds the
obtained level at a significance level $< .10$.

3. At Week 0 the across-floor attraction is significantly lower
than at Week 15; $\chi^2 = 7.96$, and $p < .02$, with 2 df. No other
week-to-week differences are significant; there is a general increase
in across-floor attraction after Week 0, and subsequent changes are
very slight indeed.

4. At no time do the sums of all within-floor attractions differ
significantly in level of attraction from those at any other time; the
level is highest at Week 0.

Our null hypothesis is thus reasonably well supported: at no time after the earliest days of acquaintance does high attraction vary with residence on the same floor.

ROOMMATES

Ten of the 136 pairs in each population were roommates. Of these ten, six pairs were made up of two sets of triplets, and the other four represented four doubles. As elsewhere noted, rooms and roommates were arbitrarily assigned as the men first entered the House.

The significance of roommateness, for our purposes, is of two kinds. First, it is likely that roommates will become more rapidly acquainted with each other, during the earliest days, than with most of the other men. This in itself does not, of course, guarantee high attraction, but the probabilities are in favor of relatively high attraction—if for no other reason, on first acquaintance, than that unknown Ss are apt to be ranked toward the bottom. In addition, person-to-person interaction tends, actuarially speaking, to be rewarding—especially when one has recently been introduced into a community of strangers. Hence we predict a higher level of attraction among roommates than among others, on very early acquaintance.

Second, roommates are likely, more than other pairs, to exchange intimacies of a kind that are trust-engendering. Insofar as this is true, each member of such pairs is likely to assume that the other's attitudes toward himself are somewhat similar to his own attitudes toward himself. Hence we predict that, throughout the entire period of acquaintance, the attraction level between pairs of roommates will be higher than for other pairs.

Both of these predictions may be tested by the data in Table 11.2. In Year I, according to these data, attraction level is at no time higher for roommates than for other pairs, with the single (and partial) exception that, at the extreme level of the highest 8 percent of expected frequencies (or about the highest 16 percent of obtained frequencies), at Week 0 only, there are significantly more roomates than other pairs; the distribution is $\begin{smallmatrix} 4 & 14 \\ 6 & 112 \end{smallmatrix}$, and $p = .028$ by exact test. In Year II, however, the relationship be-

Table 11.2. Numbers of Roommates and of Other Pairs
at Four Levels of Attraction

	Attraction level	Week 0		Week 1		Week 2		Week 5		Week 15	
		Rm	Others	Rm	Others	Rm	Others	Rm	Others	Rm	Others
Year I	≦20 (high)	4	14	2	17	1	18	2	13	1	19
	21–48	1	11	0	13	1	9	3	20	2	15
	49–128	1	41	4	34	4	35	1	26	2	25
	≧129 (low)	4	60	4	62	4	64	4	67	5	67
	TOTAL	10	126	10	126	10	126	10	126	10	126
Year II	≦20 (high)	5	15	4	12	5	13	6	15	5	14
	21–48	1	7	2	14	2	17	1	12	3	11
	49–128	0	37	2	34	2	26	2	32	1	32
	≧129 (low)	4	67	2	66	1	70	1	67	1	69
	TOTAL	10	126	10	126	10	126	10	126	10	126

tween roommateness and attraction is significantly in the predicted direction—dichotomizing either at the same high level of attraction or at the midpoint of the distribution—at all times. What is more interesting, the relationship increases with acquaintance, reaching its highest point at Week 2, and dropping off only slightly by Week 15. At Weeks 2, 5, and 15, all p values, according to either point of dichotomizing, are considerably beyond .01.

Thus neither of our predictions is fully supported. The first of them—that roommates will be more highly attracted to each other than are other pairs, on first acquaintance—is well supported by the Year-II data but only partially so in Year I. The second—that this relationship will persist—is well supported in Year II and not at all in Year I. In Year II the relationship increases, and in Year I it decreases—though in neither case significantly, Ns of roommate pairs being very small.

We have noted other respects in which the two populations differ, and some of these may suggest some clues that help to account for this difference. One possible clue is the fact of considerably greater homogeneity in ordering the attractiveness of all Ss (excepting the respondent himself) among the entire population in Year II than in Year I. Table 11.3 shows the differences in magnitude of agreement, on the part of all pairs, in ranking the remain-

Table 11.3. NUMBERS OF PAIRS OF Ss AT VARIOUS LEVELS OF AGREEMENT IN RANKING ATTRACTIVENESS OF REMAINING 15 Ss (WEEK 15)

Rho *of agreement*	*Year I*	*Year II*
$\geq .60$ (high)	10	40
.40 to .59	30	45
.20 to .39	34	37
.00 to .19	27	11
$< .00$ (low)	35	3
TOTAL	136	136

ing 15 Ss, at Week 15. Dichotomizing the total distribution as nearly equally as possible, the distribution becomes $\begin{smallmatrix} 40 & 85 \\ 96 & 51 \end{smallmatrix}$, $\chi^2 = 28.66$ and $p < .001$ with 1 df.

Since we have hypothesized that attraction varies with perceived (and, after acquaintance, with actual) agreement, it is predictable that, if roommates in one population agree with each other about the other House members more closely than in the other population, then the first set of roommates will also be more highly attracted to each other. In terms of absolute level of agreement, the two sets of roommates differ dramatically, the evenly divided distribution being $\begin{smallmatrix} 9 & 1 \\ 1 & 9 \end{smallmatrix}$ and $p = .001$, by exact test.

In terms of attraction level relative to their own populations, however, the roommate pairs in the two populations differ less, as shown in Table 11.4. Comparing roommate pairs in the two populations, the distribution is $\begin{smallmatrix} 6 & 9 \\ 4 & 1 \end{smallmatrix}$, the p value of which is .13, by exact

Table 11.4. NUMBERS OF ROOMMATE AND OF OTHER PAIRS AT TWO LEVELS OF AGREEMENT ABOUT HOUSE MEMBERS (WEEK 15)

	Year I			*Year II*	
Agreement rhos	*Rm*	*Others*	*Agreement* rhos	*Rm*	*Others*
$\geq.22$	6	63	$\geq.49$	9	59
$\leq.21$	4	63	$\leq.48$	1	67
TOTAL	10	126	TOTAL	10	126

test. The significant finding, however, is that in spite of the higher general level of agreement in Year II, the Year-II pairs of roommates nevertheless exceed that general level by a higher margin than that by which the Year-I roommates exceed the general level in their population.

Other bases for attitudinal agreement on the part of roommates (which for the most part are not comparable for the two populations) are not very revealing. Perhaps the most interesting finding from the attitudinal data concerns the accuracy of roommates' estimates of each others' ordering of Spranger Values in Year II. In spite of their relatively high attraction toward each other, they do not tend to overestimate agreement, either at Week 2 or at Week 14—if anything, the reverse. Using individual ranks of accuracy (rather than absolute levels, with regard to which individuals are different), roommates at Week 2 estimate each other significantly more accurately than the same individuals rate non-roommates ($\chi^2 = 4.05$, and $p < .05$, with 1 df); at Week 14 the difference is in the same direction, but is no longer significant.

The fact that roommates' attraction toward each other at Week 15 is higher in Year II than in Year I, although at Week 0 they hardly differed at all, is not the consequence of any artifact that we can discover. For example, it could have happened—though it did not—that the individuals who happened to occupy single rooms, and were thus excluded from roommateship, were very unpopular ones in Year II but not in Year I, in which case roommates in Year I but not in Year II would have included several pairs necessarily at low attraction levels. But the difference between the two populations is in the opposite direction: there was 1 very unpopular individual in each population who occupied a single room, but in Year II there were also 2 highly popular Ss and in Year I only 1 who had single rooms.

A second artifactual possibility stems from the fact that in Year I each of 2 highly unpopular Ss was 1 member of a set of 3 roommates; thus unpopular Ss were involved in 4 of the 10 pairs in Year I, as compared with only 2 such pairs in Year II. But this could only in small part account for the differences between the two populations: in Year II both the pairs involving unpopular Ss were at fairly high attraction levels (pair scores of 48 and 27.5), whereas in Year I all 4 of the comparable pairs were in the lower half of the total distribution in attraction (pair scores 252.5,

184.5, 133.5, and 151.5). Nevertheless, the fact remains that there were 4 such pairs in Year I, and if there had been more than 2 in Year II they *might* have been like those in Year I.

It is in their common relationships to other men that the pairs of roommates in the two populations seem to differ most. We have already noted (Table 11.4) that Year-II roommates are in closer agreement about remaining House members than those in Year I. Analogous differences appear if we consider only the high-attraction relationships that roommates have in common with other men. Such shared relationships with *more than one* third person are more frequent on the part of Year-II than of Year-I roommates. This, of course, is equivalent to saying that Year-II but not Year-I roommates tend to be members of two or more (perhaps overlapping) high-attraction triads.[1] The fact is clear enough, as shown in Table 11.5, but the connection between the fact and the dif-

Table 11.5. NUMBERS OF ROOMMATE PAIRS BOTH OF WHOSE MEMBERS HAVE HIGH-ATTRACTION RELATIONSHIPS WITH VARYING NUMBERS OF OTHER PERSONS (WEEK 15) [a]

Number of high-attraction persons	Number of roommate pairs	
	Year I	Year II
0	7	4
1	2	1
2	1	2
3	0	3
Sum of products	4	14

[a] "High attraction" is defined as meeting the 95-percent criterion, as members of a pair or of a larger set (pp. 169–170).

ferences between the two populations in roommate attraction is not self-evident.

We believe that the relationship has much to do with the different structuring of the two total populations. In Year II this tends to be centrally organized—there is a large, close-knit subgroup to which all other subgroups are rather closely attached. In Year I, on the other hand, there are two almost unconnected

[1] For present purposes a high-attraction triad is one that meets the 95-percent criterion described on pp. 169–170.

subgroups (see Figs. 9.3, 9.6). Given this difference, the probabilities that both members of any pair will be included in two high-attraction triads are of course greater in Year II than in Year I, and roommates are apparently affected by these probabilities just as other pairs are.

The divisive structure of Year I, as contrasted with the central one of Year II, also has the consequence, as already noted, that the general level of pair agreement about other House members is much higher in Year II than in Year I. This fact, together with the consideration of probabilities of being included in more than one high-attraction triad, would seem to account for the differences in roommate attraction in the two populations. That agreement about other House members, together with inclusion in more than one high-attraction triad, should affect the within-pair level of attraction is directly derivable from our general hypotheses. The closer the agreement between two House members about all the remaining ones, and in particular about those to whom they are strongly attracted, the stronger the attraction between those two persons is likely to be.

These considerations inevitably raise hen-and-egg questions of dependent-independent relationships. We have already indicated (pp. 183–188) our belief that the different structurings of the two populations may be traced to the fact that in Year II the individuals with highest attraction power were attracted to one another, as was not the case in Year I; and that this difference, in turn, resulted from an essentially fortuitous combination of factors: in Year II but not in Year I those persons whose personal characteristics tended to make them popular also shared, and discovered the fact of sharing, a set of attitudes of importance to them. Hence we are inclined to solve the hen-and-egg problem by concluding that this combination of circumstances was responsible *both* for the different modes of population structuring and for the different levels of attraction between roommates.

The Roommate Experiment

There is also a possibility that our second-year experiment in assigning roommates, as described below, might have contributed to the difference in roommates' attraction level in the two populations.

In Year II—in contrast to Year I, when roommate assignments

were literally picked out of a hat—we had, for experimental purposes, predetermined room assignments before the men's arrival. On the basis of replies to the miscellaneous inventory of 85 attitudinal items, returned by mail before the men were to arrive in Ann Arbor, we selected, as best we could, the following combinations of persons: a set of 3 maximally and another of 3 minimally agreeing Ss; two sets of 2 maximally and two sets of 2 minimally agreeing persons. The procedures by which we devised the index of agreement, for these initial assignments, were necessarily hasty; the early index was crude, compared to that later developed, but it resulted in the following degrees of agreement among roommates, according to the latter index, which was computed long *after* the room assignments had been made: [2]

	Category of agreement	N of pairs	Index of Agreement
Triple #1	high	3	.99, .98, .87
Double #1	high	1	.99
Double #2	high	1	.27
Triple #2	low	3	.12, .04, .03
Double #3	low	1	.06
Double #4	low	1	.05

Our purpose in planning this experiment was to test the prediction that, following acquaintance, the attraction level between the first five pairs of roommates would be higher than that of the second set of pairs. We failed, completely, to find support for the prediction: four out of *each* set of five pairs ended up at high attraction levels—i.e., in about the highest one-sixth of all pairs, and three of *each* set of pairs in about the highest 6 percent of all pairs. If it had not been for the totally different results in Year I, we should have had to conclude that the way to create high attraction among pairs of strangers is simply to make roommates of them. Such, we may add, are the advantages of replication.

At any rate it seems safe to conclude that the second year's experiment in roommate assignment did not contribute to the differences in roommate attraction in the two populations: even

[2] See pp. 77–78 for description of the index of agreement, according to which a high value indicates improbably high agreement.

among the five pairs of roommates whose attraction we expected to be low, it was higher in Year II than in Year I. Thus we have no reason to revise our earlier conclusions.

Because of our interest in the experimental failure, we made some informal analyses of roommate relationships, based in part on interviews held after all the data had been gathered. We are reasonably confident of the following probable bases of compatibility or noncompatibility among the ten pairs in Year II, but they are offered only as illustrative pair histories.

Pairs selected as in close agreement. The men in *Triple #1* came to constitute a close-knit subgroup (part of a pentad that met the 95-percent criterion). In interviews, all three of them specifically mentioned common intellectual, "philosophical," and/or literary interests ("we liked to talk about books"). One of them stressed "rationality," one "intellectuality," and one liberal-political attitudes as a common basis of compatibility with the other two.

The attraction relationship of *Double #1* was the highest of all 16 for one of the pair, and the fourth for the other, at Week 15. Both their own interview responses and spontaneous comments by other men indicate a rather unusual relationship of complementarity between them. One of them was a veteran, older than the other, and generally regarded as dominating; the other was never sure of his own acceptance by most of the other men, and described himself as often disturbed by the "wild arguments" of the "eastern sophisticates," especially with regard to "moral standards." After such episodes, "I'd go back and have a talk with my roommate, get a lecture from him, and feel good about my own opinions again."

Double #2 was made up of the only pair of roommates in Year II whose final attraction toward each other was in the lower half of the total distribution (barely below the median). In interviews, one of them (a veteran) described the other (who was much younger) as "a Joe College playboy," and indicated that he much preferred older and more serious companions; the younger man mentioned sports (in which the older one was not at all interested) as being very important to him, but avoided any other comment about his roommate. The younger was described by others as an extroverted practical joker, and the older as sensitive, serious, retiring. It was quite evident that few of the issues on which they had agreed, on the initial inventory, were of much importance to the younger man.

Thus, for the five pairs for whom high attraction had been predicted, three developed a relationship of high attraction based in considerable part on the kinds of attitudes that we had measured; one became a fairly high-attraction pair on the basis of both attitudinal similarity and personal complementarity; and one a low-attraction pair on the basis of rather extreme differences in interests and in personality.

Pairs selected as in low agreement. Two of the members of *Triple #2* were veterans, Catholics, and Engineering students; the third was much younger, Jewish, and a student in the Arts College. On the initial inventory no two of them were in even moderately close agreement. The relationship between the two older men began at a very low level of attraction, but gradually increased to a very high level; their interviews indicated a good deal of condescension toward the younger men—with the single exception of their younger roommate. They also had in common the values of "seriousness" and quiet attention to work—virtues which both attributed to their younger roommate; in addition, they regarded him as "intellectually mature," and rather admired his verbal facilities. He, according to interview statements, had appreciated their "protectiveness," and had felt loyal to them, but toward the end of the semester (and especially afterward, when by common consent he moved into another room with a different man) he began to recognize an intellectual incompatibility, and felt the need to be independent of them.

Both members of *Double #3* were low in popularity status—one of them very low. By Week 15 their level of attraction had started to decline, and two or three weeks later they ceased to be roommates. In the interviews, neither of them was at all enthusiastic about the other, and it was commonly believed (both by staff and by other House members) that their rather close relationship (during most of the semester) was a *faute de mieux* phenomenon stemming from the withdrawal tendencies of one of them and the personal unacceptability of the other.

The two members of *Double #4* were about as different as any two individuals in either population, except in age (both under 20). One, an eastern Protestant, was regarded as sophisticated, urbane, and likable, well read, liberal in politics, and an Arts College student. The other was Catholic, of rural background, of generally conservative tendencies, and an Engineering student.

The first of them ranked second in popularity at nearly every week, and the other at twelfth or thirteenth. Yet their attraction to each other was consistently high. Neither of them succeeded, in their interviews, in pointing to any special basis for this relationship. The first of them put it this way: "It's hard to explain. We never had much in common, but we got along extremely well; I've *always* got along *really* well with every roommate I ever had; we disagreed about many things, but never got mad about it." An important factor, almost certainly, was the fact that the less popular of them spent comparatively little time in the House (for reasons of employment elsewhere), and probably knew his roommate far better than he knew any one else; his own statement supports this interpretation.

Among the five pairs whose eventual attraction to each other we expected to be low, two proved to be very high: one pair in Triple #2 had many attitudes in common, though they did not correspond closely to the items on our initial inventory; and Double #4 had a close relationship of personal symbiosis, though little else in common. Two other pairs had a moderately close relationship: one of the pairs in Triple #2 was characterized by considerable complementarity of personal needs; and the men in Double #3 were, so to speak, thrown into each others' arms by their relative isolation from others. A fifth pair, included in Triple #2, was barely above the average in attraction to each other, and had virtually no attitudes in common. By the end of the semester these pairs, as a group, were somewhat less close than the other five pairs, and it is possible that, over a longer period of time, they would have been much less so.

By way of rough summary, (1) four of the five cases of very high actual relationships of attraction at Week 15 (Triple #1, and one pair in Triple #2) are understandable in terms consistent with predictions based upon similarity of attitudes (whether or not known before room assignment), and one of the five (Double 4) primarily in terms of personality factors. (2) One of the three pair-cases of moderately high actual attraction (Double #1) seems explainable in both sets of terms, and the other two (Double #3, and one of the pairs in Triple #2) primarily in terms of personality factors. (3) Of the two roommate pairs whose final attraction was lowest (both near the average for the total population), the relationship of one pair in Triple #2 is consistent with the notion of attitudinal similarity, while that of Double #2 is not, appearing to rest rather upon rather extreme personality incompatibility. In short, four of the five very high-attraction relationships are consistent with predictions based upon attitudinal similarity, as are two of the four relationships at moderately high or above-average attraction; the one instance of below-average attraction appears not to be consistent with such predictions.

The Contribution of Personal Characteristics to Attraction   **12**

We have shown in various ways that interpersonal attraction varies with perceived similarity of orientations, according to the hypothesized dynamics of individual systems, at all stages of acquaintance. On late but not on early acquaintance, it tends to vary with actual similarity of orientations, so that collective systems become balanced. This state of affairs—whereby individual balance is maintained while collective systems change from imbalance to balance—necessarily requires a good many changes in attraction, and we shall show that such changes are in fact considerable.

In treating attraction as a system component, we have of course considered it as neither an independent nor a dependent variable, in any inherent sense. From other points of view, however, either attraction or agreement may be considered to be dependent. In particular, it seems likely that orientations toward persons will vary, dependently, with the characteristics that the recipients of attraction present to be observed by others. Thus, in general terms, questions arise about the attainment and maintenance of balanced states *within* systems of orientation, while at the same time some of those orientations (attractions) are presumably influenced by individuals' characteristics, which are *extra*-system in nature.

Personal characteristics, however, are apt to be differentially observed by others, and they are notoriously susceptible to differential evaluation. We shall assume *both* that attraction may be influenced by the perceived characteristics of others *and* that the latter may be influenced by existing attraction. In this chapter, therefore, we shall test the general hypothesis that, while attraction toward others is presumably influenced by their observable characteristics, nevertheless the perception of such characteristics changes in such manner as to remain closely associated with attraction—which, as we have shown, changes in balance-maintaining manner.

Procedures

Our one objective source of information (in the sense of providing comparability for all Ss) concerning observable personal characteristics was the adjective check-list (see pp. 35–36), which we used only in Year II. All Ss, at several stages of acquaintance, checked all adjectives which they regarded as applicable to all other Ss. From these responses we computed an index of *favorability*, which was simply the number of favorable adjectives—as reported by Gough (1955)—applied by any S to any other S.[1] In view of the fact that different respondents varied considerably in the number of adjectives checked, these frequencies were converted into ranks, for each respondent. These ranks, like those of attraction, could be treated either aggregatively (i.e., sums of ranks received by any S) or in person-to-person terms.

Relationship of Attraction and Favorability

In *aggregative* terms, the two variables are very closely associated, both early and late. If the attraction ranks received by each S are summed and correlated with the sum of his favorability ranks received, the coefficients (*rho, $N = 17$*) are .84 at Week 14 and .82 at Week 1—almost as high as the test-retest coefficient of the summed scores of either instrument between Weeks 12 and 14 (.90 for favorability and .95 for attraction). Further, *individuals'* rankings of the other 16 Ss, according to the two indices, are significantly correlated: the mean of the 17 individual coefficients is .63 at Week 1 and .70 at Week 14—again approaching fairly closely the individual test-retest reliability of either instrument (.81 and .76 for favorability on late and on early acquaintance, and .90 and .86 for attraction). Thus the two indices may almost be regarded as alternative measures of the same

---

[1] We also developed an index based upon the ratio of favorable to unfavorable adjectives. Both because of problems of equating ratios based upon widely differing frequencies, and because of Ss' reluctance to apply unfavorable adjectives, particularly on early acquaintance, we concluded that it was less useful than the index based only upon favorable adjectives.

thing, and therefore we shall regard both of them as expressions of the orientation of attraction.

Continuity of Early Attraction Relationships

It seems reasonable to assume that, on earliest acquaintance, perceived favorability is to a considerable extent the independent and attraction the dependent variable in this close relationship. The degree to which we can make this same assumption several months later depends upon the stability of individuals' rank-orderings of other Ss in both favorability and attraction. That is, if the early, and necessarily impressionistic, indices of favorability remain relatively unchanged, then—since favorability and attraction are still highly correlated on late acquaintance—it would seem necessary to conclude that final attraction was considerably influenced by stable perceptions of others' personal characteristics. But insofar as individuals' rank-orderings of other change, it becomes less plausible to interpret the later relationship as one in which favorability is the independent variable. If both attraction and favorability are unstable, it is likely that there are effects in both directions.

Both indices are in fact rather unstable. The mean of the 17 Ss' individual correlations between attraction ranks assigned to others at Week 0 and Week 15 is a nonsignificant .31. Between Week 1 (when favorability responses were first obtained) and Week 14 (when they were last obtained) the test-retest coefficients are .54 for attraction and .44 for favorability. The null hypothesis of no relationship between Ss' earliest and latest rank-orderings of other Ss cannot be rejected; and the degree of stability after ten days of acquaintance is barely significant, for the total population.

Thus, while the relationship between the two indices remains constantly high, each of them changes with continued acquaintance.

Changing Perceptions of Favorability and Constancy of Balance

We have previously shown that attraction changes in such ways as to maintain balance. The relationship between attraction and favorability, while high, is not perfect (even with corrections for attenuation), and so we must inquire whether favorability also changes in balance-maintaining ways. We shall therefore test a prediction analogous to an earlier one that was well supported: high-attraction pairs are in significantly closer agreement as to the attractiveness of the remaining Ss than are other pairs. The present prediction is that high-attraction pairs are in significantly closer agreement, following acquaintance, as to the favorable characteristics of the remaining Ss than are other pairs. As shown in Table 12.1, we have tested this prediction not only by comparing the

Table 12.1. NUMBERS OF HIGH-ATTRACTION PAIRS, AT WEEK 14, WHO ARE IN UPPER AND LOWER HALVES OF THE DISTRIBUTION OF ALL PAIRS AT WEEKS 1 AND 14 IN AGREEMENT ABOUT THE FAVORABLE CHARACTERISTICS OF OTHER Ss (YEAR II) [a]

Agreement level	Week 1	Week 14	Total
Upper half	14	25	39
Lower half	11	0	11
TOTAL	25	25	50

[a] The pairs included in this table are the 25 whose pair-scores of attraction (on the 256-point scale) are highest among all 136 pairs. The cutting points for upper and lower halves of the distribution of agreement correlations are not the same at the two times, since the general level of agreement is higher at the later time (mean *rhos* are .42 and .20 at Weeks 14 and 1, respectively).

obtained with the expected frequency of high-attraction pairs whose agreement concerning the favorability of other Ss is in the upper half of the distribution for all pairs at Week 14; but also by indicating the degree of change in agreement, between Weeks 1 and 14, on the part of those same pairs. Both the obtained-expected difference and the changes between Weeks 1 and 14 are significant at $<.001$ (the respective χ^2 values are 23.05 and 11.65, with 1 df). Thus we may conclude not only that high-attraction pairs, on final acquaintance, tend significantly to be in agreement with each other about the favorable characteristics of other Ss, but also that this agreement represents a change from an earlier state of affairs when their degree of agreement did not differ significantly from chance expectations.

Thus we conclude that the favorability index, like the index of attraction, changes with continued acquaintance in balance-maintaining fashion.

Individual Differences in Favorable Characteristics

Among the population as a whole, individuals' personal characteristics are sufficiently ambiguous so that the perception of them changes a good deal. But it is to be expected that individuals will differ as to the clarity or conspicuousness of the traits included on the adjective check-list. And insofar as some Ss are consensually judged—particularly if such judgments remain stable throughout the acquaintance period—then we may consider attraction toward such individuals as dependent, and their personal characteristics as independent. If attraction toward them is both consensual and unchanging, it can hardly be treated as adaptive in balance-promoting ways.

The fact is that there are 4 Ss in this population who meet this criterion, rather conspicuously. At Week 14 the ranks of favorability that each of them received from the other 16 Ss are concentrated in either the highest or the lowest quartile (Ranks 1–4 or 13–16); in all four cases, 14 or more of the 16 ranks are thus concentrated,[2] and the remaining one or two ranks are in the immediately adjacent quartile. None of the other 13 Ss approaches this degree of consensuality of judgment; the individual who comes closest to it receives nine ranks in the highest quartile, but the other seven are scattered among the other three quartiles. In terms of mean ranks received, these 4 Ss may be compared with the other 13 as follows:

most favorable S	2.12
intermediate 13 Ss	4.62–10.87
3 least favorable Ss	13.75–15.00

Such extreme scores presuppose considerable consensuality of judgments.

Judgments of favorability concerning these 4 Ss, moreover, are highly stable. Though the Week-1 judgments are less extreme than those at Week 14, these 4 Ss occupy almost exactly the same rank positions of favorability at both times, as shown in Table 12.2, in

---

[2] There is no reason, a priori, why ranks received might not be concentrated in one of the intermediate quartiles, but this does not in fact happen.

Table 12.2. RANK POSITIONS IN FAVORABILITY AND IN ATTRACTION, AS RECEIVED BY 4 Ss EXTREME IN FAVORABILITY JUDGMENTS AT WEEK 14

| | Week 14 | | Week 1 | |
| | Favor- ability | Attrac- tion | Favor- ability [a] | Attrac- tion [a] |
Subject				
#34	1	1	1	1
#48	15	15	15	14
#35	16	16	13	15
#41	17	17	17	16

[a] The individual ranked seventeenth in attraction and sixteenth in favorability at Week 1 was a particularly retiring person who, according to interview responses, was still almost totally unknown at about the tenth day of acquaintance.

which rank positions in popularity (according to mean attraction rank received) are also presented. Since judgments about these four individuals are homogeneous, extreme, and stable, we may conclude that attraction toward them is to be accounted for in terms of individual characteristics rather than in terms of the maintenance of balance.

Analogous individual differences in Year I. The adjective check-list was not used in Year I, but in view of the close relation between aggregative indices of favorability and of attraction in Year II, we may inquire whether, according to the latter, there were individuals in Year I also who were judged in consensual and stable ways. The answer is that there was relatively little consensuality in Year I, according to attraction ranks. At Week 14 there was no S whose ranks did not range over at least three of the four quartiles, and only two whose ranks did not span all four quartiles. Stability between Weeks 1 and 14 was also low for this population: the correlation of popularity ranks at these two times was only .16 (as compared with .79 for Year II). There was no individual who ranked as high as fourth in popularity at both times; the Ss who ranked 1, 2, 3, and 4 at Week 14 ranked 15, 5, 9.5, and 14, respectively, at Week 1. There were, however, 4 Ss who ranked comparatively low in popularity at both times; the Ss who ranked 13, 14, 15, and 16 at Week 14 ranked, respectively, at 12, 17, 13, and 16 at Week 1. Two of these, however, were not judged with much consensuality at Week 14: each of them received five responses in each of the second, the third, and the fourth quartiles, and the sixteenth in the first quartile. Hence we conclude that in this population, by this measure, there were not more than two individuals who met the criterion of consensuality and stability—as compared with four in Year II.

Conclusions

The general tendency is for perception of the favorability of others' personal characteristics to change, as does attraction more directly measured, with acquaintance. And, like attraction, it changes in balance-maintaining ways. In view of these changes, we conclude that perceived favorability functions not only as an independent but also as a dependent variable. On earliest acquaintance, presumably, attraction is very considerably influenced by perceived favorability, as independent, but during the acquaintance process it changes in balance-maintaining ways. As a general tendency, individuals come to see others as possessing favorable characteristics in ways that are influenced less by their initial impressions than by the present impressions of other individuals to whom they are highly attracted.

Individuals differ, however, with respect to the favorability and the attraction that is accorded them. In each population there were some persons—probably four of them in Year II and perhaps two in Year I—who were responded to by consensual, stable, and extreme judgments of favorability and/or attraction. Attraction toward them is probably to be accounted for in terms of personal qualities rather than in terms of maintaining balance. With regard to the remaining five-sixths of the two populations, however, judgments were neither very stable nor consensual, and changes occurred in balance-maintaining ways.

Group Stereotypes of Individuals' Agreement in Values* **13**

There was a good deal of consensuality, following a few weeks of acquaintance, about interpersonal relationships of attraction among House members—as shown, for example, in Ss' direct reports of subgroup structuring (pp. 35–36). Not surprisingly, since the relevant facts were readily observable, these consensual judgments were pretty accurate. We have elsewhere shown that similarity of individuals' values, and especially perceived similarity, is related to attraction, and this fact raises the question whether, following acquaintance, such similarities were also generally recognized, even though less observable than manifestations of attraction. Our purpose in raising the question is not so much to test propositions concerning balance (which are better tested in more direct ways) as to inquire into the possibility that the subgroup structuring that actually emerged may have been influenced by consensual stereotyping (of whatever degree of accuracy) about individuals' similarities and differences in values.

CLUSTERS OF SUBJECTS PERCEIVED AS DISTINCTIVE

Nature of the Data (Year II only)

Since every subject twice estimated every other S's ranking of the six Spranger Values, it was possible to compute for each estimator the 120 rank-order correlations corresponding to the 120

* Many of the analyses reported in this chapter were made by Mr. Richard Wagner.

pairs of Ss not involving himself. Such a set of correlations represents the estimator's map of the agreement structure of the population, excluding himself. There are 17 such maps, altogether, and each pair of Ss is thus mapped 15 times. If each set of 15 indices of judged agreement on the part of each pair is averaged, we have a pooled estimate of pair agreement. The range of these 136 pooled estimates of agreement, in terms of *rhos,* at Week 2 was from .01 to .79, and from .00 to .78 at Week 14, their respective means being .34 and .37. The mean *rhos* of *actual* agreement of all 136 pairs, based upon own responses rather than upon estimates by others, was .13 and .15; thus the degree of actual agreement was somewhat overestimated.

Identifying Distinctive Clusters of Subjects

By way of discovering whether, within this range between about .00 and about .80, there were sets of Ss who were judged as being in high agreement with one another, and perhaps also in low agreement with other sets, we used the following procedure. (1) The 136 mean *rhos* of estimated agreement were divided into high, above-average, below-average, and low quartiles. (2) Individuals who were involved in one or more pairs in the highest quartile of estimated agreement were identified; at Week 2 there were 11 of them, and at Week 14 there were 13. (3) A matrix was constructed for these individuals, the *rho* of each pair's estimated agreement being entered at the intersection of the appropriate row and column. (4) For each S included in this matrix, a distribution of the *rhos* of his estimated [1] agreement with all other Ss in the matrix was drawn up, in terms of quartiles of the total distribution. (There is no reason, a priori, why an individual selected as being in high agreement with one or more of the others in the matrix should necessarily be in high agreement with *all* of them.) Finally (5), we chose, as a criterion for inclusion in a high-agreement cluster, the requirement that at least two-thirds of each S's pair-scores of agreement be in the higher half of the distribution.

Thus at Week 2, when there were 11 Ss included in the matrix, a high-agreement cluster consists of the largest number of Ss for each of whom at least seven (two-thirds of ten) of his *rhos* of agreement were in the upper two quartiles. As shown in Table

[1] Henceforth, since we shall be dealing exclusively with *estimates* of agreement, we shall dispense with the word "estimated."

13.1, 10 of the 11 Ss meet the criterion. At Week 14, using the same procedures, 16 of the 17 Ss were included in the matrix (i.e., were involved in at least one high-quartile pair). Among these 16, there was a set of 9 each of whom met the criterion that at least six (two-thirds of eight) of his *rhos* of agreement with all others be in the upper half of the distribution; and there was an-

Table 13.1. FREQUENCIES OF FOUR DEGREES OF GROUP-ESTI-MATED AGREEMENT ABOUT SPRANGER VALUES, ON THE PART OF ALL 136 PAIRS (WEEK 2, YEAR II) [a]

Agreement quartile	Pairs in Cluster A [b]	Pairs in Cluster B [c]	Across-cluster pairs	#39 with Cluster A	#39 with Cluster B	Total
Highest	30	0	3	1	0	34
Second	13	6	9	4	3	35
Third	2	5	21	2	3	33
Lowest	0	4	27	3	0	34
TOTAL	45	15	60	10	6	136

[a] See text for description of procedures.
[b] Ten Ss: 34, 35, 37, 38, 40, 41, 43, 44, 48, 50.
[c] Six Ss: 36, 42, 45, 46, 47, 49.

other set of 7 who met the same criterion, each of them being in the upper half of the distribution in agreement with at least four (two-thirds of six) of the remaining set-members.

At Week 14 but not at Week 2 it thus happened that the high-agreement pairs broke down into two sets of Ss, each set character-ized by high within-set and low between-set agreement, as shown in Table 13.6. Since at Week 2 all possible sets larger than 2 Ss are included in a single cluster of 10, the remaining 7 Ss constitute a residual category of individuals who tend not to be in high agree-ment with anyone. One of these, however, is a partial exception: he neither meets the criterion for inclusion in the high-agreement cluster nor resembles the other 6 nonagreeing Ss, and hence is con-sidered as belonging neither to the agreeing nor to the nonagree-ing cluster. At Week 14, for a different reason there is also a category consisting of a single S; he is the only one who fails to meet the criterion of inclusion in either of the high-agreement clusters.

Characteristics of the Group-perceived Clusters, Week 2

As indicated in Table 13.1, there are 10 *S*s who are regarded as being in substantial agreement with one another; we shall refer to them as *Cluster A*. There are also 6 *S*s each of whom is viewed as an individualist, in high agreement with no one; they are labeled *Cluster B*. A seventeenth subject does not quite fit in either camp. Neither of the two clusters—each of whose distributions is such that there is not a single score in one of the extreme quartiles —could have emerged without a good deal of consensual stereo-typing on the part of the total population of estimators. Since, after only two weeks of acquaintance, the estimates of others' rank-ordering of Spranger Values must have been highly impressionistic, one wonders what might have been the bases for the stereotyped estimates. Several indications appear.

First, all but two of the ten Cluster-A members were enrolled in the Engineering School, and all but one of Cluster B in the Arts College. Second, all four of the "vets," who were almost immedi-ately identified as older and more experienced than others, were included in Cluster A. Third, in *actual* response to four of the six Spranger Values, the two clusters were quite different, as shown in Table 13.2. Cluster-A members, relative to those in Cluster B,

Table 13.2. FREQUENCIES OF RANKS ACTUALLY ASSIGNED BY MEMBERS OF CLUSTERS A AND B TO FOUR SPRANGER VALUES (YEAR II, WEEK 2)

Rank assigned	Theoretic Cl.A	Cl.B	Economic Cl.A	Cl.B	Esthetic Cl.A	Cl.B	Religious Cl.A	Cl.B
1, 2	5	5	4	0	1	2	5	0
3, 4	2	1	5	1	5	4	2	1
5, 6	3	0	1	5	4	0	3	5
TOTAL	10	6	10	6	10	6	10	6

are high in economic and religious, and low in theoretic and esthetic values. The first two of these considerations (college of enrollment and veteran status) were surely known to all by Week 2. Subjects' actual preferences among Spranger Values were not, however, well known at this time; group estimates correctly distinguished the two clusters in respect to religious and theoretic values, but wrongly concerning economic value.

Inspection of Table 13.2 suggests that Cluster B—contrary to group estimates—is more homogeneous concerning these four Spranger Values than is Cluster A. Table 13.3, in which numbers

Table 13.3. NUMBERS OF WITHIN-CLUSTER AND BETWEEN-CLUSTER PAIRS AT VARIOUS LEVELS OF ACTUAL AGREEMENT IN ORDERING SPRANGER VALUES (WEEK 2, YEAR II)

Agreement quartile	Within Cluster A	Within Cluster B	Across clusters	Involving #39	Total
Highest	11	13	7	1	32
Second	13	2	16	3	34
Third	6	0	25	3	34
Lowest	15	0	12	9	36
TOTAL	45	15	60	16	136

of pairs at various levels of actual agreement appear, shows that this is indeed the case.

Cluster-B members are in fact in very close agreement with each other, whereas Cluster-A's within-member agreement is hardly greater than for the total population of pairs. Moreover, Cluster A's distribution does not differ significantly from that of across-cluster pairs ($\chi^2 = 1.81$, with 1 df). The difference in agreement level between the two clusters is highly significant: $\chi^2 = 15.64$, with 1 df, and $p < .001$.

In short, the group-estimated clusters are correctly differentiated in only one respect: the across-cluster pairs do not agree with each other quite as well as other pairs ($\chi^2 = 3.74$; $p = .05$ when $\chi^2 = 3.8$, with 1 df). In other respects, the group judgment is exactly reversed: Cluster B's members actually agree with each other very well, and Cluster A's do not.

Our interview data provide us with another clue to the bases for stereotyping. During the early weeks, certain individuals came to be referred to by some others (we have no way of knowing how generally) as "Eastern sophisticates." All but one of Cluster B were in fact from urban centers in Atlantic seacoast states, and only two from Cluster A, and these exceptions are revealing. They suggest that the perceived agreers in Cluster A included every one who was not an urban Easterner, except 2 Ss who associated frequently with those who were, together with 1 Eastern urbanite who was mature, socially extroverted, and a good athlete.

There is also an amazingly sharp distinction between the F-score distributions of the members of two clusters, as shown in Table 13.4. That a personality test, the significance of which is pre-

Table 13.4. DISTRIBUTION OF F-SCORE RANKS OF MEMBERS OF TWO PERCEIVED-AGREEMENT CLUSTERS (YEAR II, WEEK 2)

Ranks of non-authoritarianism	Cluster A	Cluster B
1– 5	0	5
6–12	5	1
13–17	5	0

$p = .001$ (exact test; ranks dichotomized between 5 and 6.)

sumably not self-evident, should agree so closely with a set of group judgments after relatively brief acquaintance seems surprising. This correspondence may result from the fact, as previously reported (see Christie and Cook, 1958), that authoritarianism tends to be inversely associated with urban residence, together with the fact that the importance of a certain urban-rural dimension "happened" to become prominent (and thus exaggerated) in this population, in its early weeks of acquaintance.

We must also ask whether the members of Clusters A and B, as distinguished by estimates of all 17 Ss, contributed about equally to the cluster distinction. The answer is that they did: the proportions of within-cluster pairs appearing in the four quartiles of the total distribution, as shown in Table 13.1, hardly differ at all from the proportions resulting from separate poolings of Cluster A's and of Cluster B's estimates. Both clusters, as estimators, agree that Cluster-A members tend to agree with one another and that other Ss tend to agree with no one. But one important difference between the two sets of cluster members, as estimators, emerges when we examine individuals' estimates of their own agreement with others, as shown in Table 13.5. Cluster-B members clearly see themselves

Table 13.5. Numbers of Estimates of Own Agreement with Cluster Members about Spranger Values by Members of Two Group-perceived Clusters (Week 2, Year II)

| | Estimates of own agreement with | | | | | |
| Quartile | Cluster-A members | | Cluster-B members | | Pairs Involving #39 [a] | Total |
	by Cl.A	Cl.B	by Cl.A	Cl.B		
Highest	23	5	15	9	13	65
Second	22	11	12	10	10	65
Third	30	21	15	4	6	76
Lowest	15	23	18	7	3	66
Total	90	60	60	30	32	272

[a] An examination of these 32 estimates shows that #39 perceives slightly closer agreement with Cluster B than with Cluster A, whereas Cluster-A members consider themselves more closely in agreement with #39 than do Cluster-B members, by a significant difference ($p = .024$, by exact test).

as agreeing more closely with each other than with Cluster-A members: the χ^2 value of the distribution $\begin{smallmatrix} 19 & 16 \\ 11 & 44 \end{smallmatrix}$ is 9.72, significant at $<.005$ with 1 df. Cluster-A members see themselves as agreeing more or less equally with each other and with Cluster-B members.

One other finding regarding a possible basis for group estimates —namely, existing attraction—may be presented. The 10 Ss estimated as being in close agreement were not, in fact, closely attracted to one another. Only 20 of the 45 pairs were in the upper half of the distribution of pair scores of attraction. Perversely enough, the 6 "individualists" (perceived as agreeing neither with one another nor with any one else) were already rather closely attracted to one another: 11 of their 15 pair scores of attraction were in the upper half. This fact, however, was not yet generally known to others, judging from Week 2 responses to questions about who constituted natural subgroups of two or more (see Chap. 3). The proportions of pairs within Cluster A, within Cluster B, and between the two clusters that were included in the 44 percent of all pairs mentioned by three or more respondents as belonging together differed hardly at all; and, as a matter of fact, 10 of the 14 most frequently cited pairs (8 or more times), instead of the 6.2 to be expected by chance, were cross-cluster pairs, and only 3 (instead of 6.2) were within-cluster pairs. Whatever it was that determined the estimates of agreement at Week 2, it was not knowledge of existing attraction.

In sum, all of these findings together suggest the following interpretation of the Week-2 state of group stereotyping concerning Spranger Values. A group of 10 subjects were more or less universally thought of as being in general agreement about Spranger Values, and the other seven were generally considered as being individualists, in this respect. Most of the 10 perceived agreers, who were high in authoritarianism, thought of most of the others as "Eastern sophisticates" and probably thought of themselves as solid, hard-headed, mature, God-fearing "regular guys." Most of the perceived individualists probably thought of most of the other men as somewhat "corn-fed," and of themselves as intellectually sophisticated and nonconforming. Thus at the outset there existed, potentially, two rather different subgroups.

Though our primary concern is whether this generally accepted early version of social reality affected the subsequent structuring of the total population, we shall first present the Week-14 data concerning group-perceived clustering.

Characteristics of the Group-perceived Clusters, Week 14

As shown in Table 13.6, which is exactly analogous to Table 13.1, Week-14 estimates of agreement about Spranger Values also resulted in two distinguishable clusters, including 16 of the 17 Ss. The principal changes that have occurred since Week 2 are the

Table 13.6. FREQUENCIES OF FOUR DEGREES OF GROUP-ESTIMATED AGREEMENT ABOUT SPRANGER VALUES ON THE PART OF ALL 136 PAIRS (WEEK 14, YEAR II)

Agreement quartile	Pairs in Cluster A [a]	Pairs in Cluster B [b]	Across-cluster pairs	#36 with Cluster A	#36 with Cluster B	Total
Highest	24	8	0	2	0	34
Second	9	7	9	3	5	33
Third	3	5	23	3	1	35
Lowest	0	1	31	1	1	34
TOTAL	36	21	63	9	7	136

[a] Nine Ss: #35, 37, 38, 40, 41, 43, 44, 48, 50.
[b] Seven Ss: #34, 39, 42, 45, 46, 47, 49.

following: (1) Cluster A consists of its original ten members minus #34, who is now clearly established in Cluster B. Cluster A's internal agreement is still seen at the same high level as at Week 2. (2) Cluster B consists of five of its original members (all except #36, who has now become marginal) plus #34 (who has shifted from Cluster A) plus #39 (who was previously marginal). Cluster B's internal agreement is now seen as a good deal higher than at Week 2, though still much lower than that of Cluster A at either time; its agreement level with Cluster A, however, is now seen as somewhat lower than before. In short, the division between the two clusters has changed slightly in personnel but has become sharper. The two clusters are now seen as entirely nonoverlapping, in the sense that there is no across-cluster pair that is perceived as being in the highest quartile; and 31 (instead of the expected 15.7) of the 34 pairs perceived as in the lowest quartile are across-cluster pairs.

Cluster B, following the addition of two individuals and the loss of one, is still composed largely of nonauthoritarians, their ranks on this variable being 1, 2, 3, 4, 5, 9, and 10. The first five of these, incidentally, are actually in extraordinarily close agreement: eight of their ten agreement *rhos* are in the top quarter, and the other two just below that point; the mean *rho* of actual agreement is .715. The two *S*s whose *F*-scores are intermediate do not agree with the others, and their mean *rhos* of actual agreement with the five low *F*-scorers are +.20 and —.03.

The pair-attraction scores within and between the two clusters appear in Table 13.7, where it is shown that, in Cluster B, 20 of 21 pairs are in the upper half of all attraction scores, as compared with only 11 of 36 in Cluster A; the difference is highly significant.

Table 13.7. FREQUENCIES OF PAIR-ATTRACTION SCORES AT VARIOUS LEVELS, WITHIN AND BETWEEN CLUSTERS (WEEK 14, YEAR II)

Pair attraction	Within Cluster A	Within Cluster B	Across clusters	#36 with Cluster A	#36 with Cluster B	Total
Highest quartile	6	15	13	1	0	35
Second quartile	5	5	18	2	3	33
Lower half	25	1	32	6	4	68
TOTAL	36	21	63	9	7	136

What is perhaps more interesting is that there are proportionally more high-attraction pairs across the two clusters than within Cluster A; the members of Cluster A are more attracted to Cluster-B members than to each other, though not significantly so.

If we assume that by Week 14 House members' levels of attraction toward one another are rather well known, then it is possible to test, from the data in Table 13.7, the prediction that group-perceived agreement will vary with group-perceived attraction. The data provide little support for the prediction; the perceived high-agreement Cluster A is characterized by low attraction, and the high-attraction Cluster B is only moderately high in perceived agreement. Again, as at Week 2, estimates of others' ordering of the Spranger Values are not much influenced by notions of who is attracted to whom.

As these findings suggest, the two clusters differ in popularity status: Cluster A includes the three least popular Ss, and Cluster B the four most popular ones.

The question arises (as it did concerning Week-2 data) whether the group-estimated distinctiveness of the two clusters, with respect to agreement on Spranger Values, is contributed to by members of both clusters. If this distinctiveness results primarily from the estimates of either cluster alone, it represents a special sort of self-image, or other-image. If not, it represents population-wide consensus. The facts are quite unambiguous: members of the two clusters agree very well about the matter. Both sets of subjects estimate that there is more agreement within Cluster A than within Cluster B; the significance levels are $<.01$ for estimates by members of Cluster A, and $<.05$ for members of Cluster B. The lesser level of significance on the part of Cluster B's estimates derives, in part at least, from the fact that these subjects tend to see (by significant differences) more agreement within *both* clusters than do the members of Cluster A.

Does this mean simply that the members of Cluster B see agreement everywhere? Table 13.8 shows the total frequencies with which members of each cluster judge various degrees of agreement between all 63 pairs composed of one member from each cluster. It is quite clear that Cluster-B members see *less* agreement *between* members of the two clusters than do Cluster-A members, by a highly significant margin. This total set of facts indicates not that Cluster-B members see agreement everywhere, but rather that they

Table 13.8. FREQUENCIES WITH WHICH MEMBERS OF TWO GROUP-PERCEIVED CLUSTERS ESTIMATE VARIOUS DEGREES OF AGREEMENT ON THE PART OF ALL BETWEEN-CLUSTER PAIRS (WEEK 14, YEAR II)

Rho of agreement	Frequencies as judged by members of		
	Cluster A	Cluster B	Total
$\geq .60$	158	75	233
.14–.59	185	102	287
$\leq .13$	161	201	362
TOTAL	504 [a]	378 [a]	882

$\chi^2 = 50.11; p < .001$ (2 df)

[a] The total frequency of 504 equals 63 (the number of across-cluster pairs) multiplied by 8 (the number of Ss in the cluster, less 1, since 63 of the across-cluster comparisons involve the estimator himself). Similarly, $378 = 63 \ (7–1)$.

are more discriminating than Cluster-A members: they see, more than do Cluster-A members, each cluster as agreeing within itself and disagreeing with the other cluster. Table 13.9 (which corresponds exactly to Table 13.5) provides additional support for this statement. Cluster-A members, as shown in this table, do see themselves as agreeing more closely with each other than with Cluster-B members, but by a barely significant margin (the χ^2 value of the distribution $\begin{smallmatrix} 43 & 26 \\ 62 & 37 \end{smallmatrix}$ is 3.87, the value of 3.8 being required

Table 13.9. NUMBERS OF ESTIMATES OF OWN AGREEMENT ABOUT SPRANGER VALUES BY MEMBERS OF TWO GROUP-PERCEIVED CLUSTERS (WEEK 14, YEAR II)

	Estimates of own agreement with					
	Cluster-A members		Cluster-B members		Pairs in-	
Quartile	by Cl.A	by Cl.B	by Cl.A	by Cl.B	volving #36	Total
Highest	23	8	14	19	8	72
Second	20	11	12	13	8	64
Third	18	15	19	4	12	68
Lowest	11	29	18	6	4	68
TOTAL	72	63	63	42	32	272

at the .05 level with 1 df). Cluster-B members, however, see themselves as agreeing far more closely with each other than with Cluster-A members: the χ^2 value of the distribution $\begin{smallmatrix} 19 & 32 \\ 44 & 10 \end{smallmatrix}$ is 19.57, significant beyond the .001 level with 1 df.

Are the Week-14 estimates any more accurate than those at Week 1? Table 13.10 (which is to be compared with Table 13.3)

Table 13.10. NUMBERS OF WITHIN-CLUSTER AND BETWEEN-CLUSTER PAIRS AT VARIOUS LEVELS OF ACTUAL AGREEMENT IN ORDERING SPRANGER VALUES (WEEK 14, YEAR II)

Agreement quartile	Within Cluster A	Within Cluster B	Across clusters	Involving #36	Total
Highest	10	10	9	4	33
Second	12	5	15	4	36
Third	8	2	17	5	32
Lowest	6	4	22	3	35
TOTAL	36	21	63	16	136

shows that the original error still persists, though less egregiously: Cluster B is still, in fact, characterized by closer agreement than is Cluster A.[2] Both clusters are still wrong in attributing more agreement to Cluster A than to B.

Two sets of findings, each apparently inconsistent with other evidence, may now be brought together. First, both clusters agree that there is more agreement within Cluster A than B, and both are wrong. Secondly, Cluster-B members see *more* agreement within each cluster than do members of Cluster A, but *less* agreement on the part of between-cluster pairs. Is there any way in which all of these findings can be accounted for?

The latter set of findings is consistent with the interpretation that Cluster-B members are more interested in, more sensitive to, and more aware of subjects' positions on Spranger Values than are Cluster-A members (see pp. 240–241). But this would not account for their being wrong in seeing more agreement within Cluster A than within their own cluster—though it is not incon-

[2] As shown in Table 13.10, the differences between the two clusters are not significant, but if the distributions are trichotomized they become so, at <.05.

sistent with the fact, since they are not quite as wrong about it as are the members of Cluster A.

By way of further interpretation, the following considerations are at least plausible. First, the members of Cluster B, being both relatively concerned about Spranger-like values and aware of their own disagreement with Cluster-A members, tend to exaggerate this disagreement. Secondly, Cluster-B members generally held Cluster-A members in rather low esteem and, being relatively popular and thus "in a position to choose," spent little time with them. Thus their autistic exaggerations of disagreement were nourished by noncommunication. Simultaneously, constant communication amongst themselves increased their store of information about each other, and increased awareness of within-cluster differences. Thus, as is so often the rule, groups which are socially distant seem more homogeneous and more different from one's own group than they really are, whereas small differences within one's own group are noticed, and even become important.

Why do not these same considerations apply also to Cluster A which, contrary to Cluster B, overestimates its own and underestimates the other cluster's degree of internal agreement? There are two kinds of considerations which together produce this result. First, the members of Cluster A are (relatively speaking) unfamiliar with and/or indifferent to other individuals' preferences on Spranger Values—including those of other members of Cluster A. Secondly, it is not to be expected that the pooled estimates of Cluster-A members would have distinctive properties comparable to those of Cluster B, because Cluster A does not constitute a cohesive group; it includes a cohesive triad (#38, 46, 50), and two members (#40, 44) of a second cohesive triad which is not at all close to the first one, together with the three most unpopular of the seventeen members (#35, 41, 48) and one relatively unpopular individual (#37) whose extra-House ties appeared to be closer than his ties within the House. It is hardly surprising that such a set of individuals is characterized by relative randomness of pooled estimates, on the one hand, nor that, on the other, their pooled estimates do not show the characteristics to be expected of a cohesive group.

The evidence for Cluster A's relative ignorance of or indifference to others' preferences in Spranger Values is as follows. First, Cluster-A members tend to be less accurate than Cluster B, as estimators. Ignoring #36 (who is in neither cluster), three of Cluster A's nine members (or 33 percent) are in the upper half of the 17 *S*s in accuracy, and five of Cluster B's seven members (or 71 percent) are in the upper half. Second, Cluster-B members are more discriminating; the distributions of their estimates are often bimodal—they tend to see much agreement and also much disagreement—while those of Cluster A reveal almost no bimodality: they tend to see either high agreement (J-curves) or moderate (bell-shaped curves) agreement as characteristic of the entire population. Third, if instability over time in rank-ordering the Spranger Values may be taken as an indicator of indifference to those values, than by this criterion also Cluster A exceeds Cluster B in indifference. Cluster B's mean self-correlation (*rho*) over a three-month interval is .89, and Cluster A's is .68; for no member of Cluster B is this index lower than .77, whereas it is lower than .77 for four of Cluster A's nine members, and actually negative for one (#35). And, finally, Cluster B is in fact relatively distinctive and homogeneous in rank-ordering Spranger Values, while Cluster A is not. The mean *rho* of actual agreement among Cluster-A pairs is .17, and among Cluster-B pairs .39. (If a single individual, #39, is excluded from Cluster B, its mean *rho* of actual agreement rises to .70, whereas there is no single member of Cluster A whose subtraction makes much difference, and in Cluster A individual members' *rhos* of mean agreement with other members ranges between —.08 and .40.)

Early Group-perceived Agreement as a Predictor of Subsequent Attraction Structure

Figure 13.1 presents a sociogram, in which all pairs of *S*s whose pair scores of attraction at Week 15 reach the 95-percent criterion, or which are included in triads or larger sets that meet the same criterion, are connected by straight lines; and in which a wavy line separates the two group-perceived clusters, as of Week 2. The sociogram illustrates the rather considerable accuracy with which Week-2 stereotypes predicted to subgroup structuring, nearly four months later. There are at Week 15 more high-attraction bonds within than not within the two Week-2 clusters—14 of a possible

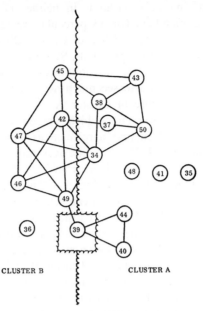

Fig. 13.1. Sociogram showing high-attraction bonds at Week 15, as related to group-perceived agreement clusters at Week 2. See text for details.

31 as compared with 10 of a possible 47; the difference is significant at $< .05$.[3]

At Week 2, as shown in Fig. 13.2, S #34 had been assigned (erroneously) to agreement Cluster A. At some time between then and Week 14 (probably rather soon, though the relevant data were not obtained during the interval) #34 came to be seen, correctly, as more closely in agreement with Cluster B.[4] Figure 13.3 shows the relationship between the Week-14 perceived-agreement clusters and the actual subgroup structuring at Week 15. We believe that the same sociogram would be essentially accurate for Week 5 or 6. As of a time not much later than that, at any rate, the group-perceived agreement structure must have corresponded rather closely to the attraction structure, as the latter was

[3] This computation is based upon only the 13 Ss who were involved in one or more pairs reaching the 95-percent level of pair attraction. See p. 243 for a rationale for this procedure.

[4] Early in this interval it became generally known that #34 had shifted from the Engineering to the Arts College, and this may well have coincided with changing stereotypes about him.

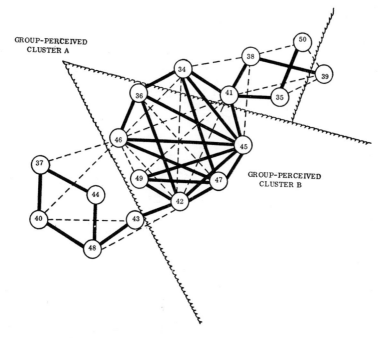

Fig. 13.2. Sociogram of actual agreement about Spranger Values (Week 2, Year II). Heavy solid lines indicate actual agreement in highest quarter of total distribution; dashed lines indicate agreement in second quarter. Wavy lines separate group-perceived agreement clusters (second-quarter agreements are indicated only if they complete a triad including at least one highest-quarter agreement).

becoming stabilized. And by Week 14 the correspondence pictured in Fig. 13.3 is as shown, quantitatively, in Table 13.11A. In Table 13.11B the same relationships are shown, with the single exception that all Ss who are involved in no attraction pairs that reach criterion are excluded; the rationale for this procedure is simply that considerations of low popularity status are irrelevant to the hypotheses that we are interested in testing. That is, we wish to test the prediction that, among all Ss who are involved in one or more high-attraction pairs, more of the latter will be found within the group-perceived agreement clusters than across them. We have no theoretical basis for predicting which Ss' personality characteristics will be such that they are included in no high-attraction pairs at all.

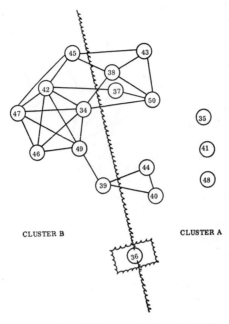

Fig. 13.3. Sociogram showing high-attraction bonds at Week 15, as related to group-perceived agreement clusters at Week 14.

Table 13.11. NUMBERS OF PAIRS AT TWO LEVELS OF ATTRACTION WITHIN AND ACROSS GROUP-PERCEIVED AGREEMENT CLUSTERS (WEEKS 14, 15, YEAR II)

	A. Including all 16 Ss in the two clusters.			*B. Including only 13 Ss in $\geqq 1$ high-attraction pair.*		
	High-attraction pairs	*Other pairs*	*Total*	*High-attraction pairs*	*Other pairs*	*Total*
Within-cluster	18	39	57	18	18	36
Across-clusters	7	56	63	7	35	42
TOTAL	25	95	120	25	53	78
	$\chi^2 = 6.40$			$\chi^2 = 8.52$		
	$p < .02$ (1 df)			$p < .005$ (1 df)		

Sources of the Stereotypes

The Week-2 estimates of agreement, in combination with the Week-14 patterns of high attraction, present an interesting problem. According to the early group estimates, Cluster-A members are in rather close agreement about Spranger Values and Cluster-B members are not. Both judgments are in error: the facts are exactly the reverse. Why, then, should these erroneous early estimates predict so well to attraction relationships nearly four months later?

The most likely interpretation, we believe, is somewhat as follows. First, in one fundamental respect the early estimates were not in error—namely, that they distinguished between two sets of individuals whose values were in fact different. The sociogram of actual agreement at Week 2 (Fig. 13.2)—in which all pairs in the highest quarter of all 136 pairs in actual agreement are shown by heavy connecting lines, and those in the second quarter by lighter ones, while the boundaries between the group-perceived clusters at Week 2 are marked off by wavy lines—illustrates the essential correctness of the perceived clusters. Apart from Ss #34 and 41, whose actual agreements are closer with Cluster B than with A, it is clear that Cluster B is correctly distinguished from the remaining individuals. Ignoring these two misplaced Ss altogether, for the moment, there is only 1 of a possible 48 across-cluster pairs that are in fact in the highest quarter of agreement, as compared with 13 of 15 possible within Cluster B, and 8 of a possible 28 within Cluster A. With the exception of two "misplaced persons," then, the group estimates corresponded to real differences.[5]

From this essentially correct base, in the second place, the Week-2 estimators seem to have made some erroneous inferences —to the general effect that "nonurbanites think alike," and, correspondingly, that urbanites neither think alike nor agree with nonurbanites. The interesting thing about these inferences (which we, in turn, can only infer) is that they seem to have been made in

[5] The subsequent fate of these two Ss is interesting. One of them, whose general popularity became conspicuously highest among all Ss, developed very high (95-percent criterion) pair-attraction relationships with three members of the Week-2 Cluster B, and with two members of Cluster A. The other, whose popularity status became the lowest of all 17 Ss, developed high pair-attraction relationships with no one. Thus, in opposite ways, both of these misplaced individuals later became marginal to the two clusters.

Group Stereotypes of Individuals' Agreement ——————— **245**

similar ways by members of both clusters. Why such inferences should have been made by either cluster is a bit of a problem, but why the two clusters should have agreed so well about it is a still more difficult one.

Our evidence is consistent with the interpretation that most Cluster-A members were, in characteristically ethnocentric manner, devoted to a set of rather conventional values which its members tended to attribute to one another and which Cluster-B members also attributed to them. What neither set of estimators realized, at this time, was that (as shown in Figure 13.2) Cluster A was in fact divided into two subclusters of agreement. Ss #34, 35, 38, 41, 50 actually ranked religious values low and (except for #34) economic value high, while Ss #37, 40, 43, 44, 48 reversed these rankings. Thus both clusters, as sets of estimators, were essentially correct about the general conventionality of most Cluster-A members, but wrong in viewing them as homogeneous in ranking these particular values.

The evidence suggests, similarly, that the members of Cluster B tended to regard themselves (and to be regarded by the others) as unconventional.[6] To Cluster-A members, unconventionality apparently connoted idiosyncracy; moreover, they were decidedly inaccurate in estimating Cluster-B members, with almost perfect uniformity attributing extreme disagreement with themselves to those to whom they were least attracted. Cluster-B members, on the other hand, were quite accurate in estimating each other, but tended to underestimate their own actual agreement—thus preserving the self-image of nonconformity.

These interpretations would account, in a consistent way, for the fact that members of both clusters exaggerated agreement in Cluster A and underestimated it in Cluster B.

Consequences of the Stereotypes

A more interesting question has to do with the *consequences* of the consensual stereotypes at Week 2, whatever their sources. It

---

[6] Among other evidence for this statement, and also for comparable ones in the preceding paragraph, are self-checks on the adjective check-list, responded to by all Ss at several scattered times. The adjectives "unconventional," "progressive," and "sophisticated" were self-checked almost exclusively by Cluster-B members, and one or more of these three were self-checked by every member of Cluster B. The same adjectives were applied more frequently by others *to* Cluster-B than to Cluster-A members, also.

seems likely that the early stereotyping reflected existing loyalties, on the part of most members of both clusters, to value systems associated both with previously known groups (family and community, for example) and with subgroups within the House. We think it also likely that the stereotyping heightened such loyalties, vis-à-vis subgroups in the House, and it is even conceivable that it in some cases created new loyalties of this kind. If so, this is equivalent to saying that the new systems of orientation—both individual and collective—that inevitably evolved while making new acquaintances tended to focus on sets of values associated with the stereotyping that we have described, and that subsequent relationships of interpersonal attraction were influenced by this fact.

Perhaps the most significant thing about the collective stereotypes is that they changed so little between Weeks 2 and 14. Only three individuals show any change during this interval in assigned cluster membership: two of these three are marginal at one time or the other, and only one is changed from one cluster to the other (having been grossly misplaced, initially). Further, both sets of estimates are characterized by the same errors: the actually nonagreeing Cluster A is consensually viewed as agreeing closely at both times, while the actually agreeing Cluster B is not so viewed (though more nearly so at the later time). Errors and all, the stereotypes remained almost unchanged.

Things persist, however, not merely because they got started but rather because of a persisting balance of forces by which they are maintained. In spite of the group's errors in differentiating cluster members' Spranger Values, we have maintained that the cluster differentiation corresponded to something real—something more closely resembling authoritarianism (with all its syndrome implications) than Spranger Values. We suspect that estimates of almost any other set of generalized values would have shown about the same cluster differentiations as those resulting from estimates of Spranger Values, which served as a sort of projective device for eliciting latent rather than manifest values. If so, then the fairly close relationship between the group-perceived clustering and the actual attraction structure of the total group can best be understood by assuming that both are influenced by reasonably accurate group judgments as to some fundamental values held by its members.

Viewed in this light, our question whether early stereotyping had subsequent effects upon the group's attraction structure breaks down into two questions: the effects of the *early* emergence of the stereotyping, and the effects of the *consensual* nature of the stereotypes. To both questions we propose a qualified affirmative. The basis for our considering it probable that the earliness of the stereotype formation had effects is simply the general proposition that early perceptions of things tend to preempt the field; granted only that the early ones provide a viable basis for adaptation to the phenomenon perceived, later ways of perceiving things, if they conflict with original ones, tend not to be accepted. The principal implication of this proposition for our present problem is as follows. Insofar as individuals, at an early stage of acquaintance, fitted themselves as well as others into the group-perceived stereotypes, their early attraction choices would be thereby influenced; and insofar as such early attraction choices proved balance-inducing, they would tend to be permanent (and, incidentally, the stereotypes would tend to persist). We think it altogether likely that the early and prominent emphasis, in this population, upon whether or not one was an "Eastern sophisticate" influenced several, if not many, individuals to assess themselves and others in terms relevant to that distinction; and that this way of looking at things persisted —partly because it had a basis in fact. At any rate the gradually emerging attraction structure was such that it fits in well with such reasoning.

Our conclusion that the consensual nature of the stereotyping probably had effects upon subsequent attraction structuring rests, similarly, upon a general proposition, sometimes referred to by the phrase "social reality." When our impressions (for example, of nonmaterial things) cannot readily be verified by direct sensory processes, we tend to rely upon consensual validation: if every one says it is so, then for all practical purposes it *is* so. There are many areas of life (such as agreeing to drive on the right side of the street) where the *fact* of consensus is more important than its content, and the tendency to accept consensus as adequate validation often extends into areas where other means of validation are actually available. We suspect that the ways in which our subjects assessed each other (and even themselves) were in many cases affected by the kind of consensus that was reflected in the stereotypes about who agreed with whom. The observed "fact" of consensus created a world of social reality which could hardly have failed to influence attraction choices.

Thus the early stereotypes about value agreement, which in a literal sense were rather inaccurate, could hardly have been *directly* responsible for the subsequent attraction structure. Rather, they revealed a general recognition of individual differences concerning rather basic values, and it was these differences—which in any case would have been discovered, in some degree, sooner or later— that contributed directly to the attraction structure. The effects of the early stereotyping, we suspect, were to hasten the recognition of individuals' values of a certain kind, and to intensify their importance. In these indirect ways the early stereotyping had effects upon attraction structure.

THE ACQUAINTANCE PROCESS VIEWED AS INTERACTION AMONG PERSONS

To say that the attraction structure in Year II came to parallel both the perceived and the actual agreement structure with respect to Spranger Values (as illustrated in Figs. 13.2 and 13.3) is equivalent to saying that individual and collective systems tended toward balance—which is the central thesis of the present study. But we do not wish to leave the impression that the only common object of orientation that was involved in balanced systems, in this population, was this particular set of values. Indeed, we suspect (particularly in view of the considerable inaccuracy of the estimates) that the Spranger Values served as a projective device, so that responses to it were determined in considerable part by response sets quite irrelevant to the ostensible basis for the estimates. As to what determined these response sets, there is substantial evidence to suggest that they were associated with urban background, with maturity, and with college of enrollment (which were known to all) and also with authoritarianism, which was presumably not known.

Regardless of the exact nature of their actual determinants, the estimates had two properties that are central to our problem: they were highly consensual, and they divided the population into two subpopulations. We may, in fact, treat these two properties as one: the consensually viewed division of the population. And since, as we have shown, this consensual division (or stereotyping, as we have called it) has a good deal to do with the eventual structure of interpersonal attraction, the question of the sources of the consensually perceived division of the population is an important one.

It is evident, in the first place, that the degree of consensuality exceeds that which would be predicted from our propositions about balance. There are many pairs of individuals whose attraction toward each other is low (as well as many high-attraction pairs) who make similar estimates of others' Spranger-Value responses. The consensus is essentially population-wide.

It seems to us improbable that this degree of consensuality could have occurred—especially if, as we have argued, the responses by which the consensus is revealed were of somewhat projective nature—in the absence of any one of three conditions. First, there must have been some set of personal characteristics that was salient for the whole population, regardless of consensuality in evaluating those characteristics. Nearly all House members must have been more or less agreed on a basis for categorizing each other. If so, there was consensus about the basis for categorizing. Second, such consensual salience—on the part of a group of initial strangers with respect to each other—presupposes communication sufficient in volume and of such nature that the mode of categorizing each other became accepted by nearly all individuals. And, third, such general acceptance of the mode of categorizing could not have occurred in the absence of some factual (or apparently factual) basis—such as urban background, maturity, and college of enrollment. We have presented presumptive evidence to suggest that all these conditions were met in this population. The consequence was that the House members, through the communication process by which the categories became salient, *created* a set of norms for judging each other. As such, it helped to determine interpersonal attraction, and thus served as one of the bases for achieving system balance.

We stress the point that House members themselves *created* this set of norms because we believe that the process by which certain among various potential alternatives are made salient and consensual is an essential ingredient of the acquaintance process. These norms were presumably specific to this particular population, and their content did not correspond to anything that we observed in Year I. They evolved, we believe, because our subjects presented some rather obvious differences (especially those related to urban sophistication as opposed to nonurban conventionality), and because such differences were noted, talked about, and made salient. In other populations other differences might be noted. We even suspect that different ones might have been noted in this one. At any rate, the evolvement of certain kinds of acceptable norms was made possible by the selection of our subjects (e.g., the fact that actual urban-nonurban differences were associated with college of enrollment), and was made certain by their behavior (e.g., certain individuals conspicuously called attention to such differences).

The fact that one set of norms rather than some other was created almost certainly meant that some sets of interpersonal attraction developed while others that might have developed did not. Although we have shown (in Chapter 5) that in a statistical sense it was possible to predict high attraction from pre-acquaintance information, this success may have been made possible by certain unpredictable aspects of the process by which population norms were created. The success of the prediction depends *both* upon the properties that individuals brought with them—including their orientations, of course—*and* upon the not altogether predictable circumstances by which certain among those properties became the basis for a salient and consensual set of norms.

Finally, these considerations have a bearing upon the place of our theory in accounting for the outcomes of acquaintance. We have no reason to revise our initial assumption that, regardless of the content of sets of norms that groups create for themselves, their members adapt to each other and to their common world in balance-promoting ways. But balance-promoting adaptations, as we think we have learned from evidence like that presented in this chapter, are not just automatic outcomes, passively experienced, of the given packages of orientations that strangers present to one another. Also included in the packages are individual histories and individual properties which, in a formal sense, are irrelevant to our particular theory but which may be crucial determinants of the interactional setting within which balance-promoting adaptations occur. The achievement of balance is a consequence not just of disembodied forces—which are only abstractions helpful in accounting for palpable events—but, in fuller perspective, of the multiply-determined behavior of individuals and groups as they respond to and are responded to by one another.

PART SIX

The Acquaintance Process

We introduced the formulation in terms of which this study was planned with the truism that stable systems are likely to be balanced systems. Our objective has been not to defend a truism that in any case is logically unassailable, but rather to provide empirical support for a particular set of propositions concerning what constitutes balance in interpersonal systems.

In the first of our two chapters devoted to a final overview we shall attempt to assess our findings, selectively—rather than to review them (summaries appear in the several chapters in Parts Two to Five)—in the perspective of a general theory of the changes that occur as individuals become acquainted with one another. And in the final chapter we shall briefly point to some ways in which an understanding of the phenomena of acquaintance may contribute to the more general problem of human interaction.

Individual Changes toward
Balanced Collective Systems

14

CHANGES IN INDIVIDUAL ORIENTATIONS

We shall begin with individuals' changes—not because they are more basic in any causative sense than group changes (we regard the two as continually interdependent), but simply because, according to our formulation, individual orientations are the elemental components of systems, both individual and collective. Thus the most elementary way of describing changes in either kind of system is in terms of individual orientations.

We found little change in individuals' attitudes during the four months of our data-gathering—or, more accurately, we found little change in those attitudes that were systematically related to attraction. We may have sampled too limited a range of attitudes, but there are good grounds for suspecting that most attitudes of sufficient importance to our subjects to influence their attraction toward others had already achieved such stability, before they met each other, that not much change was to be expected during so brief a period.

House members' orientations toward each other—that is to say, their attractions—had, however, no previous history, and they changed a good deal from first to last. These changes accounted in considerable part for the maintenance of individual balance and the achievement of collective balance. That is, as individuals acquired more information about each others' attitudes, their high-attraction preferences tended to change in favor of individuals with whom they were more closely in agreement.

Such balance-promoting changes in attraction presuppose one other kind of change—namely, in judgments of others' orientations. With the acquisition of new information about each other, estimates of others' orientations tended to become more accurate, and the preponderance of changes in attraction were thus influenced by considerations of reality. But estimates also changed in ways that were balance-promoting without being more accurate; in such cases the changed estimates served to maintain balance in individual systems involving highly attractive others without lowering the level of attraction.

Thus, among the three components of individual systems—attraction, attitudes, and perceived orientations of others—only the first and third changed very much. If a balance-maintaining change in *either* of these occurs, in an individual system, then a change in the other is not necessary for the maintenance of balance. By the same token, if balance is disturbed by the receipt of new information about another person, a change in one or the other, or in both, is required if balance is to be restored. We found evidence to suggest, if not to prove, that some individuals (especially those low in authoritarianism) tended to achieve balance by increasing the accuracy of their estimates of others' orientations and changing their attraction preferences accordingly. Others tended to maintain high-attraction preferences that had been established early, and to maintain balance by autistic distortions of others' orientations. A few individuals seemed relatively immune to considerations of balance, though not with complete consistency. In general, however—as shown by changes of either kind, separately—it must be concluded that nearly all members of each population made balance-maintaining changes of both kinds.

In sum, nearly all of our subjects organized their first impressions of each others' attractiveness and of each others' orientations in such ways that, given their own existing orientations, individual systems were in balance at the outset. And in general they processed subsequent information about each other in ways that resulted in *changing* attraction preferences and in *changing* perceptions of each others' orientations—while simultaneously *maintaining* balanced individual systems. Thus changes which might otherwise appear haphazard come to be seen as orderly, and in some degree predictable.

CHANGES IN COLLECTIVE SYSTEMS

The components of collective systems, as we noted in Chapter 2, are relationships among analogous orientations of individuals—orientations toward each other, toward other persons, or toward nonperson objects. Since actual (as distinguished from perceived) changes in orientations toward objects other than House members were slight, our discussion of changes in collective systems will be limited to interpersonal attraction among our subjects. Such changes may be regarded as changes in within-population structuring, which appear in the form of increasing numbers of increasingly large and increasingly stable high-attraction subgroups. These changes occur as a special case of the general principle of balance, which may be stated as follows: pairs of persons who are highly attracted toward the same person(s) tend to become highly attracted toward each other. Thus high-attraction triads form around high-attraction pairs as (sociographically portrayed) the unconnected ends of a three-person chain close to form a triangle. Similarly, individuals whose bonds of attraction to one or two members of a high-attraction triad are strong tend to be "adopted" by the other members. Such are the consequences of the principle of balance for high-attraction structuring of a population.

There are limits, however, to this process—limits imposed, in particular, by demands for balance with regard to objects other than House members. We found that this accretive process developed further in one of our populations (which eventually developed a centrally organized structure) than in the other (which developed a more divisive structure). This difference is pretty well accounted for by the fact that the highly popular individuals (whose personal characteristics were such that nearly all others were positively attracted toward them) in the former population but not in the latter were highly attracted toward each other. And this in turn we accounted for by the fact that in the former population but not in the latter the popular individuals shared many values of importance to them. Thus population structuring is determined by changes in attraction that are balance-promoting not just with respect to House members but also with respect to pre-acquaintance values, and by interaction effects between these sources of change and the personal characteristics of members.

Our evidence appears to show, nevertheless, that in general the contribution of individuals' personal characteristics to population structuring did not outweigh that of balance-promoting influences. In each population there were a few individuals whose characteristics were so conspicuous that they were judged in extreme, consensual, and stable manner by their peers. Personal evaluations of the great majority of our subjects were not highly consensual, however, and changed a good deal from first to last. They changed, moreover—as did the more direct indices of attraction—in balance-promoting ways. Hence we conclude, not that personal characteristics made no contribution to the eventual attraction structure, but that the perception of personal characteristics became fitted into, and in some degree determined by, balance-promoting tendencies.

Unpredictable events, too—such as those which resulted in the early, persistent, and stereotyped categorizing of House members by each other in one population—have their effects upon the structuring of attraction. But these effects, like those of personal characteristics, seem not to be opposed to those of balance-promoting tendencies—tendencies, which may, in fact, help to precipitate the "unpredictable" events. In any case their effects are guided and probably enhanced by tendencies toward balance.

GROUP PROPERTIES AS VARYING WITH STAGES OF ACQUAINTANCE

We have from time to time pointed out certain differences between our two populations, because we wish to guard against oversimple generalizations about developmental stages throughout the acquaintance process. But it is equally important, we believe, not to overlook genuine developmental phenomena, if such there be. Since we cannot, in any event, generalize from only two rather special populations of very similar nature, we shall be content to point out that such changes as we have found in either or both of our populations *might* also occur in others. And insofar as some of these changes prove, through subsequent evidence, to be rather dependable ones then, *a fortiori,* generalizations about group properties must take groups' acquaintance histories into account.

We have found, for example, that in some respects there is a closer resemblance between very early and final population structuring than between second- or third-week and final structuring—though when one takes into account the stability of such structuring the discontinuities disappear. We have seen that it takes time for the divisiveness of one population, and the centrality of the other, to develop. Consensuality within a population tends to increase with continued acquaintance, perhaps for the population as a whole or perhaps only for subgroups within it; in either case group norms change. Most importantly, from our theoretical point of view, the achievement of balance in collective systems presupposes sufficient time for group members to explore each others' orientations. Thus—though not necessarily in standard, universal ways—generalizations about interpersonal relationships or structure or norms within a given group at a given time are dependent (whether or not the fact is stated) upon conditions which vary with the interactional history of that group's members.

Social-psychological propositions, as they appear in the literature, are often based upon findings (particularly experimental ones) from groups whose acquaintance history scarcely exceeds one hour. Others are supported by observations of groups (especially "natural" ones) whose history is long but relatively unknown. Perhaps longitudinal studies, like the present one, which begin at the point of first acquaintance but do not end there, can be of service in sorting out those propositions which are dependent upon given stages of acquaintance. Such studies might, in fact, contribute propositions of their own.

The Acquaintance Process as a Prototype of Human Interaction

15

In almost any face-to-face encounter of two or more human beings, processes occur that are acquaintance-like. Participants, however familiar with one another they may already be, acquire information about each other, assess one another's attitudes, and either reinforce existing states of orientation toward each other and toward the common world, or change them, or develop new ones. Such, according to our point of view, are the components of the acquaintance process. We have already made it clear that we view these subprocesses as interdependent, in ways that are governed by the principles of balance in individual and collective systems. But our present, and final, concern is to portray the general principles of balance as subsidiary to still more general ones.

La condition humaine, as we view it, is such that individuals continually face a three-pronged problem of adaptation. Each of us must somehow come to terms, simultaneously, with the other individuals and groups of which our interpersonal environment is constituted, with the world that we have in common with those persons and groups, and with our own, intrapersonal autistic demands. Were it not for this ever-present, triple confrontation, problems of strain and balance would not arise—and the acquaintance process might prove simpler to account for.

We face, in each of the three directions, forces that are ineluctable. We ignore properties of the "real" world at our peril. Stones will bruise, and fire will burn—these things we learn by direct, sensory experience, aided and abetted by the teaching of others. So far, there is no problem in confronting the interpersonal world and the world of common objects, but nevertheless a future problem is in the making. As we find that our own experience and the testimony of persons whom we trust are mutually reinforcing, we tend to rely on the latter—it short-circuits trial and error, enables us to avoid painful experiences, often leads to direct satisfaction. And so their testimony, too, is ignored at our peril. But the time comes when the two sources of evidence do not reinforce each other, but yield conflicting evidence: our senses, or our own inferences therefrom, tell us one thing and our associates another. Or—especially when direct sensory experience is limited, or inaccessible—two trusted human sources give different testimony. How then shall we know the "real" nature of things? It is out of such a history—presumably universal to all humans, and perhaps unique to them—that intrapersonal demands for balance arise. The world is at odds if one's own sources of conviction are contravened by those whom one has reason to trust.[1] Thus we become sensitive to the acquired, drive-like state of strain, and it, too, is ineluctable in that for most individuals it is potentially ever-present; like other states of drive, it may be tolerated, for a time at least, but whether endured or appeased it influences behavior.

Thus we view balance-promoting changes in orientations as adaptations to the triple confrontation of immediate interpersonal environment, common world, and acquired sensitivity to strain. Insofar as such adaptations minimize the testimony of one's senses and maximize the testimony of trusted others, we are apt to regard them as overconforming (see Asch, 1951). If these tendencies are reversed (or if there are no trusted others), we regard the adaptations as individualistic, unsocialized, or even antisocial. Insofar as they are characterized by distortion of the testimony of others in balance-maintaining fashion—so that one's orientations neither toward those others nor toward the common world need be changed —we have referred to them as autistic. And insofar as balance is achieved by changing one's own orientations (either attitudes or attractions) rather than by distortions of others' orientations, the adaptations may, contrariwise, be regarded as realistic.

Finally, there is a special consequence of continued acquaintance—or even, not infrequently, of brief episodes of interaction—which, while neither inevitable nor universal, is so common and

---

[1] With respect to our own measures of attraction, as reported in this monograph, we have assumed that high-attraction preferences have, as one of their determinants, at least a moderately high degree of trust.

so important—and so closely associated with the principles of balance—that we regard it as a kind of theoretical capstone. We have, implicitly at least, regarded the process of reciprocal scanning of each others' orientations as a crucial part of the interactional behavior that goes on between persons who are getting acquainted. The consequence of this process is some delineation, however, partial, of the *area of mutually shared orientations.* (The term "shared" may be defined either individually, as that which a person experiences as common to himself and others; or collectively, as that which all of a set of persons experience as common to all of them. We refer to the former as *subjectively* and to the latter as *mutually* shared. See French, 1959, p. III, 13; Newcomb, 1950, pp. 35 ff.) Following any opportunity for reciprocal scanning—even a brief one on early acquaintance—there is apt to be some delineation on the part of the interacting persons of the area of mutually shared orientations—of at least some small sector about which they agree that they agree or disagree. With repeated opportunities for reciprocal scanning, the lines of delineation become increasingly clear; as each of the interacting persons becomes more certain of just what its confines are—as they become more sure of a larger area of agreements and disagreements—they "know" each other—including each others' orientations—increasingly well.

Among other possible outcomes of an increasingly clear delineation of the area of mutually shared orientations is one that is of crucial importance to our problem, as presented in our opening pages: the understanding of the development of stable interpersonal relationships. This possible outcome is an area of mutually shared orientations *including those of high importance* to those who share them. Collective systems may be in balance—or at any rate not out of balance—without mutually shared orientations of importance, providing attraction is not high, whereas high-attraction collective systems will not remain in balance without them. And it is high-attraction systems that are most dependably stable throughout the vicissitudes of time and space.

The most stable of interpersonal relationships, in short, are those characterized by both system balance and high attraction—a combination that presupposes an area of mutually shared orientations of importance to system members.

APPENDIXES

The Attitude Items ──────────── **I**

The following battery of items was responded to in its entirety at Weeks 0 and 15, and in part at various intervening times—in particular at times when an evening discussion had dealt with an issue closely related to one or more of the items. Each item was responded to at least three times between Weeks 0 and 15. The 35 items were arranged in seven families of five issues each. The descriptive labels for each of the seven families of issues, as they appear below, did not appear on the questionnaires.

DIRECTIONS

On the following pages 35 questions are asked. Below each question you will find five alternative answers. In the spaces at *the far left* you are to check those answers which are acceptable to you as answers to the questions. It may be that none of these answers are acceptable to you; it may be that they all are. You are to *check those which are acceptable* answers to you.

In the next spaces (*second column*) you are to *rank-order* the five alternatives in terms of their acceptability. That is, put a "1" before the alternative that is most acceptable to you, a "2" before the alternative that is next most acceptable, and so on until you have put a "5" before the alternative that is least acceptable to you.

I. House Policies

1. How should this group set up its cooking and eating arrangements?
   a. Everyone eat out; use dining room as a lounge.
   b. Hire some one to cook, serve, and clean up.
   c. Hire a cook, and all members pitch in and serve and clean up.
   d. Members cook and eat in groups of 3 or 4, working separately.
   e. Members all eat together; groups of 3 or 4 take turns cooking, serving, and cleaning up.
2. How should this group arrange for care and cleaning of the House, outside of kitchen and own rooms?
   a. Hire a maid to do all the cleaning, everyone chipping in to pay her.
   b. Everyone pitch in and do his share where he can; make no assignments.
   c. Entire group work together at specified times every week.
   d. Divide into teams, one team doing all the work for a week or so, another for the next week or so, and so on.
   e. Divide into teams, and give each team part of the work, with teams rotating jobs every week or so.
3. About what kinds of things will formal rules be needed in the House?
   a. No formal rules; everyone just respect everyone else's rights.
   b. Only rules about work assignments in the House.
   c. Rules about work assignments and about study hours.
   d. Rules about work assignments, study hours, and methods of handling any grievance that a member may have.
   e. Rules about all of the above, and also some formal rules about penalizing members who break rules.
4. To what extent should the House be formally organized to handle its problems?
   a. No organization needed; decide things as they come up, as a group.
   b. No permanent organization; set up committees to work out problems as they come up.
   c. Elect a permanent House committee, to work out problems that arise, and make recommendations to the group.
   d. Elect one man to be president or House chairman, and let him set up committees to take care of problems that arise.

The Attitude Items ———————————————————— **265**

e. Elect one man president or chairman; also elect permanent House committees; these people will work out problems and decide about them as they come up.

5. To begin with, rooms have been assigned at random. What should be the policy about changes in room assignments?

a. Leave them alone; make no changes and permit none.

b. Make random re-assignments, so no one gets stuck with a poor room.

c. Everyone indicate his preferences in a secret ballot, and let the research team work out a "best" solution.

d. Everyone indicate his preferences in open session, and work out a plan to suit all as well as possible.

e. Let members work out "switches" among themselves.

II. University Policies

1. The University publishes *The Michigan Daily*, a newspaper managed and edited by students. How much control should the University exercise over *The Daily*?

a. No control over student publications.

b. A very limited control—only to the extent of insisting on decency and good taste in what is published.

c. A fair amount of control—to insure decency and good taste, and to see that University officials and policies are not unduly criticized.

d. Tight control—as to good taste and as to any criticism of University policies and officials.

e. Complete control over student publications, checking all material before it is printed, and directing editorial policy.

2. What should be the University's policy concerning student use of cars?

a. No restrictions; students have as much legal right to drive as anyone else.

b. No restrictions except for students who have a history of misdemeanors or undesirable behavior.

c. Permission to drive cars only for "business" purposes, not for pleasure driving.

d. Permission to drive cars restricted to those few who have exceptionally good reasons for needing a car.

e. No students permitted to drive cars at this University.

3. What should the University's policy be concerning fraternity bias clauses which bar racial and/or religious groups from their membership?

   a. Strictly hands off; students have a right to choose those whom they want to associate with, in any way they want to.
   b. Encourage fraternities to remove such bias clauses if their national organization will permit it.
   c. Strongly urge fraternities to remove such bias clauses, and refuse to permit any new fraternities to come on campus if they have such bias clauses.
   d. Order fraternities to remove such bias clauses within the next couple of years or else be banned from the University.
   e. Order fraternities to remove such bias clauses immediately or else be banned from the University.

4. The student government at the University of Michigan is called the Student Legislature. How much power or authority should the Student Legislature have?

   a. It should be abolished; let students study and let the administration and faculty run the University.
   b. It should be continued, but only as a forum for airing student opinion.
   c. It should function as an advisory body for the administration and faculty.
   d. It should have some authority in matters directly related to student affairs.
   e. It should have complete authority in matters related to student affairs.

5. How closely should the University supervise women students regarding hours, conduct, etc.?

   a. No supervision; college students should be mature enough to run their own lives.
   b. The same supervision as men students.
   c. Supervision when and only to the extent that the girl's parents request it.
   d. Fairly close supervision of all women students who are not yet 21, but very little of those who are 21 or older.
   e. Close supervision of all women students, since the University is responsible to their parents for their conduct.

The Attitude Items ———————————————— **267**

III. Personal Behavior

1. What should a young man do if his boss has given him what seems like a raw deal?
   a. Go to him, tell him off, and quit.
   b. Let the boss know how he feels, and give warning that he won't stand for such treatment again.
   c. Go to him and talk it over; try to see the boss's side of it, and try to make the boss understand how he feels about it.
   d. Forget it; getting sore about it just makes things worse.
   e. Accept it and realize that the boss probably did it for the employee's own good and for the good of the job and the company.

2. How should male students dress on campus?
   a. They should dress entirely for personal comfort.
   b. Personal comfort is the primary consideration, but with some attention to appearance.
   c. Personal comfort and appearance should be considered equally.
   d. Good appearance is the primary consideration, but with some attention to personal comfort.
   e. Personal comfort should be sacrificed to good appearance.

3. What should be the reading habits of undergraduate men, with respect to extra-curricular (non-required) reading?
   a. Mostly light reading; required reading is enough to take care of the serious side of life.
   b. More light reading than serious reading, but some of both.
   c. A judicious mixture of light and serious reading.
   d. More serious than light reading, but some of both.
   e. Mostly serious reading; students have all the rest of their lives for light reading.

4. To what extent should a person try to become close friends with others?
   a. Be self-sufficient and don't form close ties with anyone; one doesn't get hurt that way.
   b. Form close ties with only a few people who are really understanding and can be trusted.
   c. Become close friends with anyone you trust; a lot of people can be trusted but a lot cannot.
   d. Try to become close friends with all the people you know; most

people will be loyal friends if they know they are trusted, though a few may take advantage of such trust.

e. Let people know you trust them and want to be close friends with them; they will respond in kind.

5. Suppose a man is acting as a student proctor in an examination for some large, introductory course. He sees that his roommate and best friend is cheating in the exam. The roommate is a hard-working though not a brilliant student, and desperately needs a good grade in this course. The decision as to what to do about it is entirely in the proctor's hands, for no one else sees the cheating. What should the proctor do?

a. Take away his exam book and report him for cheating.

b. Prevent him from cheating further, let him finish the exam, and report him for cheating.

c. If he can be led to withdraw from the exam on some excuse, treat him as absent; otherwise report him for cheating.

d. Prevent further cheating but let him finish the exam, and not report him for cheating.

e. Act as if nothing had happened, and not report him for cheating.

IV. Sex and Family

1. How much sex education should parents give their children?

a. None is needed; the child will find out all he needs to know about sex, and soon enough, from his playmates, books, etc.

b. Parents should give their children sex education prior to marriage; before that none is needed.

c. Parents should instruct their children in matters of sex before they are adolescents, so that they will have all the facts before they need them.

d. Parents should answer honestly any questions that their children ask them about sex, at any age.

e. Parents should begin at a very early age to educate their children thoroughly in matters of sex.

2. Who should make family decisions?

a. The husband has responsibility for the family, and therefore should have authority to make all family decisions.

b. The husband should make all family decisions except those involving the care and training of children, in which the wife should share.

   c. The husband should make all family decisions except those about the care and training of children and those of a household nature, which should be the wife's responsibility.

   d. Family decisions should be made by joint agreement of husband and wife, but the husband should make the decisions in cases where they cannot reach an agreement.

   e. Family decisions should all be made by joint agreement between husband and wife.

3. Is it a good idea for a man to marry before finishing college?

   a. No; college students are too young, too financially insecure, and too inexperienced to know what they want.

   b. Usually it's a bad thing, because the husband cannot be the major financial support, and he is not situated in a permanent job.

   c. It depends entirely on the individual case; for some couples it works out well and for others it does not.

   d. Usually it's a good thing, because college couples can pool whatever resources they have, and generally are mature enough to know what they want.

   e. Yes; it should be encouraged because the experience of marriage is good for the student and usually helps him settle down to work harder.

4. What are the proper standards concerning pre-marital and extra-marital sexual activity?

   a. Sexual activity for either men or women before marriage, and extra-marital sexual activity after marriage, are wrong.

   b. Some sexual freedom for men but not for women should be permitted before marriage, but not after marriage for either.

   c. Freedom in sexual activity for both men and women should be permitted before marriage but not afterward.

   d. Both sexes should be allowed sexual freedom before marriage, and some extra-marital activity is OK after marriage for men but not for women.

   e. Both sexes should be allowed sexual freedom both before and after mariage, provided both partners agree on the arrangement.

5. How important is the sex relationship in building a good marriage relationship?

   a. Good marriages are built entirely on grounds other than sex; the sex relationship is of minimal importance.

   b. Good marriages are built primarily on grounds other than sex, but sex is an important factor.

c. Good marriages are built on several grounds, one of which is the sex relationship.

d. Good marriages are built on several grounds, but the sex relationship is the most important factor.

e. Good marriages are based almost entirely on the sex relationship; other factors will be OK if the sex relationship is OK.

V. Religion

1. How should differences between the findings of modern science and religious beliefs be resolved?
   a. Religious viewpoints that differ with the findings of modern science should be abandoned.
   b. Religious viewpoints that differ with the findings of modern science should be re-examined and probably modified to be made compatible with our best current knowledge.
   c. Science and religion each has its own area of applicability, and each is valid only within these limits; let the two get along together, even if in seeming contradiction.
   d. When a scientific finding seems to contradict religious principles, one must find an interpretation of the finding which is compatible with known religious truths.
   e. When a scientific interpretation is not in accord with known religious truths, it is therefore not valid and should be abandoned.

2. How should one regard religious beliefs other than one's own?
   a. With complete appreciation and respect; the powers of the universe reveal themselves in different ways to different people.
   b. With appreciation and respect, but with recognition that some religions are better than others.
   c. With appreciation and respect for the most part, but recognizing that there are some points about which one can only be tolerant.
   d. With tolerance but not appreciation; conflicting beliefs cannot all be right, and it is wrong not to follow the best.
   e. With no tolerance for beliefs that are in error, but with tolerance for the people who mistakenly hold them.

3. To what extent should various religious sects join together, cooperate, or compete with one another?
   a. All should get together, iron out their minor differences, and consolidate into a united religious force.

b. All should get together and work in cooperation, but not unite.

c. Religious groups holding similar views ought to work out differences and consolidate; but others hold totally different views, and thus could not so combine.

d. Different religious groups ought to maintain their own views, and remain separate; but they should not transgress the right of other groups to do the same.

e. If a religious group is convinced of the rightness of its creed, it must try in all peaceful ways to spread that creed to all, and thus may have to compete with other groups for members.

4. How important is being a member of a church or religious organization in leading a good life?

a. To lead a truly religious life, one must be a member of a religious group dedicated to that purpose.

b. Maybe a few exceptional men can lead virtuous lives apart, but for most men it is necessary to share their religious beliefs with others of like mind.

c. One may lead a good life alone, but belonging to a religious group makes it easier and more satisfying through sharing beliefs with others of similar viewpoints.

d. Leading a religious life is a matter of following personal conscience in every-day behavior; there is no need to belong to a formal religious group to do so.

e. Belonging to a formal religious organization can be a hindrance to leading the best religious life, by forcing a man to abandon his own convictions in favor of views which he does not really believe.

5. What should be the place of religion in every-day life?

a. Religion should pervade every area of life, and determine all life decisions.

b. Religion should provide the underlying guiding principles of life, and thus ought to help people make all kinds of decisions.

c. Religious ideals should influence many life decisions, but they do not always provide useful guides for every-day matters.

d. There are definite areas of life where religious ideals should prevail, but there are other areas where decisions must be based on reason and experience.

e. Religious views offer only ideals; real life decisions have little to do with religion, but must be judged entirely on the basis of reason and experience.

VI. Public Affairs

1. What should be our policy toward Russia?
    a. We should try to reach an understanding with Russia, avoiding war if at all possible, exercising great patience.
    b. We should try to get along with Russia, and avoid war unless she directly attacks our own territory.
    c. We should try to avoid war, but also try to keep Russia from further expansion by going to war if necessary.
    d. We should be ready to go to war any time Russia starts or causes trouble anywhere in the world.
    e. We should wage a preventive war against Russia now, while we still have the advantage of superior weapons.
2. What should the United States do in regard to sharing atomic-energy information and resources?
    a. We should keep all atomic information resources strictly to ourselves.
    b. We should share non-military atomic information and resources, but only with our allies.
    c. We should share non-military atomic information and resources with all non-Communist countries.
    d. We should share non-military atomic information and resources with all countries.
    e. We should share non-military atomic information and resources with all countries, and share military atomic information with our allies.
3. How good a president has Eisenhower been?
    a. An excellent president; one of our best.
    b. A generally good president; most of his policies have been good.
    c. A fair president; his policies have been good at times and poor at others.
    d. Not a particularly good president; his policies have been bad more often than good.
    e. A generally poor president; almost all his policies have been bad ones.
4. In general, how successful has Senator McCarthy been in exposing Communist operations in this country?
    a. The harm he has done is far greater than the good, if any.
    b. He has probably done more harm than good.

c. The good and the harm he has done are about equally matched.

d. He has probably done more good than harm.

e. The good he has done is far greater than the harm, if any.

5. What selective service regulations does this country need?

   a. No selective service; the armed forces should recruit men entirely by volunteers.

   b. Limited selective service; any man who has good cause should be permanently deferred.

   c. All able-bodied men should be subject to selective service, but should be able to defer their service for good cause.

   d. All able-bodied men should serve their time in the armed forces when their number is called; there should be no deferments, temporary or permanent, for anything but physical health.

   e. All able-bodied men in the country should serve their time in the armed forces, and then remain permanently on call for service.

VII. RACE RELATIONSHIPS

1. In what ways, if any, can Federal laws aid in handling problems of Negro-White conflict?

   a. Make it illegal for persons to discriminate against Negroes in any manner.

   b. Make it illegal for persons to discriminate against Negroes in the areas of housing, employment, and education, but otherwise leave things alone.

   c. Make a few general laws, but mostly we should leave the problem up to individuals.

   d. Make no laws concerning discrimination, but leave it to the people to work out their own ways of handling this conflict.

   e. Accept the fact that there will always be Negro-White conflict, and make realistic laws calling for segregation.

2. How should the problem of assigning Negroes and Whites to schools be handled?

   a. No segregation of schools; Negroes and Whites should attend the same schools and be treated equally by teachers and by other children.

   b. Separate schools for those who want them, whether Negroes or Whites, and unsegregated state-supported schools for all others.

   c. Negroes and Whites should attend the same schools and be

treated equally for academic purposes, but separated for social functions.

    d. Negroes and Whites should attend the same school buildings, but should have separate classrooms and other facilities within those buildings.

    e. Negroes and Whites should have separate, state-supported schools, but the state should rigorously enforce real equality in facilities.

3. What about laws concerning marriages between Negroes and Whites?

    a. There should be strict laws against Negro-White marriages in all states.

    b. Laws against Negro-White marriages are good for southern states, but are not needed elsewhere.

    c. No laws against Negro-White marriages, but both parties to such marriages should be condemned.

    d. Laws against Negro-White marriages are wrong, but such marriages should be discouraged, since the children of them will suffer.

    e. Laws against Negro-White marriages are wrong; every man has a right to marry anyone he pleases without social disapproval.

4. Who is to blame for continuing conflict between Negroes and Whites?

    a. Negroes are entirely to blame; their "slave complex" has made them very hostile to Whites.

    b. Negroes are mostly to blame, but attempts by Whites to "keep them in their place" are also partly to blame.

    c. Negroes and Whites are equally to blame for the continuing conflict.

    d. Whites are mostly to blame, but Negroes have invited this treatment, by their behavior.

    e. Whites are entirely to blame; they have imposed discrimination, and justify any device to keep Negroes from getting ahead.

5. Whites should be willing to accept Negroes into relationships of what degrees of familiarity?

    a. To close kinship by marriage.

    b. To close personal friendship.

    c. To the same street as neighbors.

    d. To membership in the same profession.

    e. To admission in the same movie theatres.

YEAR II

The following questionnaire was responded to in its entirety at Week −1 (i.e., before coming to the University, by mail) and at Week 15. Certain selected items were also responded to at various times during the interval, especially at times when an evening discussion dealt with an issue closely related to one or more of the items.

DIRECTIONS

Below you will find a list of "things"—objects, persons, ways of behaving, ideas, etc. For each of these, please indicate *how strongly favorable or unfavorable* you are.

If your feeling about it . . .

is strongly favorable, then write in the blank space	6
is moderately favorable, then write in	5
tends to be slightly favorable, then write in	4
tends to be slightly unfavorable, then write in	3
is moderately unfavorable, then write in	2
is strongly unfavorable, then write in	1

Occasionally you may have to pause, in making up your mind between "4" and "3." Even if you do not feel very certain about these "4" and "3" responses, please make one choice or the other, and be sure to write in one of the six numbers before each item.

1. being well educated
2. being free from organized religions
3. being loved and having warm personal relationships
4. being active in helping to bring about changes for the improvement of society
5. living a life that promotes good physical health
6. participating keenly and successfully in economic competition
7. attaining a high degree of efficiency in everyday activities
8. being free from having to take the worry and responsibility for things on your own shoulders
9. being a person who is able to influence other people
10. not having to conform to the opinions of others
11. working cooperatively with people
12. having plenty of opportunity for privacy or being alone

13. being assured of financial security
14. being able to appreciate beauty
15. being creative in your work
16. having a chance for new experiences
17. doing a thorough and careful job
18. being a leader
19. having a family, children, and a secure home
20. being in the company of many people
21. getting high grades
22. believing in a life after death
23. attending a church
24. being tolerant of beliefs other than your own
25. praying for guidance
26. believing in punishment for sin
27. marrying a person of a different religion
28. going to bed early most of the time
29. making your bed every morning
30. lending your personal belongings
31. having a radio going while you are trying to sleep
32. rules prohibiting cars on the Michigan campus
33. being in a school which does not require military training
34. choosing the medical profession as a career
35. mathematics as a major
36. social studies (social sciences)
37. choosing a business career
38. being a natural scientist
39. taking courses in art
40. Dwight D. Eisenhower as President
41. the United Nations
42. Adlai Stevenson as a future President
43. removing from their jobs persons *suspected* of being communists
44. Senator Josephy McCarthy
45. C.I.O. labor unions
46. going to war, if necessary, to save Formosa from Red China
47. The Republican Party
48. being in the same house or dorm with Negro students
49. segregating White and Negro children in schools
50. having close friends who are Jewish
51. Negro-White marriages
52. playing chess

The Attitude Items ——————————————— **277**

53. playing card games
54. listening to jazz records
55. playing football or baseball
56. dancing
57. listening to classical recorded music
58. watching football or baseball games
59. going to movies
60. reading books

persons who . . .
61. smoke 1–2 packs of cigarettes a day
62. drink regularly, though not excessively
63. are careless in picking up clothing, personal effects, etc.
64. tell risqué ("dirty") stories
65. type, or play music, while you are studying
66. are very neat and orderly about personal effects
67. are sincerely very religious
68. like to discuss with you the intimate facts of their love life

men who . . .
69. make a point of standing up for their rights
70. are careless in personal dress
71. don't take their studies very seriously
72. are always polite and respectful toward authorities
73. like to be very friendly with nearly every one
74. would report a friend seen cheating in an exam
75. are practical jokers
76. never get angry and lose their tempers
77. like poetry and ballet

at the Project House
78. having a formal set of officers to run the House
79. taking a turn at washing dishes
80. having quiet hours in the House
81. keeping your own room clean
82. having parties, as a House, on week-ends
83. having pets in the House
84. imposing fines on House members who break rules
85. being able to lock your door when you go out

The Adjective Check Lists

II

During Year II only, *S*s responded to lists of adjectives [1] by checking those that they thought applied either to themselves or to other House members, or both. At Weeks 0 and 13 a list of 180 adjectives, selected from Gough's list of 300, was responded to as applying to the respondent himself. At Weeks 1 and 14 a shorter list of only 60 adjectives (because of the time required for going through the list 16 times) was responded to by each *S* in terms of applicability to each of the other *S*s. Half of these 60 adjectives were "favorable," and half "unfavorable." The basis of selecting the 60 adjectives was somewhat arbitrary, representing only our own judgment (following our experience with the Year-I population) as to the personal traits that seemed either to be relevant to our hypotheses or to have been somewhat prominently noticed in the first population.

The findings reported in Chapter 12 are based upon simple counts of "favorable" and of "unfavorable" adjectives, with no differentiation as to content.

The 60 adjectives included in the shorter list appear on page 280.

[1] The adjectives were selected, by kind permission of Dr. Harrison G. Gough, from *The Adjective Check List,* and were used in the light of information supplied in the accompanying *Reference Handbook* (Gough, 1955). Our distinction between "favorable" and "unfavorable" adjectives is based directly upon the latter source, according to which "Thirty judges rated each of the 300 adjectives for its favorability. The highest-rated 25% of them were selected for a favorability key [and] the least favorable 25% were selected for an unfavorability key" (pp. 32, 33).

FAVORABLE ADJECTIVES

adaptable	frank	modest
calm	friendly	natural
capable	good-looking	practical
cheerful	honest	progressive
clear-thinking	industrious	resourceful
conscientious	intelligent	sociable
considerate	kind	sympathetic
cooperative	loyal	understanding
dependable	masculine	warm
fair-minded	mature	witty

UNFAVORABLE ADJECTIVES

bitter	immature	snobbish
boastful	intolerant	stingy
bossy	irresponsible	superstitious
coarse	noisy	suspicious
complaining	prejudiced	tactless
demanding	quarrelsome	unintelligent
egotistical	queer	unkind
evasive	resentful	unscrupulous
foolish	self-pitying	unstable
hostile	selfish	weak

Instructions, whether for description of self or others, included the following, taken directly from Gough (1955): "There follows a list of adjectives. Please read them quickly and put a check-mark in front of each one you would consider to be (self-descriptive) (descriptive of the person listed at the top of the page). Do no worry about duplications, contradictions, and so forth. Work quickly and do not spend much time on any one adjective. Try to be frank, and describe (you as you really are) (him as he really is), not as (you) (he) would like to be."

Indices of Agreement Concerning Lists of Specific Attitude Items

Though the natures of the 35 issues in Year I and the 85 specific items in Year II were quite different, the following procedure for developing an index of agreement was employed in both cases.

Step 1. Since our predictions have to do with agreement about objects of importance to both members of any pair of Ss, a criterion of importance is required. For Year-I responses, which involved the ranking of five alternatives to each of 35 items, we chose as the criterion of importance a Rank-1 or Rank-2 response by both members of a pair. For Year-II responses, each of which involved a forced choice among 3 degrees of favorable and 3 degrees of unfavorable attitude, we considered any item to which both members of a pair responded by 1, 2, 5, or 6 as important to that pair (there were in fact comparatively few extreme responses at 1 or 6).

Step 2. A criterion of agreement on the part of any pair of Ss, with regard to any single item of importance to both, was determined upon. For the Year-1 data, Rank-1 or Rank-2 responses by both pair members constituted the criterion; and, for the Year-II data, responses either of 1 or 2 by both members, or of 5 or 6 by both members.

Step 3. A criterion of disagreement was also required; it need not include all instances that failed to meet the fairly high standard of agreement just described, but it should be such as to include items of importance to one or both pair members. For the Year-I data, we considered any pair as disagreeing about any item when the sum of the following discrepancies exceeded 4 (the maximum possible being 8): the rank assigned by pair-member A to pair-member B's Rank-1 alternative, minus 1 ("1" being B's ranking of that alternative); and the rank assigned by pair-member B to pair-member A's Rank-1 alternative, minus 1 (A's ranking of that alternative). Since the analogous sum of discrepancies for pairs considered to be agreeing could not exceed 2, this meant that all pairs whose summed discrepancy scores were 3 or 4 were considered as neither agreeing nor disagreeing.

For the Year-II data, where a forced-choice technique had been employed, and neutral responses excluded (as described under Step 1) all pairs of responses which met the criterion of importance and which were not agreeing responses were considered disagreeing responses.

Step 4. For each of the 136 pairs, the numbers of items with regard to which these criteria of agreement and of disagreement were met were counted. (One qualification was added, in the case of the Year-I data: the numbers of items with regard to which disagreement was extreme—i.e., discrepancy scores of 7 or 8—were doubled before computing the sum of disagreements.) Thus, for each pair of Ss, the following ratio was computed:

$$\frac{N \text{ of agreeing responses to items of importance to both members}}{N \text{ of disagreeing responses to items of importance }[1]}$$

Step 5. In arriving at a final index, we were governed by the following considerations. From any list of attitude items, not all would be of importance to any individual, and no two individuals are likely to select exactly the same items as important. It follows that for any pair of Ss the number of responses entering into an index would be a good deal smaller than the total number of items responded to. Further, the number of responses from which the index is to be computed will vary greatly from one pair to another. In view of this latter fact, one further step—stemming from the fact that the significance of a given ratio of agreements to disagreements (say 3/1) varies with the absolute numbers involved—was required in computing the index. That is, the probabilities of pair agreement in 18 of 24 responses are far less than those of agreement in 3 of 4 responses, even though the ratios are the same. The final index was therefore computed as a p value, representing the probability of the obtained frequencies for each pair taken from a population of pairs whose total frequencies of agreeing and

---

[1] I.e., of importance to both, in Year II, and to one pair member in Year I, as explained above; and weighted as noted above, in Year I.

disagreeing responses were those actually obtained.[2] As noted on page 77, high numerical values represent improbably high ratios of agreements to disagreements.

At week 0 of Year I, for example, 43 percent of all item-pair responses (that is to say, 43 percent of 3940, the sum of all items considered as in agreement or in disagreement for each of the 136 pairs) were in disagreement, according to the criterion described earlier. Under these conditions, the probability that 14 or more of 29 item responses on the part of a pair of Ss will be disagreeing ones is .347; and the probability that 8 or more of 26 will be disagreeing ones is .930. These p values thus become our indices of agreement on the part of these two pairs of Ss in this population at this time.[3]

---

[2] The p values were taken from tables presented in National Bureau of Standards (1949). We are greatly indebted to Dr. Richard Savage, formerly of the Center for Advanced Study in the Behavioral Sciences, not only for pointing out the advantages of this procedure but also for lending us the volumes from which the p values could be read off.

[3] It is necessary to make this statement in terms of *dis*agreements since our tables included proportions only up to 50 percent, and our obtained proportions of agreements always exceeded 50 percent. Since our predictions had to do only with improbably high (and not improbably low) agreements, we were interested only in the p value of the obtained number or more (and not in the obtained number or less) of disagreements.

On the Use of Chi-square In Estimating the Significance of Relationships between Pair Agreement and Pair Attraction

Questions arise concerning the justification for employing x^2 as a test of significance since, given a matrix of 136 pair scores derived from rank-order correlations, there necessarily are dependencies among those scores. These dependencies show up in the skewed distributions of the marginal totals. We must therefore ask whether, given such marginal distributions, the allocation of the indices of agreement follows a pattern dictated by the indices of attraction. We have no grounds for assuming that the occurrence of the two indices in different cells of the matrix, given their occurrence in the marginal distributions, constitute mutually independent events.

There are conditions, however, under which the assumption of independence is not necessary in order to carry out a valid x^2 test (see Roy and Mitra, 1949), and our data apparently meet these conditions. When the row and column marginals are thought of as fixed, then we may ask not about the independence of the row and column attributes but rather about the assortative combinations of indices in the several cells. If we then test the null hypothesis that any observed arrangement in cells is one of a large number of random arrangements, there is no special constraint that the cell entries be independent of one another. We are thus asking: What, given the obtained marginal distributions on both dimensions, is the probability that an arrangement in cells that differs this much or more from strict proportionality would occur, by a purely random cell arrangement? If, as we believe, it is legitimate to ask the question in this form, then the inferences drawn from our x^2 tests, as reported in the text, appear to be justified.

These conclusions, however, conceal a more troublesome question.

It may occur, among a population of 136 pair relationships or a population of 272 responses, that a significant χ^2 results from the contributions of only a part of the individuals each of whom has made 16 responses that appear, directly or indirectly, in the table. That is, the frequency with which some individuals' responses appear in the diagonal cells of a fourfold table may greatly exceed chance expectations, whereas the frequency of other Ss' appearance in these cells may not exceed them at all. In that case, the inferences that we wish to draw for an entire population should properly be applied to only a fraction of the individuals therein, who are in fact responsible for the significant χ^2.

It is because of this problem that we have, in Chapter 6, attempted an analysis of the differential contributions that individuals make to our findings, especially concerning tendencies toward balance and toward accuracy. We do not regard the evidence presented in this chapter as decisive. The fact remains that the findings of this study, which in general support our predictions, are a joint resultant of two factors. The first is a general, more or less population-wide tendency for *different* responses by the *same* individuals to be so related to *corresponding* responses by *other* individuals that the population's total set of responses supports the predictions. That is, the "typical" S's responses of attitude and of attraction are so related to other "typical" Ss' responses of attitude and of attraction as to indicate balance-promoting tendencies. The second contributing factor must be described in terms of personality-related differences: whatever the intrapersonal determinants, individuals differ in their tendencies to maintain balance. Our generally significant findings are consequences of both factors.

Hence the inferences we may draw from our tests concerning the properties of pairs of persons are limited, insofar as they apply to total populations. Our evidence—since it comes from two different populations, responses by each of which were made to widely different objects of orientation—indicates that the predicted tendencies are population-wide in one sense but not in another. We did not find, unambiguously, that the predicted tendencies were universally found in all subjects. We did find that they were characteristic of enough subjects, in each population, to justify the conclusion that the emergence of the characteristics of the population as a whole was significantly influenced by forces toward balance.

On the Significance of Correlations between Scores of Mutual Pair Attraction and Pair Agreement about the Attractiveness of Other House Members

We have for various purposes correlated pair scores of mutual attraction with scores of actual agreement, on the part of the same pairs, about the attractiveness of the remaining 15 Ss. In assessing the significance of the resulting coefficients, the question arises whether it is proper to base the significance estimates on an N of 136, in view of the fact that all responses are made by only 17 Ss. Thus in Table 5.1 (p. 75) all coefficients, for both populations at all times on and after Week 2, are significant at less than .001 if we use an N of 136, but even the highest coefficients reach the level of only .02 if we use an N of 17 (see Walker and Lev, 1953, p. 470).

One way of resolving the problem is to compute analogous correlations for each S, separately. Insofar as nearly all Ss contribute to the positive correlations reported in Table 5.1, the significance of the trend for the total population can be estimated by a sign test. The individual coefficients which have been summarized in Table A-1 were computed as follows. (1) all 16 pairs scores of mutual attraction (that is, all possible pairings) were rank-ordered for each S; (2) all 16 pair scores of actual agreement with other individuals were similarly rank-ordered, for each S; (3) these two sets of ranks were then correlated. (By this procedure any given pair score is included among the 16 scores for each S involved in the pair, though of course the same pair score does not necessarily receive the same rank for the 2 Ss.)

The finding is that at no time later than Week 1, in either population, are there fewer than 14 of the 17 Ss whose individual coefficients are not positive. According to the tables of cumulative binomial probabilities, the *p* value when 14 of 17 coefficients have the same sign, and when $Q = P = .5$, is .006; and when all 17 coefficients have the same sign it is less than .001. Since these values are consistent with those derived from the use of an N of 136, but not with the use of an N of 17, we conclude that the former is more appropriate.

Table A-1. DISTRIBUTIONS OF INDIVIDUALS' CORRELATIONS BETWEEN MUTUAL PAIR ATTRACTION AND PAIR AGREEMENT ABOUT THE ATTRACTIVENESS OF THE REMAINING 15 *S*s.

Rank-order correlation	Week 0		Week 2		Week 15	
	Year I	*Year II*	*Year I*	*Year II*	*Year I*	*Year II*
>.500 [a]	3	3	6	5	7	12
.001 to .500	12	8	11	9	10	2
≦.000	2	6	0	3	0	3
TOTAL	17	17	17	17	17	17
MEDIAN	.18	.10	.35	.24	.46	.57

[a] Significant at less than .05, with 14 df. $N = 16$ for each coefficient.

There are two additional points about Table A-1 that are worth comment. (1) Only one *S* (#41) shows a negative correlation at all three times, and only two *S*s (#35 and 48) at two of the three times. All of these individuals are in the Year-II population, and all are highly unpopular (though one of them, #35, ends up with a significantly positive coefficient). (2) In Year I but not in Year II the sign test is highly significant at Week 0 (based on responses made on the third day of acquaintance). This finding is associated with the fact, elsewhere reported (pp. 162–3), that in Year I there was a very early but highly unstable structuring—apparently based upon very limited early contacts—of relatively distinct subgroups.

Distributions of Pair Scores of Attraction,* at First and Last Measurements, Both Years

Raw score	Rank-order scale	Year I		Year II	
		Week 0	Week 15	Week 0	Week 15
486–510	1.0– 16.5	16	20	18	17
462–485	18.5– 32.0	9	8	5	9
440–461	33.0– 48.0	5	10	5	7
422–439	49.0– 63.5	10	6	3	5
396–421	65.5– 80.5	10	4	20	5
376–395	82.5– 95.5	4	4	5	9
355–375	97.5–111.5	9	5	7	10
332–354	113.5–128.5	10	9	7	6
312–331	130.5–143.0	5	11	6	9
291–311	145.5–158.5	7	5	8	8
270–290	161.5–175.0	3	5	5	5
251–269	176.5–190.5	5	10	11	8
223–250	193.5–207.5	12	7	6	6
192–222	209.5–223.5	6	13	10	12
143–191	225.5–238.5	14	3	8	9
0–142	240.5–256.0	11	16	12	11
Total		136	136	136	136

* The categories in this table are so arranged that, by chance expectations, the frequencies should be as nearly equal as possible (in view of tied scores); the expected frequency in each category is about 8.5 ($\frac{1}{16}$ of 136).

Procedures for Identifying High-attraction Units

The basic datum is the pair-score of attraction, as indexed by the 256-point scale (see Appendix IX). The basic criterion of *high* attraction is 95 percent of the maximum possible mean score for a unit of any given size; as explained on page 169, the maximum possible mean score declines with increasing size of the unit.

The steps involved in isolating units of any size that meet this criterion are as follows.

1. Any pair score at 95 percent of the highest possible score of 1 on the 256-point scale automatically meets the criterion. Although (for purposes of convenience) the highest possible pair score has been assigned the value of 1 and the lowest possible the score of 256 (rather than the other way around), it is necessary to reverse this order to obtain a percentage base; thus the cutting point becomes $257 - (95$ percent of 256, or 243.2) $= 13.8$. Any pair with a score of $\geqq 13$ is therefore a high-attraction unit of two.

2. A triad consists of three pairs, and a high-scoring triad is identified by adding to a high-attraction pair (as already identified) another S whose pair scores with each of the two Ss in such a pair are high enough that, when averaged together with the initial pair's score, the mean of the three reaches the 95-percent criterion. Given a high-attraction pair, there are 15 other Ss and so 15 possible sets of three pair scores to be averaged. (In actual practice, however, it is not necessary to compute all fifteen of these means, since it is obvious by inspection that many of them would not meet the criterion.) The maximum possible average value for a unit of three is 2.5, since the attraction ranks exchanged in such a unit would be 1, 1, 1, 2, 2, and 2, and—no matter

how combined—the three resulting pair scores would total 7.5,[a] averaging 2.5 for three pairs. Applying the same formula as for pairs, the percentage base becomes $257 - 2.5$, or 254.5, and the cutting point is $257 - (95$ percent of 254.5, or 241.8$) = 15.2$. Thus any set of 3 Ss with a mean score of $\geqq 15$ is a high-attraction triad.

3. When all possible three-person units have been identified, the analogous procedure, whereby all possible fourth persons are added to make four-person units, is carried out. The maximum possible mean score for a four-person unit is 5.0 (derived from exchanged attraction ranks of 1, 1, 1, 1, 2, 2, 2, 2, 3, 3, 3, 3) and the cutting point is $257 - (95$ percent of 252, or 239.4$) = 17.6$, so that all four-person units with a mean score of $\geqq 17$ meet the criterion.

Exactly the same process could, in principle, be carried out for progressively larger units; in practice, we have never found a unit of larger than five that met the necessary criterion.

This is not, of course, a procedure for identifying uniquely optimal "placements" for each individual, but rather one for identifying all sets of persons—including the possibility of overlapping sets containing one or more of the same individuals—that meet a stated criterion.

This procedure has been followed in identifying the units that appear in both the tables and the figures in Chapter 9.

[a] The highest of all pair combinations of attraction ranks is 1-1, which occurs but once in the 256-cell matrix, and is therefore equivalent to Rank 1 on the 256-point scale, as described in Appendix IX. The next highest combination is 1-2, which occurs twice, and is thus equivalent to Rank 2.5. Then comes the combination 2-2, which occurs only once, and is therefore equivalent to Rank 4 on the 256-point scale. The only possible combinations of attraction Ranks 1,1,1,2,2,2 into three pair scores are 1-1, 1-2, 2-2 and 1-2,1-2,1-2; and these combinations are equivalent, respectively, to Ranks (on the 256-point scale) of $1 + 2.5 + 4 = 7.5$, and to $2.5 + 2.5 + 2.5 = 7.5$. Thus the maximum possible mean score for a triad is 2.5.

Indices of Interunit Attraction

For the purpose of noting between-unit relationships it would be convenient, if it were not otherwise troublesome, to assign each person to a single unit. The fact is, however, that there are often individuals who have strong connections with different units which are otherwise loosely connected, or not at all. We have therefore adopted the following procedures.

1. As in other cases, every S is assigned to every unit in which it is possible for him to have membership at or above the 95 percent criterion level; and each unit is extended to its maximum size, in the sense of adding every S whose inclusion does not reduce the mean within-unit attraction below the 95-percent criterion.

2. This procedure results, in some instances, in the inclusion of one or more of the same pairs of Ss in more than one unit, as in the following example from Year II, week 1:

> Tetrad composed of Ss 34-42-44-47
> Triad composed of Ss 44-47-49

In this case, the pair score of the pair 44-47 would appear not only as part of both within-unit values but also as part of the between-unit value, unless the procedures noted below are adopted.

3. In the case of *nonoverlapping* units the between-unit value is simply the mean of all between-unit pair scores; in the following example, this value is 700/4, or 175:

	S #51	S #52
S #53	100	150
S #54	200	250

In the case of *overlapping* units, the number of pair-scores to be averaged varies with the number of overlapping individuals. If there is a single S who appears in both units, the number of pair-scores is one less than the product of the numbers of individuals in the two units, as in this example, where the mean value is 450/3, or 150:

	S #55	S #56
S #55	X	100
S #57	150	200

In case two units have two or more overlapping members, the pair-score of the two Ss included in both units is counted but once, as in this illustration, in which only six pair-scores are averaged in computing the between-unit value of two units of three persons each, and in which the value is 900/6, or 150:

	S #53	S #54	S #57
S #53	X	100	150
S #54	X	X	200
S #58	50	150	250

The 256-Point Scale of Reciprocal Pair Attraction

As elsewhere explained (pp. 72–74), raw pair scores were so computed that the most extreme degree of reciprocally high attraction (ranks of 1 and 1 given by members of a pair to each other) received the highest possible score of $512 - (1^2 + 1^2)$, or 510, while the most extreme degree of reciprocally low attraction (ranks of 16 and 16) received the minimum score of $512 - (16^2 + 16^2)$, or 0. This procedure was determined upon not in order to achieve a metric of attraction, but only to determine an order that would take into account both rank level and degree of mutuality.

It is possible, however—once an order has been determined—to achieve an ordinal metric, based upon the frequencies with which each possible combination of sums of squared ranks would occur under a stated set of assumptions. The simplest such assumption is that according to chance expectations every possible combination of reciprocated ranks would occur with equal frequency. A 16×16 matrix was therefore constructed, such that each of 16 rank values was paired with each of 16 rank values. In each of these 256 cells the sum of the squared rank-values was entered, and these sums-of-squares were then arranged in rank order. Certain of these sums resulted from a unique combination of reciprocal ranks (e.g. the sum of 8 results only from $2^2 + 2^2$, which appears but once in the matrix); others resulted from two, from three, and even from four different cell entries (e.g., the sum of 65 results from $8^2 + 1^2$, which appears twice in the matrix, and also from $7^2 + 4^2$, which also appears twice). Since—given the previously determined order—there is a fixed rank-order position (e.g., 43.5 for the raw summed-squares value of 65, since there are 41 higher combinations) for every possible combination of reciprocal ranks, this rank-order position, from 1 to 256, becomes an ordinal measure of pair attraction.

The advantages of this measure (referred to as the 256-point scale) are that any distribution of scores thus obtained may be interpreted in the light of expected frequencies, and that a rationale is provided whereby differences between pair scores at different points on the continuum may be compared. For these reasons we have, through our tables of distributions, used the 256-point scale rather than the raw sums of squared ranks.

Individuals' Week-to-Week Rhos of Attraction Ranks *

Sub-jects, Year I	0–1	1–2	5–6	6–7	7–8	8–9	11–12	12–13	13–14	14–15	Mean
							Weekly intervals				
14	.45	.75	.80	.43	.74	.84	.68	.87	.91	.81	.73
15	.86	.91	.94	.96	.94	.97	.94	.92	.96	.98	.94
16	.46	.91	.95	.95	.96	.97	.94	.94	.94	.97	.90
17	.35	.93	.70	.62	.89	.71	.69	.77	.86	.97	.76
18	.27	.90	.89	.93	.84	.84	.67	.77	.97	.86	.80
19	.59	.83	.67	.77	.55	.70	.94	.78	.84	.89	.76
20	.42	.76	.11	.84	.95	.88	.56	.67	.80	.67	.68
21	.49	.78	.97	.93	.97	.98	.92	.93	.82	.95	.88
22	.54	.88	.79	.93	.97	.98	.99	.99	.99	.98	.91
23	.24	.87	.93	.88	.95	.98	.92	.94	.88	.97	.86
24	.57	.85	.89	.88	.95	.96	.65	.87	.96	.93	.86
25	.83	.88	.78	.92	.83	.66	.48	.83	.80	.80	.79
26	.21	.72	.88	.98	.92	.98	.99	.98	.95	.99	.87
27	.74	.79	.92	.95	.97	.93	.96	.97	.95	.95	.92
28	.44	.89	.85	.87	.93	.93	.68	.85	.84	.85	.82
29	.66	.49	.83	.82	.96	.91	.74	.84	.87	.85	.80
30	.42	.75	.84	.77	.92	.77	.94	.94	.90	.92	.82
MEAN	.51	.82	.81	.85	.90	.89	.81	.88	.91	.91	.83

Sub-jects, Year II	0–1	1–2	2–3	3–4	4–5	5–6	6–7	7–8	10–11	11–12	12–13	13–14	14–15	Mean
								Weekly intervals						
34	.86	.89	.88	.95	.89	.87	.92	.92	.97	.90	.92	.92	.98	.92
35	.79	.74	.84	.85	.84	.89	.81	.96	.92	.97	.96	.95	.95	.89
36	.62	.63	.92	.56	.61	.72	.71	.88	.79	.85	.77	.90	.82	.76
37	.51	.39	.70	.73	.65	.88	.85	.70	.82	.89	.86	.76	.82	.74

* From Nordlie (1958), pp. 135–136.

Sub-jects, Year II	Weekly intervals													
	0–1	1–2	2–3	3–4	4–5	5–6	6–7	7–8	10–11	11–12	12–13	13–14	14–15	Mean
38	.52	.85	.70	.93	.90	.97	.96	.93	.97	.95	.94	.95	.94	.89
39	.54	.73	.91	.97	.96	.97	.95	.95	.98	.98	.99	.97	.98	.92
40	.90	.83	.89	.97	.96	.94	.92	.87	.95	.87	.93	.99	.88	.92
41	.68	.90	.83	.34	.88	.81	.84	.77	.66	.67	.93	.69	.66	.75
42	.58	.81	.85	.95	.87	.94	.98	.95	.97	.98	.97	.97	.85	.90
43	.76	.80	.89	.88	.97	.91	.91	.84	.86	.95	.94	.90	.98	.89
44	.75	.86	.86	.97	.94	.96	.96	.96	.77	.87	.83	.76	.78	.87
45	.57	.92	.78	.91	.98	.98	.98	.99	.98	.99	.98	.96	.95	.92
46	.32	.90	.85	.90	.96	.93	.97	.97	.97	.97	.93	.97	.98	.90
47	.47	.92	.91	.93	.95	.97	.95	.93	.93	.92	.97	.97	.92	.91
48	.75	.92	.77	.68	.74	.88	.93	.79	.90	.71	.91	.79	.87	.82
49	.81	.89	.79	.75	.95	.82	.92	.91	.97	.94	.93	.98	.98	.90
50	.47	.66	.99	.93	.85	.99	.99	.97	.59	.70	.82	.85	.85	.83
MEAN	.65	.81	.85	.84	.88	.91	.92	.90	.89	.89	.92	.90	.90	.87

References

Adorno, T. W., E. Frenkel-Brunswik, D. J. Levinson, and R. N. Sanford, 1950. *The Authoritarian Personality*. New York: Harper.

Allport, G. W., P. E. Vernon, and G. Lindzey, 1951. *A Study of Values* (revised edition). Boston: Houghton.

Asch, S. E., 1951. Effects of Group Pressure upon the Modification and Distortion of Judgments. In H. Guetzkow (ed.), *Groups, Leadership and Men*. Pittsburgh: Carnegie Press.

Atkinson, J. W. (ed.), 1958. *Motives in Fantasy, Action, and Society*. Princeton, N.J.: Van Nostrand.

Burdick, H. A., 1956. *The Relationship of Attraction, Need-achievement, and Certainty to Conformity under Conditions of a Simulated Group Atmosphere*. Unpublished doctoral dissertation, University of Michigan.

Burdick, H. A., and A. J. Burnes, 1958. A test of "strain toward symmetry" theories. *J. Abn. Soc. Psychol.*, 57, 367–370.

Christie, R., and Peg Cook, 1958. A guide to published literature relating to the authoritarian personality through 1956. *J. Psychol.*, 45, 171–199.

Coombs, C. H., 1952. *A Theory of Psychological Scaling*. Ann Arbor: Engineering Research Institute, University of Michigan, Bulletin 34.

Edwards, A. L., 1954. *Statistical Methods for the Behavioral Sciences*. New York: Holt, Rinehart and Winston.

Festinger, L., 1957. *A Theory of Cognitive Dissonance*. Evanston, Ill.: Row, Peterson.

Festinger, L., K. Back, S. Schachter, H. H. Kelley, and J. Thibaut, 1950. *Theory and Experiment in Social Communication*. Ann Arbor: Institute for Social Research, University of Michigan.

Festinger, L., S. Schachter, and K. Back, 1950. *Social Pressures in Informal Groups*. New York: Harper.

French, J. R. P., Jr., 1959. *The Effects of the Industrial Environment on Mental Health: Working Paper I*. Ann Arbor: Institute for Social Research, University of Michigan (mimeographed).

Gough, H. G., 1955. *Reference Handbook for the Gough Adjective Checklist*. Berkeley: Institute of Personality Assessment and Research, University of California (mimeographed).

Heider, F., 1958. *The Psychology of Interpersonal Relations.* New York: Wiley.

Homans, G. C., 1950. *The Human Group.* New York: Harcourt.

Kendall, M. G., 1948. *Rank Correlation Methods.* London: Charles Griffin.

National Bureau of Standards, 1949. *Tables of the Binomial Probability Distribution.* Applied Mathematics Series #6. Washington: Gov. Print. Off.

Newcomb, T. M., 1943. *Personality and Social Change.* New York: Holt, Rinehart and Winston.

Newcomb, T. M., 1947. Autistic hostility and social reality. *Human Relations,* 1, 69–86.

Newcomb, T. M., 1950. *Social Psychology.* New York: Holt, Rinehart and Winston.

Newcomb, T. M., 1953. An approach to the study of communicative acts. *Psychol. Rev.,* 60, 393–404.

Newcomb, T. M., 1958. Review of Heider, *supra. Amer. J. Sociol.,* 23, 742–3.

Newcomb, T. M., 1959. Individual systems of orientation. In S. Koch (ed.), *Psychology: A Study of a Science.* Study I. Conceptual and Systematic, Vol. 3, Formulations of the Person and the Social Context. New York: McGraw-Hill.

Nordlie, P. H., 1958. *A Longitudinal Study of Interpersonal Attraction in a Natural Group Setting.* Unpublished doctoral dissertation, University of Michigan.

Roy, S. N., and S. K. Mitra, 1949. An introduction to some non-parametric generalizations of analysis of variance and multivariate analysis. *Biometrika,* 43, Parts 3 and 4, 361–376.

Samuels, Ina, 1956. *The relation of motivational variables to distortion on relevant response dimensions.* Graduate thesis on file in Psychology Department, University of Michigan.

Smith, C. G., 1961. *Autism, Realism, and System Balance in a Student Population.* Unpublished doctoral dissertation, University of Michigan.

Spranger, E., 1928. *Types of Men.* Translated by P. J. W. Pigors. Halle: Niemy.

Tagiuri, R., R. R. Blake, and J. S. Bruner, 1953. Some determinants of the perception of positive and negative feelings in others. *J. Abnorm. Soc. Psychol.,* 48, 585–592.

Walker, Helen M., and J. Lev, 1953. *Statistical Inference.* New York: Holt, Rinehart and Winston.

INDEX

Abravenel, E., vi, 30
Accuracy of estimates
   individual differences in, 98–102, 106–109, 113–115
   related to authoritarianism, 123–126
   related to tendencies toward balance, 111
Acquaintance
   group properties as varying with stages of, 257–258
   process and systems of orientation, 20–23
   process viewed as interaction, 249–251, 259–261
Adjective check-list, 35, 222, 279–280
Adorno, T. W., 43, 123, 132
Affiliation, need for
   related to strain and balance, 139–143
Agreement
   about House members, 72–76, 202–207
   about specific attitudes, 76–77, 189, 281–283
   about values, 82–84, 190
   among floormates, roommates, 211–215
   group stereotypes of, 228–251
   inferred from objective variables, 85–95
   as predictor of attraction, 80–82, 241–246
   see also Attraction, Perceived agreement, and Systems of orientation
Allport, G. W., 40

Alter, Elaine, vi
Asch, S. E., 20, 260
Atkinson, J. W., 43
Attitudes
   families of, Year I, 37–38, 264–275
   measures of, 36–42
   miscellaneous list of, Year II, 38–39, 276–278
   nature of, 7
   stability of, 79–80
   see also Values
Attraction
   interunit, 175–180, 291–292
   measures of, 32–36, 291–292
   mutual, index of, 72–74, 293–294
   nature of, 6–7
   see also Agreement, Balance, Pair attraction, Perceived agreement, Popularity, Triads, Structuring, Systems of orientation, and Units
Attraction choices
   measures of, 32–36
   related to personal characteristics, 221–227
   stability of, 195–202, 223, 295–296
   see also Popularity
Attraction power, 183–188
Authoritarianism, as related to
   accuracy, 123–126
   autism, 132–139
   group-perceived clusters, 233, 235
   sensitivity to strain, 129–132
   tendency toward balance, 126–129
   see also Adorno
Autism, 132–139, 259

Personality variables, 42–44
Popularity
  differentiation with respect to, 148–149
  of group-perceived clusters, 237
  related to agreement, 202–205
  related to stability of attraction, 197–202
  see also Attraction power and Personal characteristics
Population differences
  in agreement about lists of items, 77–79
  in centrality of structuring, 182–183
  in sensitivity to others' attitudes, 92, 138–139
  in triad structuring, 164–165
Pre-acquaintance attitudes, as predictors of attraction, 80–82
Predictors of final attraction
  from early stereotypes, 241–246
  from pre-acquaintance attitudes, 80–82

Reality forces, 16, 259–260
Relevance, common, as system parameter, 13
Roommates
  attraction among, 210–220
  experimental assignment of, 215–220
Rooms, assignment of, 28, 87
Roy, S. N., 284
Runkel, P. J., vi

Sallade, G. W., 30
Saltzstein, H., 30
Samuels, Ina, vi, 141
Savage, R., vii, 283
Scarr, H., vi
Schachter, S., 20
Schmuck, R., vi
Significance
  of correlations between pair agreement and attraction, 286–287
  of relationships by X^2, 284–285
Smith, C., vi

Spranger, E., 40
Spranger Values
  actual responses, 82–84, 231
  estimates of others' responses, 52–53, 69, 113–121, 124–126, 128–130, 133–139, 228–251
  manner of obtaining responses, 40
Stability
  of attraction responses, 195–202, 223, 295–296
  of mutual attraction, 157–160
  of popularity, 197–202
  of systems, modes of maintaining, 17–18
Staff members, roles of, 30–31
Stalker, Willodean, vi
Stereotypes, group-perceived
  consequences of, 246–249
  sources of, 245–246
  about value agreement, 228–244
Strain
  individual sensitivity to, 118–120, 129–132
  nature of, 12–14
  test of hypothesis alternative to, 68–70
  see also Balance
Strangership as criterion for selection, 3
Strong, E. K., Jr., 44
Structuring of populations
  centrality of, 180–191
  early-late changes, 167–191
  see also Differentiation, Population differences, and Units
Subjects
  characteristics of, 86–87
  perceived clusters of, 228–241
  selection of, 24–26
Systems of orientation
  and acquaintance process, 20–23, 259–261
  collective, 11–12, 14–15, 71–96
  individual, 9–11, 12–14, 50–70
  individual changes toward collective, 254–258
  individual as related to collective, 18–20